D0593978

SWIFT

AND THE

CHURCH OF IRELAND

Oxford University Press, Amen House, London E.C.4

GLASGOW NEW YORK TORONTO MELBOURNE WELLINGTON

BOMBAY CALCUTTA MADRAS KARACHI CAPE TOWN IBADAN

Geoffrey Cumberlege, Publisher to the University

SWIFT

AND THE

CHURCH OF IRELAND

BY

LOUIS A. LANDA

OXFORD
AT THE CLARENDON PRESS
1954

PR 3726
.L3

INDIANA
UNIVERSITY
LIBRARY

NORTHWEST

PRINTED IN GREAT BRITAIN

To my wife

Who shared in the making
of this book

Preface

M OST of the research for this book was done in 1947–8 when
I was a Guggenheim Fellow, privileged to spend the year in
Ireland and England. To the Guggenheim Foundation I owe,
as do so many others, my most profound thanks. I am equally
grateful to my own university for constant generous treatment
manifested in a variety of ways, particularly for granting me
leave of absence. In Ireland I received countless courtesies
from institutions and individuals. The Very Reverend David
F. R. Wilson, then Dean of St. Patrick's, welcomed me
with old-world courtliness to Swift's realm and gave me
permission to use the chapter minutes and the cathedral
manuscripts. His vicar, the Reverend J. W. Armstrong,
a canon of St. Patrick's, displayed infinite patience and
searched among the archives at my whim. I shall not forget
the pleasant hours in the cathedral. I acknowledge with
special thanks the kindness of Mr. Newport White, who has
dominion over Marsh's Library, which played its part in
Swift's life. Miss Geraldine Fitzgerald aided me again and
again, both when I worked in the Library of the Representative Church Body (Dublin) and later when I bombarded her
by post. The Reverend John Brady of Dunboyne, Co. Meath,
supplied me with useful historical information concerning
Co. Meath. I wish particularly to single out among the
individuals to whom I am obligated Dr. Richard Hayes,
Director of the National Library of Ireland. I can never thank
him adequately for his generosity and thoughtfulness; I will
merely say, feebly in view of what he has done, that I am
deeply appreciative. I am also grateful to the authorities and

the members of the staffs in various institutions: The
Diocesan Library of Down and Connor, the Public Record
Office of Northern Ireland, the Armagh Public Library, the
Royal Irish Academy, the Pearse Street Library (Dublin),
the Public Record Office of Ireland, and—above all—the
Library of Trinity College, Dublin.

I was not treated less kindly in England. I acknowledge
gratefully permission to use certain manuscripts at Lambeth
Palace, the Public Record Office (London), and the Victoria
and Albert Museum. Christ Church, Oxford, and Mr. W. G.
Hiscock, its Librarian, deserve very special thanks for
permitting me to use the invaluable Wake correspondence.
Lord Rothschild kindly permitted me to use the manuscripts
in his collection at Merton Hall, Cambridge. Mrs. A. M.
Blake, of Bramerton Hall, Norwich, graciously gave me
access to the papers of Sir William Temple remaining in
her family. I owe much of course to the British Museum
and the Bodleian.

An appointment in 1952 under the Fulbright Act, as a
visiting lecturer at the Universities of London and Oxford,
gave me an opportunity to finish this book. Professor James
Sutherland of the University of London considerately
arranged a schedule that permitted ample time for my own
work; and Oxford was likewise understanding in this respect.
Finally, I owe an immeasurable debt of gratitude to Dr.
Herbert Davis of the University of Oxford and Professor
Irvin Ehrenpreis of Indiana University. They read the book
in manuscript and gave me the benefit of their exceptional
knowledge of Swift.

L. A. L.

PRINCETON UNIVERSITY
May 1953

Contents

ABBREVIATIONS   xi

INTRODUCTION   xiii

I PRIEST AND PREBENDARY   1
   i ORDINATION AND KILROOT   1
   ii LARACOR   25
   iii PREBENDARY OF ST. PATRICK'S   44

II THE DEAN AND HIS CHAPTER   68

III TEMPORALITIES   96
   i THE CLERICAL LANDLORD   97
   ii RESIDENCE   111
   iii THE SACRED TENTH   123
   iv THE LEGION CLUB   135

IV THE STATE OF THE ESTABLISHMENT   151
   i THE LAITY   151
   ii IMPROPRIATIONS   159
   iii THE IRISH INTEREST   169
   iv THE BISHOPS   177

CONCLUSION   189

INDEX   197

Abbreviations used in the Notes

Auto. Frag.	'The Family of Swift' in the Appendix of Deane Swift, *Essay upon the Life, Writings, and Character of Dr. Jonathan Swift*, 1755. Written by Swift, *c.* 1728. Forster, *The Life of Jonathan Swift*, 1875, p. 4, prints a version with additions by Dr. John Lyon: 'Fragment of Autobiography'.
Boulter, *Letters.*	*Letters written by His Excellency Hugh Boulter . . . to several Ministers of State in England,* Dublin, 1770.
Chap. Min.	St. Patrick's Cathedral, Dublin: Minutes of the Chapter.
Corresp.	*The Correspondence of Jonathan Swift, D.D.,* ed. F. Elrington Ball, London, 1910–14.
Deane Swift, *Essay.*	*Essay upon the Life, Writings, and Character of Dr. Jonathan Swift,* London, 1755.
Delany, *Observations.*	Patrick Delany, *Observations upon Lord Orrery's Remarks on the Life and Writings of Dr. Jonathan Swift,* London, 1754.
Dobbs, 'Brief Description'.	Richard Dobbs, 'A Brief Description of the County of Antrim' [1683], in Appendix II of George Hill, *An Historical Account of the Macdonnels of Antrim,* Belfast, 1873.
Forster.	John Forster, *The Life of Jonathan Swift,* London, 1875.
Gilbert Collection.	Letters (holographs and transcriptions) of Irish clergymen in the Gilbert Collection, Pearse Street Library, Dublin (MSS. 27 and 28).
Journal to Stella.	*Jonathan Swift, Journal to Stella,* ed. Harold Williams, Oxford, 1948.
King Corresp.	The correspondence of Archbishop William King, Trinity College, Dublin. Holographs, contemporary copies and transcriptions (by T. Fisher).
Lawlor, *Fasti.*	Hugh Jackson Lawlor, *The Fasti of St. Patrick's, Dublin,* Dundalk, 1930.
Lyon, Hawkesworth.	The annotations by Dr. John Lyon of John Hawkesworth, *Life of the Revd. Jonathan Swift, D.D.,* 1755, in the Forster Collection (579, M. 48. D.), Victoria and Albert Museum, South Kensington.

Monck Mason.	William Monck Mason, *The History and Antiquities of the Collegiate and Cathedral Church of St. Patrick*, Dublin, 1820.
Orrery, *Remarks.*	John Earl of Orrery, *Remarks on the Life and Writings of Dr. Jonathan Swift*, London, 1752.
Poems.	*The Poems of Jonathan Swift*, ed. Harold Williams, Oxford, 1937.
Prose Works.	*The Prose Works of Jonathan Swift, D.D.*, ed. Temple Scott, London, 1897–1908.
Prose Works, ed. Davis.	*The Prose Works of Jonathan Swift*, ed. Herbert Davis, Oxford, 1939– .
Wake Corresp.	The Correspondence of Archbishop William Wake, in Christ Church Library, Oxford.

Introduction

SWIFT was not, as he himself declared, 'the gravest of Divines'.[1] By his own confession he had 'composed more libels than sermons'—so Pope once remarked of him lightly but perhaps not inaccurately.[2] Nevertheless he was a formidable and, in the main, a conscientious clergyman of the Church of Ireland. 'I look upon myself, in the capacity of a clergyman,' he wrote, 'to be one appointed by providence for defending a post assigned me, and for gaining over as many enemies as I can.'[3] This suggests a sense of mission which Swift would have been the first to repudiate, yet throughout most of his clerical career he was prompted by deeply felt convictions and tenacity of purpose. It is true that this statement applies less obviously to the spiritual than to the temporal affairs of the Church, a fact which did not escape the eyes of his enemies. One of them termed him a man 'whose Affection to the Church was never doubted, tho' his Christianity was ever question'd'.[4] But Swift would not have thought the Anglican Establishment so deserving of his best endeavours had he believed it unsound in doctrine. It was his nature to defend his domain without compromise, and he would have done so in any other sphere. Be that as it may, some of the greatness which surrounds him as a writer might with justice invest him as a churchman.

In his own day such a claim would have been at once

[1] *Poems,* ii. 764. [2] *Corresp.* ii. 98.
[3] *Prose Works,* Davis, ix. 262.
[4] *A Letter to the Reverend Mr. Dean Swift, occasion'd by a Satire said to be written by him, entitled, A Dedication to a Great Man, concerning Dedications* (London, 1719), p. 16.

strongly challenged in certain quarters. A chorus of voices incessantly cried out against him. Many of these, perhaps most of them, deserve to be little heeded, yet what they said defines an atmosphere which inevitably affected him and from which he never wholly escaped. His appointment as dean left them shrill and clamorous:

> Look down, *St. Patrick*, look, we pray,
>   On thine own *Church and Steeple*;
> Convert thy *Dean*, on this *Great Day*;
>   Or else God help the People![1]

Whether these lines, as legend has it, were actually affixed to the door of the cathedral on the day of his installation is of no consequence: they do represent a prevalent sentiment. William King, Archbishop of Dublin, disturbed by rumours that Swift would receive a bishopric, was partially relieved at the news of the lesser preferment because 'a Dean could do less mischief than a bishop'.[2]

> A Place he got, yclyp'd a *Stall*,
> And eke a Thousand Pounds withal;
> And, were he a less *witty Writer*,
> He might, as well, have got *a Mitre*.[3]

Thus was the sentiment expressed in doggerel. It was poor consolation that 'the Scandal of his Cloth' should get a deanery, although it was recognized, as one disgruntled enemy wrote, that 'the minion of a great Minister . . . deeply engaged in the dirty Work of the Day' would as a matter of course be rewarded by his patron. Still he raised the question: 'What Pretence has [Swift] more than any other Man, to a Thousand a Year for doing nothing, or little more than strutting behind a Verger. . .?'[4] These were the voices of Swift's political enemies, Whigs and Low Churchmen.

---

[1] [Jonathan Smedley], *Gulliveriana: or, A Fourth Volume of Miscellanies* (London, 1728), p. 78.

[2] Gilbert Collection, MS. 28, King to Wake, 8 May 1716.

[3] [Smedley], *Gulliveriana*, p. 109.

[4] *A Letter from a Clergyman to his Friend, with an Account of the Travels of Capt. Lemuel Gulliver and a Character of the Author* (London, 1726), pp. 19–20.

Curiously they can be paralleled, though not so extensively, by some of Tory and High Church persuasion. It is in fact difficult to find anyone pleased by the appointment. The queen, herself sympathetic to the High Church, consented reluctantly, to the displeasure of certain members of that group. Robert, later Viscount Molesworth, the Irish states-man, visiting in London at the time, reported to Ireland that the appointment had vexed 'the godly party beyond expres-sion'.[1] Nor were Swift's friends gratified; they had hoped he would be placed in England. And Swift himself, long expec-tant, angry over the delays and wranglings attendant on his preferment, found his satisfaction at finally being settled greatly tempered. '... neither can I feel Joy at passing my days in Irel[an]d,' he wrote to Stella, 'and I confess I thought the Ministry would not let me go; but perhaps th[e]y cant help it'.[2]

Since he always moved in the realm of violent controversy, Swift was seldom the object of a wholly unbiased judgement. Few of his enemies achieved the objectivity of Archbishop King who, after a decade of observing Swift as a dean, praised him for his services to the Church and the nation. Increasingly the inferior clergy of the Establishment thought of him as the champion of their causes; and the formidable power he gained in 1724, when he became the Hibernian Patriot, gave him greater influence among them. The passing years added in various ways to his stature as a churchman. To this the early biographers do not fail to testify, but they have sketched his clerical activities so lightly that no clear or substantial picture emerges. With them, and with the later biographers as well, the clerical Swift has been overshadowed by the striking figure who for four brilliant and dramatic years was associated with Queen Anne's last ministry. It is worth remarking that Swift was in Orders for fifty years—eighteen before he was a dean—and was an active clergyman for forty. These years in

---

[1] *Hist. MSS. Comm., Report on Various Collections*, viii. 262 (MSS. of M. L. S. Clements, Esq.).
[2] *Journal to Stella*, ii. 662.

the Irish Establishment had their sober achievements. Although there was much of a routine nature, there were also times of struggle and excitement, not so momentous as in the last years of Anne but not lacking in either significance or drama.

Ordained in 1694, Swift rose from an obscure cleric in a remote corner of northern Ireland to a dignitary of renown who after four decades in the Irish Church vented his pessimism in a characteristic remark: 'I have long given up all hopes of Church or Christianity.'[1] Not all of his sombre remarks deserve emphasis or credence. *Gulliver's Travels* has too deeply cast its shadow over the facts of his life. The conception of Swift the misanthrope has frequently affected the interpretation of his words and behaviour by giving them an unjustifiably dark colouring. But this gloomy pronouncement of 1736, almost a valediction, is not a casual or isolated statement. It was arrived at through long experience and an accumulation of causes. It would be inaccurate to view his pessimism concerning the Irish Establishment as a reflection of misanthropy or of temperamental melancholy. It would likewise be misleading to see it merely as the result of personal failure, though the personal element played a part. Certainly there runs throughout his clerical career a note of grievance, of frustration, and defeated hopes. But there is another and a better explanation: his hopelessness derived primarily from his realistic appraisal of the Church of Ireland. He was aware of its general debility from historical despoliations, of its internal dissensions and vulnerability to external attack, and of the weakness of the Irish economy on which it depended. These of themselves are sufficient to account for his pessimistic attitude.

[1] *Corresp.* v. 351.

I. *Priest and Prebendary*

I. ORDINATION AND KILROOT

NEITHER the motives nor the circumstances which led Swift
to take Orders are wholly clear. As he approached the step,
he was a little hesitant and uncertain, not from spiritual
doubts or youthful irresolution but apparently from unwill-
ingness to forgo another promising career had the opportunity offered. It is not unlikely that his feelings were
reflected in his remark to a cousin, Thomas Swift, then rather
indecisively settling on a career: 'All that I can say is,' he
wrote to his cousin, 'I wish to God you were well provided
for, though it were with a good living in the Church.'[1] What
is obvious is that he evinced no strong compulsion to enter
the Church; and indeed he would have viewed a 'call' with
disdain as savouring of the emotionalism of the despised
sectaries. Yet undoubtedly a clerical career presented itself
early as at least a possibility. When finally he made his
decision, it was after consideration of other prospects, though
his range of choice was remarkably narrow and unimpressive.
The striking fact is that in Swift's day, for one of his birth,
education, and position, the alternatives were few. There is
some evidence that he received an offer, presumably from
King William, of a post in the army, an offer which must have
struck him (he never mistook his own talents) as singularly
unsuitable.[2] Another offer came from Sir William Temple—
this one of civil employment, in the Office of the Master of
Rolls in Ireland.[3] His refusal in this instance may have been

[1] *Corresp.* i. 365.
[2] Deane Swift, *Essay*, p. 108; Lyon, Hawkesworth, p. 17.
[3] *Auto. Frag.* sec. xxv.

B

dictated—we cannot be certain—by the paltriness and insecurity of the position, but more likely by his decision to
terminate a makeshift relationship with Temple which had
not been lacking in friction and which offered nothing stable
or permanent. Swift had reached a point where he felt that
he must finally determine on a definite career—so he indicated
in his *Autobiographical Fragment*:

Mr. Swift lived with him (sir W. Temple) some time, but resolving
to settle himself in some way of living, was inclined to take orders. [But
first commenced M.A. in Oxford as a student of Hart Hall on 5th July,
1692 (later insertion by Dr. John Lyon).] However, although his
fortune was very small, he had a scruple of entering into the church
merely for support, and Sir W. Temple then being master of the rolls
in *Ireland* offered him an employ of about 120l. a year in that office;
whereupon Mr. Swift told him, that since he had now an opportunity
of living without being driven into the church for a maintenance, he
was resolved to go to *Ireland* and take holy orders.[1]

This statement presents an interesting and rather curious
interpretation by Swift of his own motives. He was 'inclined
to take orders' but did not wish to do so until he had more
than an economic justification. As an eighteenth-century
attitude, this has a slightly quixotic ring; still it may be what
it seems, an early display of the pride and independence so
characteristic of Swift in his later career. But we must accept
this retrospective glance with caution, as possibly coloured
by the intervening years—after all, more than thirty years
separated his decision to enter Orders and the statement in
the *Autobiographical Fragment*.

Apart from motives, there are two facts of interest at this
stage: his resolution to take Orders in Ireland rather than in
England and his intention of obtaining the Master of Arts
degree from Oxford. The latter was very likely related to his
decision to enter the Church—as Deane Swift supposes,
'... upon his resolving to go into the church, he looked upon
it as a proper expedient for his advancement in the world
with a good grace, to enter himself a member of the university

[1] *Auto. Frag.* sec. xxv.

of *Oxford*, and take his master's degree in that seat of the Muses'.[1] It is quite conceivable that Swift may have had some hopes of a fellowship and of securing a clerical living attached to that status. In fact, the possibility of a fellowship at the College of Dublin (as Trinity College was then generally called) was broached in 1690 by Temple to Sir William Southwell, who was shortly to assume office as Secretary of State for Ireland. 'If you please to accept him into your service, either as a gentleman to wait on you, or as clerk to write under you . . . or upon any establishment of the College to recommend him to a fellowship there . . . I shall acknowledge it as a great obligation. . . .'[2] From this statement we may draw an obvious inference. As Swift approached 23, the canonical age at which he could be ordained, and after almost seven years at Trinity College and an additional year with Temple, he had not yet definitely resolved to enter the Church to the exclusion of other possible careers.

Swift's indecision and apparent aimlessness can be better understood if viewed in the light of a practical situation common in the period. It was a time of early matriculation in the universities, and the youth who graduated as a Bachelor of Arts at the age of 19 or 20 still faced an interval of three to four years before he was eligible for admission to Orders. Those determined on a clerical career had to make shift as well as possible while waiting for the years to pass, and there are well-known instances of men later distinguished as churchmen who, moneyless like Swift, found themselves vacillating between the Church and whatever else offered at the moment. Swift, who matriculated at the age of 14, received his Bachelor's degree before he was 19. Had he then contemplated entering Orders, for which his degree made him eligible, he would have been forced to wait over four years. Fortunately he was able to remain in the University for another three years, an expedient frequently followed by those who looked eventually to the Church. It is easy to understand

[1] Deane Swift, *Essay*, pp. 42, 45.
[2] *Corresp.* i. 2.

why there were contemporary proposals that university
graduates be admitted to the diaconate at the age of 22—and
also why there was a tendency on the part of some bishops
to exercise occasional latitude by admitting candidates to
Orders before they had reached the canonical age. Even early
in 1689, when Swift left Trinity College as a result of the
'trouble', he still faced almost two years before he could
expect to be ordained. It is therefore a reasonable surmise
that his indecision about Orders was, if not induced, at least
aggravated by these practical considerations common to him
and many other young men without means of support.[1]

Swift has himself given the impression that he took Orders
late: '... above half the clergy in this town [are] my juniors',
he wrote from Dublin shortly before his ordination in
October 1694.[2] In a sense he was late, yet his decision was
being weighed almost three years earlier. In February 169½
he wrote to a friend that he had begun 'to think of entering
into the Church'; and in June he enrolled in Hart Hall for the
Master of Arts degree, apparently in furtherance of his
design.[3] Yet there was another difficulty—the canonical injunction that no one should be admitted either deacon or
priest who could not certify that he had a living in readiness, a
dilemma feelingly expressed by one of Swift's contemporaries
who complained: '... since I have no preferment I cannot be
ordained, and because I am not ordain'd I can have no preferment'.[4] But by the end of 1692 the matter appeared to be
settled satisfactorily. Late in November he informed his uncle
William Swift that he was to delay taking Orders until the

---

[1] Norman Sykes, *Church and State in England in the XVIIIth Century* (Cambridge,
1934), pp. 195ff.; [John Johnson], *The Clergyman's Vade Mecum* (London, 1706),
pp. 37ff. Swift may have left Ireland in 1688 (see Deane Swift, *Essay*, pp. 36, 37–38).

[2] *Corresp.* i. 13.

[3] Ibid. i. 5, 9 n. Deane Swift says: 'it is plain' that Swift decided early to take
orders (*Essay*, p. 368).

[4] T. Brockbank, *Diary and Letter Book, 1671–1700*, ed. R. Trappes-Lomax,
printed for the Chetham Society, 1930, p. 74. For the canons of the Irish Establishment, which differed somewhat from those of the English Establishment, see
*Constitutions and Canons Ecclesiastical: treated upon by the Archbishops and Bishops,
and the rest of the Clergy of Ireland ... 1634 ... and ... 1711* (Dublin, [1715]).

king provided him with a prebend and that Temple gave assurance one would be provided. Sir William, he added, 'is less
forward than I could wish, because I suppose, he believes I
shall leave him, and, upon some accounts, he thinks me a little
necessary to him [at present]'.[1] When it is considered that
Swift may have expected a prebend in either Canterbury or
Westminster, his high hopes and his impatience with Temple
for not pressing the matter more urgently are understandable.
The royal prebends in these cathedrals, attractive because of
their revenues and the slight obligation on the incumbent to
reside, were much sought after, and such a benefice would
have settled Swift comfortably for life. Why the preferment,
whatever its nature, was not given we do not know. Temple,
Swift was wholly convinced, received a promise. Later in life
Swift was wont to dwell with bitterness on the folly of trusting
to the word of a prince, but the only certainty is that a year and
a half later, in May 1694, he was not yet in Orders and had
left the household of Temple, with that gentleman 'extreme
angry' and refusing, so Swift wrote to his cousin, to 'promise
any thing firmly to me at all'.[2] Thus he was disappointed in
his first expectations of preferment, missing at the very beginning of his career that opportunity for a benefice in the
Anglican Church *in England* which eluded him even at
the height of his power and influence. The delay in his ordination, viewed in the light of the circumstances just recounted,
was not therefore a matter of personal vacillation so much
as expectant waiting for an appointment which never came,
though he might have been diverted from his intention if a
satisfactory settlement had offered in another sphere. There
is little reason to doubt the words of his first biographer, the
Earl of Orrery: 'I am induced to think, that he entered into
orders, more from some private and fixed resolution, than
from absolute choice.'[3]

---

[1] *Corresp.* i. 10. See also *Corresp.* i. 157; iii. 301; *Auto. Frag.* sec. xxvi, and my
discussion below, pp. 25f. It is not clear whether the promise of a royal prebend was
made on this occasion or later, when Swift resigned Kilroot. Westminster is first
specifically mentioned in 1709 (*Corresp.* i. 157).

[2] Ibid. i. 12.   [3] *Remarks,* p. 5.

The rift with Temple left Swift with only one recourse, to leave England for Ireland where he could fulfil the conditions requisite for ordination. In Ireland he expected no difficulties. He wrote confidently to a relative in June 1694, a month after leaving Temple, that 'I design to be ordained September next, and make what endeavours I can for something in the Church'.[1] His intention was admission to Orders at the Embertides of September, one of the four periods set by the canons for that purpose, but in this hope he was disappointed. His application to certain bishops, acquaintances of his family, raised an unexpected difficulty, the insistence that he produce a certificate of behaviour because of his long absence from Ireland.[2] This request from the bishops was merely in observance of Canon XXXI, which required that a candidate for the diaconate present testimonials of his 'good life and behaviour' from responsible persons who had knowledge of him for a period of three years preceding ordination. To Swift, however, it was disconcerting that he should strike particularly conscientious members of the episcopate, since latitude and even laxity in the regulations touching ordination were notoriously prevalent. He had applied, to his inconvenience, at a moment when there was a determination to correct the abuses.[3] From the bishops Swift turned to Narcissus Marsh, Archbishop of Dublin, to find him equally unyielding. Marsh, described by a contemporary as one who 'enquired narrowly into the characters of those whom he ordained, both as to their Learning and Morals',[4] insisted not only that Swift produce a testimonial but, as was logical, a testimonial from Sir William Temple. Thus was Swift forced to write a letter he wished to avoid, the famous 'penitential' letter. Whether this letter shows meanness of spirit and servility—a matter which has

---

[1] *Corresp.* i. 12.   [2] Ibid. i. 13.

[3] See the entry in Archbishop Marsh's Diary, quoted in Richard Mant, *History of the Church of Ireland* (London, 1840), ii. 51. See also Mant, ii. 199–202, and for a similar situation in England, Edward Carpenter, *Thomas Tenison, Archbishop of Canterbury* (London, 1948), pp. 142ff.

[4] Gilbert Collection, MS. 28, Edward Synge to Wake, 4 May 1709. For Swift's characterization of Marsh, see *Prose Works*, xi. 189–90.

exercised Swift's biographers—is not our concern here. The relations with Temple being what they were, Swift obviously desired to ask no favours. He requested 'some certificate of my behaviour during almost three years in your family. . . . The particulars expected of me are what relate to morals and learning, and the reasons of quitting your Honour's family, that is, whether the last was occasioned by any ill actions.'[1] He now hoped to be ordained in November—the opportunity in September had passed—if the testimonial were forthcoming. Temple, it appears, replied immediately as requested since Swift was ordained deacon on 28 October, earlier than contemplated, by William Moreton, then Bishop of Kildare but later to become Swift's diocesan as Bishop of Meath.[2] As Bishop of Kildare, Moreton held *in commendam* the deanery of Christ Church Cathedral, Dublin; and it was here in the sister cathedral to St. Patrick's that Swift made his delayed entry into the Church.

At the time of the 'penitential' letter Swift's earlier high expectations of a royal prebend at Canterbury or Westminster were reduced to very modest proportions. A month after the rift with Temple he thought of a chaplainship in Portugal as desirable; and in Dublin, as he prepared for ordination, he discovered that he could hope for nothing more than 'some

---

[1] *Corresp.* i. 14.

[2] There has been confusion concerning the bishop who ordained Swift. Monck Mason (p. 235) and Forster (p. 77) named William King, then Bishop of Derry. But in the *Auto. Frag.* a notation was inserted, apparently by John Lyon, that William Moreton, Bishop of Kildare, had admitted Swift to both deacon's and priest's Orders. The confusion appears to have resulted from a misreading of the Letters of Orders. The title applied to the Bishop of Derry was Derensis Episcopus, to the Bishop of Kildare, Darensis Episcopus. The Letters of Orders, now in the Forster Collection at South Kensington, clearly read Darensis Episcopus (see Forster Collection 576, MS. 48. G. $\frac{6}{24}$ and 577, MS. 48. G. $\frac{6}{25}$). Moreton was Bishop of Kildare at the time of Swift's ordination. Forster later admitted his error to William Reeves, Dean of Armagh, who clarified the matter in his article, 'Observations upon a Letter from the late John Forster . . .', *Proc. of the Royal Irish Academy*, Nov. 1879, ii, ser. ii, no. 1, 4–6. Reeves refers also to a subscription role of the diocese of Kildare with a notation in Swift's hand that he was ordained by Gulielmus Darensis Episcopus. Monck Mason has corrected errors by Sheridan and Scott concerning Swift's ordination (p. 235, note w).

small reader's place' until he proved himself by occasional
preaching worthy of something better.[1] Once again he appears to have met with a stricter practice than he had expected
or at least than frequently prevailed. The intent of the canons
was that a deacon, no matter how gifted, should undergo a
trial period before being admitted to the priesthood, though
uncanonical haste was common enough. As it turned out,
his diaconate was brief—less than three months, a period of
which we have no knowledge. On 13 January 169$\frac{4}{5}$ he was
ordained priest, once again by the Bishop of Kildare and in
Christ Church Cathedral.[2] As deacon he was eligible to be
only a curate or reader (under the Act of Uniformity of 1662);
as priest he could hold a benefice with cure of souls.

    The benefice was bestowed almost at once. On 28 January,
a fortnight after admission to priest's orders, Swift was appointed to the prebend of Kilroot in the cathedral of Connor.
In the *Autobiographical Fragment* he records tersely that he
was given this prebend by the then Lord Deputy of Ireland,
Lord Capel, to whom he had been recommended.[3] By whom
he does not say, and the omission has paved the way for as-
sumptions by his biographers. It is possible that Temple, who
had served with Capel in the Privy Council of Charles II,
made an appeal in Swift's behalf. Deane Swift carried the
supposition so far as to say: 'I shall take it for granted, that he
was just coldly recommended by sir W. to the lord Capel.'[4]
This explains, he thought, why Swift received no better preferment. Monck Mason mentions, without any evidence, a
letter of recommendation to Lord Capel sent with Temple's
testimonial (for which there is only inferential evidence).[5]

---

[1] *Corresp.* i. 12, 14. Despite the canons there was latitude both in the time of
ordination and in the interval required between diaconate and priesthood (see
[John Johnson], *The Clergyman's Vade Mecum*, pp. 40ff.; William Watson, *The
Clergyman's Law: or, The Compleat Incumbent*, 2d. ed. [London, 1712], i. 251–2).

[2] Forster Collection, 577, MS. 48. G. $\frac{6}{25}$.

[3] At the time of the appointment Capel was only one of three Lord Justices, but
he had been given latitude in making such appointments (see *Cal. State Papers, Dom.,
Wm. and Mary, 1694–95*, p. 458). He was made Lord Deputy in May 1695.

[4] *Essay*, Appendix, p. 49 n.; cf. p. 106.

[5] Monck Mason, p. 235.

Forster on the other hand, equally without evidence, says that Swift was recommended by family friends.[1] However minor the point, it would be of interest to know who was responsible for Swift's first benefice. He was very likely too proud, in view of his relations with Temple at the moment, to ask outright for a testimonial *and* a recommendation for preferment; yet in the 'penitential' letter one detects what may have been a covert appeal, a hint subtly broached, in the reference to the 'small reader's place' he must accept. 'This (without great friends)', he wrote to Temple, 'is so general, that if I were fourscore years old I must go the same way....'[2] The phrase 'without great friends' was almost certainly calculated as a plea; and Temple, reserved and somewhat pompous but by no means petty or ungenerous, may have responded to the occasion. But one must weigh against this possibility Swift's failure to give Temple credit in the *Autobiographical Fragment* and the silence of John Lyon, who in his annotations of Hawkesworth's *Life of Swift* passes silently over the statement that Swift 'obtained a Recommendation to Lord Capel'. Evidence from silence is weak, yet this is the kind of information Lyon constantly supplied. Lyon's testimony, for what it is worth, militates more strongly against Temple in two further instances, where Hawkesworth refers to favours Swift received from Temple. 'It appears', Lyon notes bluntly, 'he recd no favours'; and at the second point he says that the favours 'were mere Civilitys'.[3] If Temple were not responsible, who was most likely? Forster's mention of family friends (without evidence) suggests wide possibilities, too wide for speculation; but one person hitherto overlooked ought at least to be named—St. George Ashe, Swift's college tutor. He was a person of great influence, having become Provost of Trinity College in 1692, and was thus in a position

[1] Forster, p. 77. Émile Pons follows Forster: *Swift: les années de jeunesse et le Conte du tonneau* (Strasbourg, 1925), p. 194.

[2] *Corresp.* i. 14.

[3] Lyon, Hawkesworth, pp. 12, 27. See also *Corresp.* iii. 301: Swift's letter to Viscount Palmerston, in which he omits mention of any aid from Temple in securing Kilroot.

to be helpful. The firm friendship between the two, which
never lapsed, was already established at the critical juncture
when Swift was making his decision to enter the Church.[1]
There is no one whom he was more likely to consult—and
no one more eligible for the distinction of having launched
him on the clerical journey.

Swift did not enter a healthy and flourishing diocese. The
prebendal stall of Kilroot to which he was instituted was one
of four in the Cathedral of the Holy Saviour (Sancti Salva-
toris) in the diocese of Connor, which had been united with
Down by a bull of Pope Eugenius IV in 1441.[2] At the time
of Swift's institution the parish church of Lisburn was serving
as the cathedral, the old cathedral of Down having been
destroyed in the sixteenth century.[3] Although the see of
Connor was ancient, the bishop had no chapter until 1609
when James I, a patron of the Church of Ireland, created by
letters patent certain dignities and prebends in the united see
of Down and Connor and endowed them with benefices. The
king's act was a result of his being informed of 'great decays
and unconscionable concealments and usurpations of the
Temporalities, Tithes, advowsons and other spiritualities' of
the dioceses, and it was intended to restore 'the Vicarages with
their Gleabs and mansion houses ... to the Uses of the Ministers of God's service'.[4] Kilroot was one of the prebends created
and endowed at this time. Despite the worthy intentions of
James I the diocese of Connor did not flourish. A visitation
of Ulster in 1622 revealed that of 67 parishes, chapelries, and
granges in Connor which came under observation only 7
churches were in repair.[5] In County Antrim, where Swift's

---

[1] See *Corresp.* i. 362. Ashe signed Swift's testimonium to the University of Oxford
in 1692 (see Deane Swift, *Essay*, p. 43).

[2] William Reeves, *Ecclesiastical Antiquities of Down, Connor, and Dromore, con-
sisting of a Taxation of those Dioceses in the Year MCCCVI* (Dublin, 1847), p. 156.

[3] *History of the Church of Ireland from the Earliest Times to the Present Day*, ed.
W. A. Phillips (Oxford, 1933–4), iii. 140, 277.

[4] From a letter of James I to the Lord Deputy of Ireland, in Lemuel Mathews
(?) *The General State of the Dioceses of Down and Connor, 1693*. I have used the
transcript in the Library of the Representative Church Body, Dublin, Libr/8, p. 31.

[5] See the visitation reprinted in C. R. Elrington, *Whole Works of James Ussher*

parishes lay, the dire condition of the Church in the middle
of the seventeenth century is indicated by an Inquisition of
1657, which revealed that in the 65 parishes 30 churches
were in ruins, 27 had no incumbents, 51 had no glebes, and
the tithes of 32 were impropriate to laymen.[1] And in 1693,
a bare two years before Swift's incumbency, another report
on Down and Connor emphasized its lamentable condition,
among other things the clergy wrongfully dispossessed of
their glebe lands, incumbents restrained from claiming their
legal rights for fear of offending their patrons or parishioners,
non-residence widely prevalent, churches falling into disrepair and ruin.[2]

What were Swift's impressions as he took up residence in
the north of Ireland under such conditions? What were his
reactions to the decayed temporalities of his diocese and
indeed of his own parishes? Unfortunately there is no record
of his feelings. He tarried only briefly—perhaps an eloquent
comment in itself—yet it is a reasonable surmise that these
first months of his long clerical career inspired the strong
concern for the temporalities which informs his various
Church pamphlets. The jealous guardianship which he later
came to exercise over the actual physical possessions of the
Church, his keen recognition of the vital relation between
worldly prosperity and spiritual health in the Church—
these are matters which cannot be emphasized too much in
any consideration of him as a churchman.

There is another situation which must have made a forcible
impression on Swift at this time, one which touched the entire
Church of Ireland as well as the diocese of Down and Connor
and, most striking of all, the very prebendal stall which he held.
If the decayed temporalities were before his eyes in the form
of ruined churches and alienated glebe lands, the situation now
to be recounted would impress him with the spiritual dry rot

(Dublin, 1864), i, Appendix V; Walter Mant, *Memoirs of the Right Reverend
Richard Mant* (Dublin, 1857), pp. 17–18.

[1] *An Inquisition of Parishes in Co. Antrim, 1657*, in the Library of the Rep.
Church Body, Dublin, Libr/26, pt. v (a transcript).

[2] Rep. Church Body, Dublin, Libr/8, p. 30.

in the cathedral chapter and the diocese, and even in his own parishes. It touched Swift personally with dramatic possibilities (never realized) in that his bishop, Edward Walkington, was convinced that he held his prebend illegally and that it still rightfully belonged to his predecessor, William Milne.[1] The confused circumstances are set forth in a letter Walkington addressed to Anthony Dopping, Bishop of Meath, early in 1697, calling attention to a general misapprehension that Milne had been deprived of his office as prebendary of Kilroot whereas he had been merely suspended. As a result of the misapprehension 'one Mr Jonathan Swift putt in for the poor man's living, and obtain'd the King's patent for it . . .'. Walkington was writing, he declared, in justice to Milne

who was censured by your Lordship here at Lisburn for some misdemeanours, and his penalty was a suspension from his office & benefice during the kings pleasure, this censure was by the poor man himself & by most of the hearers mistaken for deprivation, & the mistake was so current, & universall that one Mr. Jonathan Swift putt in for the poor man's living, and obtain'd the Kings patent for it, during which time the poor man has been maintain'd by the charitable contribution of the Clergy or otherwise he must have starv'd, but so it is that about a month agoe some friend or other of his, who either had retaind some faint remembrance of his cause or fancied that so severe a censure was not like the clemency & justice that was so remarkable in your Lordships, advised him to inquire a little more narrowly whether he were depriv'd or no which he accordingly did, by consulting the records of that court, from a true & authentique copy of which, he is assur'd that he is onely suspended as upon enquiry it [would?] appear to your Lordship. . . .[2]

The proceedings under which Swift's predecessor at

---

[1] Milne, a Scottish Presbyterian, came to Ireland in 1657. Ordained by the presbytery of Antrim, he held the parish of Islandmagee. In 1660 he abandoned Presbyterianism, and in 1662 he was reordained by Bishop Jeremy Taylor. A year later he became prebendary of Kilroot. See J. B. Leslie, *Biographical Succession List of the Clergy of the Connor Diocese* (transcript in Library of Rep. Church Body; see under 'Kilroot'); Henry Cotton, *Fasti Ecclesiae Hibernicae*, iii. 266; and James Seaton Reid, *History of the Presbyterian Church in Ireland* (London, 1853), ii. 256, 417.

[2] Armagh Public Library, G11, Dopping Papers, iii, Letter 301.

Kilroot was censured dated back to 1693, when an ecclesiastical commission was appointed to examine the state of the diocese of Down and Connor. This commission, composed of Dopping and William King, then Bishop of Derry, was a response to the many rumours and complaints which had been reaching authorities in both England and Ireland over a period of several years. William Milne was only one of many clergymen involved in the charges, and a comparatively minor figure. The chief complaints were directed against the incumbent Bishop of Down and Connor, Thomas Hackett, who was facetiously known as the Bishop of Hammersmith because of his prolonged residence there instead of in his own diocese. Other dignitaries involved in the charges were the Dean, the Treasurer, and the Precentor of Connor, and the Dean and the Archdeacon of Down, not to mention a number of lesser clergymen. It would be instructive to list the many charges against these churchmen, in most instances proved and acted upon by the commission, as a revelation of the sordid, scandalous, and corrupt conditions which prevailed in the diocese shortly before Swift's appearance, conditions which in the outcome paved the way for his prebendal appointment. Suffice it to say that there were suspensions, excommunications, and deprivations for such varied offences as drunkenness, fornication, adultery, neglect of cures, pluralism, diversion of funds, excessive procuration and visitation fees, non-residence, illegal use of the bishop's seal, and simony.[1]

Of Swift's predecessor and of the disposition of his case something more particular must be said, since both Milne and Bishop Walkington advanced a claim that Swift was in possession of the prebend through an error. Evidence against Milne was given to the commission by Thomas Ward, Dean of Connor, and particularly by John Winder, rector of

[1] See 'A Memorandum concerning the Diocese of Down and Connor', in the Gibson Papers, Lambeth Palace, vol. i, no. 929, fol. 55; Bodleian, Rawlinson MS. c. 926; Carte Papers 170; *Cal. State Papers, Dom., Wm. and Mary, 1694–95*, pp. 60, 69, 70, 75, 81; James Seaton Reid, *History of the Presbyterian Church in Ireland*, ii. 417–18.

Carnmoney, who was later to become Swift's friend, correspondent, and successor at Kilroot. Both charged Milne
with non-residence.[1] Had this been Milne's only abuse of
his position Swift would never have become prebendary of
Kilroot, non-residence being too widely prevalent throughout
Ireland (and frequently excusably so) to warrant severe
punishment. But the charge was aggravated by Milne's
personal behaviour, which included intemperance and in-
continence. In the end his punishment was threefold. He was
publicly admonished for his intemperance. He was suspended
during the king's pleasure for neglect of his cures. And
finally he was 'putt upon his purgation for his incontinency
of life'. In failing to meet the test of purgation he was 'declared
convict of that crime objected against him & thereupon was
deprived'. Justice, however, was tempered with mercy: '. . .in
regard of [Milne's] great age, poverty & long being in the
Church & of the Clergy the Commissioners have declard it,
in their opinion to be reasonable that he may have 20l per
anno pension out of the said Prebend during his life'.[2] There
seems to be no doubt that Milne was actually deprived, not
merely suspended, as he and Bishop Walkington believed;
nor is there any evidence that his right to reinstatement was
pressed—or any evidence that Swift was aware that his own
appointment was in question. Yet unquestionably he heard
much of the matter from his friend Winder and from others,
clergy and laymen, who had directly participated in the
inquiry. The noise and scandal did not quickly subside, in
Ireland or in England. The deprivation of a bishop was no
common occurrence; and the proceedings of the commission
were kept before the public for several years thereafter by

---

[1] Bodleian, Rawlinson MS. c. 926, fols. 37–39. A third witness against Milne,
Jasper Brett, repeated the charges of Ward and Winder.

[2] B.M., Lansdowne MS. 446, fol. 126. See also Reynell MS. II, in Diocesan
Library of Down and Connor, Belfast; *Cal. State Papers, Dom., Wm. and Mary,
1694-95*, pp. 65 ff., where Dopping reports the admonition, suspension, and
purgation, but not the deprivation; P.R.O., S.P. Ireland, nos, 29, 30, 32, 38, 40. It
may not have been clear to Milne and his friends what his failure at purgation
meant.

Lemuel Mathews, Archdeacon of Down, who appealed his cause both in the courts and Parliament and who as late as 1705 was still struggling for redress.[1] In all of this turmoil William Milne, one of the lesser figures, did not attract unusual attention; that was focused on the dignitaries. But it was Milne who had significance for the young clergyman who was to succeed him and who was destined for fame far beyond that of any of the principals in this diocesan scandal. Once the verdicts of the commission were given, the way was open for Lord Capel to appoint Swift to the prebend of Kilroot—to a benefice reduced by £20 a year, which went into the pocket of his predecessor, and to a cure disrupted by long neglect and abuse. Thus Swift entered into an atmosphere where Church and clergy were at their worst—not an auspicious beginning certainly and one likely to leave lasting and profoundly distasteful impressions.

Swift's patent to the prebend of Kilroot is dated 28 January 169$\frac{4}{5}$. In March and April he went through the required forms of induction and of reading assent and consent to the articles, canons, and liturgy.[2] It was, then, in the spring of 1695 that he made his first appearance in his parishes and received his initial impressions of the people he was to serve briefly and of the conditions under which he was to live. In the cathedral at Lisburn he might be expected to occupy his

[1] B.M. Add. MS. 21132, fol. 30; P.R.O., S.P. 63 (Ireland), 365; *Cal. State Papers, Dom., Anne, 1702–1703*, p. 424.

[2] J. B. Leslie, *Biographical Succession List of the Clergy of the Connor Diocese*, i, 55 (transcript in the Library of the Rep. Church Body, Dublin); Reynell MS. II, Diocesan Library of Down and Connor, Belfast; *Ulster Journal of Archaeology* (1854), ii. 203. According to these documents Swift was instituted to his prebend on 5 Mar., and appeared to read assent in Templecorran, 24 Mar., Ballynure, 21 Apr., and the parish church of Connor, 28 Apr. Kilroot is conspicuously not mentioned. The information was gleaned from records in the Registry Office of the Consistorial Court of Down and Connor. The records, now lost, existed as late as 1854. Present at Swift's induction were Andrew Aiton, who inducted him, William Cunningham, Osborne Ketteringham, Simon Kilpatrick. At Templecorran were Richard Dobbs and James Calhoun. At Ballynure were Henry Ellis and Henry Clements. At the parish church of Connor were Alexander Stewart, Simon Fitzpatrick, Edward Sumervall (Sumarall ?), and Osborne Ketteringham.

prebendal stall on occasions and perhaps take his turn in preaching as a member of the chapter. As required for induction, he read divine service and preached at Lisburn on 28 April 1695; but whether he ever appeared thereafter we do not know.[1] The corps of his prebend was a union of three parishes, Kilroot, Templecorran, and Ballynure.[2] From these, all located in County Antrim, Swift received his income, approximately £100, most of it, if not all, in tithes and therefore subject to the exigencies of collection, a topic upon which he was bitterly eloquent later in his career.[3] Here he experienced personally another matter which was to preoccupy him at length later, the confusion and entanglement in Church possessions resulting from the division of tithes and from impropriations, that is, Church lands and tithes in the hands of laymen. For example, in the parish of Kilroot Swift as incumbent received only the vicarial tithes, in this instance amounting to the small tithes and a third of the tithes from corn and hay, whereas the rectorial tithes went to the Earl of Donegal, the impropriator, and so were lost to the Church.[4]

---

[1] *Ulster Journal of Archaeology* (1854), ii. 203.

[2] The charter of the cathedral of Down and Connor grants to the prebendary of Kilroot 'all those our Rectories and Vicarages of Kilroigh, Templecororan, Temple Igormagan, Laughnallitten, Ballynure, Insula & Balleprior'. I have not found Temple Igormagan mentioned in connexion with the prebend of Kilroot in any of the available visitation books and inquisitions. It was probably separated from the corps very soon. Insula (Island Magee) and Ballyprior are, according to the Inquisition of 1657, interchangeable names for the same rectory or parish, also apparently lost to the corps of Kilroot before 1657. Laughnalitten was a church or chapel in Templecorran parish—'a small thing belonging to Temple-i-corran [with] noe church, nor walls', so it was reported in 1622. See William Reeves, *Ecclesiastical Antiquities*, pp. 57 and *passim* and Reeves MS. I, p. 71, in Diocesan Library of Down and Connor (a transcript of the visitation of 1622). See also the *Inquisition . . . Antrim, 1657*, Rep. Church Body, Dublin, Libr/26, pp. 26–27, 53–54; for the charter of Foundation of the cathedral of Down, Connor, and Dromore, see Pat. Roll, 7 Jas. I, pt. ii (transcript in the Library of the Rep. Church Body, Dublin, Libr/30, p. 12).

[3] *Auto. Frag.* sec. xxv; but see *Corresp.* i. 25, where Swift mentions Ballynure alone as worth 'more than a hundred pounds a year'. At the time of Milne's deprivation the value of the prebend was reckoned about £100 (see Reynell MS. II, Diocesan Library of Down and Connor).

[4] For this and the following material on tithes see *Inquisition . . . Antrim, 1657*, pp. 26–28, 53; Richard Dobbs, 'Brief Description', p. 378; *Corresp.* i. 25.

In the parish of Templecorran the incumbent also received only vicarial tithes, the rectorial tithes being in the possession of the see of Connor. It was in the parish of Ballynure that Swift was both rector and vicar, and here he received more substantial tithes.

Of Swift's three parishes the two larger ones, Templecorran and Ballynure (both two miles in length and a mile and one-half in width) are the least interesting.[1] Kilroot, however, has some claims to antiquarian and historic interest, having played a part in early Christianity in Ireland. That its past was known and appreciated in the seventeenth century is indicated by the selection of its name for one of the four prebends created in the Cathedral of the Holy Saviour in 1609. Bishop Ussher, in his investigations into Irish antiquities, reported the existence of an ancient church of Kilroot in the year 412. His authority was a Life of St. Ailbe who, thankful to God for a safe sea journey to Ireland, bade his disciple St. Colman found a church. It was presumably thus that Kilroot (Cill-ruaidh) came into existence. Though Ussher's account has been questioned, Kilroot undoubtedly had great antiquity. It was mentioned in *Fragments of Irish Annals* under the date of 725 and in the *Annals by the Four Masters* under the date of 1122. At the dissolution of the monasteries in 1536 and subsequently, the temporalities of Kilroot passed by royal grant from the Abbot of Kells to the Chichester family, who still retained possession in Swift's day. The bishops of Connor held certain mensal lands in the parish; and in the early seventeenth century Kilroot was best known as a diocesan residence.[2] A decade before Swift's incumbency the manor

---

[1] *Inquisition . . . Antrim, 1657,* pp. 26–28. The reputed sizes of the parishes as given in the visitations and even in the surveys should be accepted only with great scepticism. It is possible that the number of profitable acres was fairly accurately known, but the number of acres in waste, bogs, and wood was less likely to be accurately ascertained.

[2] For the founding of Kilroot see Reeves, *Ecclesiastical Antiquities,* pp. 60, note w, 245, and *passim;* James O'Laverty, *An Historical Account of the Diocese of Down and Connor* (Dublin, 1884), iii. 83–84; 'The Irish Itinerary of Father Edmund MacCana, translated . . . and illustrated by notes, by William Reeves', *Ulster*

house of the bishop was still an object of attention, although Richard Dobbs, the High Sheriff of Antrim, with whom Swift was acquainted, declared that 'no Bishop hath lived there, in the memory of man, that I can learn'.[1]

Kilroot was a small parish, extending 'about a mile over every way' and containing only four townlands with an unimpressive number of profitable acres.[2] Since Swift received only vicarial tithes—the whole tithes in the seventeenth century never amounted to more than £40—Kilroot brought him no substantial return.[3] There is no evidence that he had a glebe to cultivate or a manse house to live in, and there is definite evidence that he had no church to preach in. The extant visitations for Kilroot in the seventeenth century record the church as ruinous, and omit any mention of glebe or manse.[4] The report on the state of the diocese of Down and Connor drawn up in 1693 called attention to the lack of glebes and manse houses for the clergy, and the resultant failure of incumbents to reside and serve the cures. This in turn, the report pointed out, was one reason for the high incidence of dissent.[5] That Kilroot, and Ballynure as well, suffered from the inroads of dissent is apparent from the

Journal of Archaeology (1854), ii. 59. See also *Annals of the Kingdom of Ireland by the Four Masters*, ed. John O'Donovan (Dublin, 1856), ii. 1015.

[1] Dobbs, 'Brief Description', p. 387. See also *A Preliminary Survey of the Ancient Monuments of Northern Ireland*, ed. D. A. Chart (Belfast, 1940), p. 51. Chart believes that bishops resided at Kilroot until 1700 but gives no evidence.

[2] *Inquisition . . . Antrim, 1657*, p. 53; *Books of Survey and Distribution, Co. Antrim*, sec. on Kilroot (in P.R.O. Northern Ireland, 2A.2.1); Dobbs, 'Brief Description', p. 378.

[3] Transcripts of the visitation returns: Diocesan Library of Down and Connor, Reeves MS. I, p. 71 (for 1622); Trinity College, Dublin, MS. 1067 (for 1634); *Inquisition . . . Antrim, 1657*, p. 53 (for 1657); Diocesan Library of Down and Connor, Reeves MS. 16, p. 36 (for 1679). See also Richard Dobbs, 'Brief Description' (p. 378), where the whole tithes are said to be 'not worth £40'.

[4] Of the various visitations (see preceding note), that of 1657 reports the church as 'ruinated' and without 'gleab or incumbent'; the return of 1679 reports the church as 'ruinous'. Dobbs refers to an 'old Church' but I take his phrase to mean one in ruins, at least not a parish church actively in use (p. 387). The fact that Swift did not read assent in Kilroot confirms that the church was still in ruins when he became the incumbent (see above, p. 15, n. 2).

[5] Rep. Church Body, Dublin, Libr/8, pp. 29–30.

testimony of Dean Ward of Connor, given shortly before
Swift's appointment. Many cures in Connor, Ward declared,
were neglected, 'particularly the cure of Ballynure and Kill-
rott belonging to Mr Miln [is] not served by himself or any
curate . . . [so] that several considerable persons in the Parrish
of Ballynure particularly Mr Dobbs & his Lady & Mrs
Stewart & several others . . . were forced to frequent the
Presbyterian meetings for want of a fitt minister to attend
that Cure'. Similar testimony was given by others, including
John Winder.[1]

But it was not merely the failure of the prebendary of
Kilroot to serve his cure which explains the high incidence of
Nonconformity in the parishes Swift succeeded to. In view
of Swift's lifelong struggle against dissent it is of special
significance that he began his clerical career in parishes with
a long history of Presbyterianism; and there is a touch of
irony in the fact that his predecessors in these cures were of
that persuasion. The first Presbyterian minister in Ireland,
Edward Brice, held the benefice of Templecorran in 1613
or 1614 and became prebendary of Kilroot in 1619, a position
he retained until his refusal to comply with the canons of the
Church of England in 1636.[2] Swift's immediate predecessor,
Milne, was a Commonwealth minister until the Restoration,
at which time he was one of the few Ulster Presbyterian
clergymen to conform to Anglicanism. Soon afterwards he was
given the prebend of Kilroot.[3] Throughout the reigns of
James I and Charles I there was a constant influx of Scottish
Presbyterians, small farmers and colonists chiefly, into
northern Ireland, men who made no secret of their hostility
to the episcopal order and the liturgy of the Church of
England. Down and Connor received a disproportionately
large number, particularly County Antrim, where Swift's
parishes lay.[4] In Swift's period at Kilroot it was apparent for

[1] Bodleian, Rawlinson MS. c. 926, fols. 37–39.
[2] 'Edward Brice' in *D.N.B.*; W. D. Killen, *History of Congregations of the Presbyterian Church in Ireland* (Belfast, 1886), p. 30.
[3] See above, p. 12, n. 1.
[4] W. A. Phillips, *History of the Church of Ireland*, iii. 14–15; 'Origins of Presby-

everyone to see that the English government and its deputies in Ireland were committed to a policy of favouring the dissenters. King William not only renewed the *regium donum* to the Ulster Presbyterians; he increased it. Lord Capel, to whom Swift owed his appointment, vigorously pressed the claims of the Irish Nonconformists to legal toleration; in any case the Act of Uniformity was not enforced. Persistent pressure came from England to ease the dissenters where possible. In Swift's diocese the appointment of Walkington to the see was in part due to his willingness to follow a policy of moderation. The dissenters themselves, under such favourable auspices, exerted no small measure of influence in Ulster affairs, in the municipal corporations for example; and their ministers openly flaunted their power—or so it seemed to churchmen. Belfast, only a few miles from Kilroot, was the very centre of the strength and wealth of Presbyterianism; and in the diocese of Down and Connor generally the weakness of the established Church was in sharp contrast to the flourishing condition of the Kirk, which had a well-knit organization and openly held its provincial synods.[1] The fact is that the established Church did not have, as Swift must have observed, the exclusive position it was presumed to have.

In Kilroot itself, as Richard Dobbs described it in the decade before Swift resided there, the people were 'all presbyterian' except himself, some half-dozen others, and the parson, with 'not one natural Irish in the Parish nor papist'. Templecorran could not boast as many Anglicans—'all presbyterian except the parson and clark'.[2] Three years before Swift arrived in County Antrim a dignitary of the established Church registered this complaint:

The Nonconformists are much the most numerous portion of the Protestants in Ulster. . . . Some parishes have not ten, some not six, that

terianism in Co. Antrim', *Bulletin of the Irish Committee of Historical Sciences*, no. 57, pp. 6–7.

[1] See J. C. Beckett, *Protestant Dissent in Ireland, 1687–1780* (London, 1948), pp. 33ff., 106.

[2] Dobbs, 'Brief Description', p. 378.

come to church, while the Presbyterian meetings are crowded with thousands covering all the fields. This is ordinary in the county of Antrim especially, which is the most populous of Scots of any in Ulster.[1]

From Swift's own pen there is extant only one reference to the size of his congregations: in a letter to Winder soon after his resignation he refers to his sermons as 'the idlest trifling stuff that ever was writ, calculated for *a church without a company or a roof*'.[2] There can be no doubt that Swift had only a few parishioners. It would be the merest speculation to reach any final conclusions concerning the impact upon Swift of these conditions, of the striking contrast between his own moribund benefices and the vitality of the meeting houses; yet the circumstances were highly appropriate for developing his detestation of Nonconformity and his fear of its power. We must not overlook the possibility that a portion of a *Tale of a Tub* was written at Kilroot, and, if not actually there, then while he was non-resident but still prebendary of Kilroot, with the experience of Ulster Presbyterianism fresh enough to give a dark and bitter tinge to that work.

Swift's biographers have passed over his life at Kilroot with the merest mention or have had recourse to tradition and legend—and with good reason, since trustworthy evidence is scanty. Certain questions suggest themselves at once. Where did he reside when he was prebendary of Kilroot? Where did he preach? If the matter of where he resided seems of small note, one must remember that to the Irish churchmen of the seventeenth and eighteenth centuries it was of major importance, that they conceived manse houses with accompanying glebes to be a desperate need, to make residence of the parochial clergy possible, and that they attributed the comparative

---

[1] From a letter of Bishop Leslie to William King, quoted by Reid, *History of the Presbyterian Church in Ireland*, ii. 391.

[2] *Corresp.* i. 29. Italics mine. The 'Dearly beloved Roger' incident first recounted by Orrery as occurring at Laracor has been transferred to Templecorran by Thomas O'Gorman. See his interesting but highly speculative letter to Craik, now in the Forster Collection, South Kensington, MS. XXXII, 48. E. 26. R. Wyse Jackson, in *Jonathan Swift, Dean and Pastor*, 1939, mentions without evidence 'the sort of half-civilized fisherman congregation [Swift] had in Kilroot' (p. 7).

failure of Anglicanism to this deficiency. The report on
Swift's diocese in 1693 lamented the 'want of Gleab-lands &
Manse-houses'. This gave an excuse, the report added, to
many clergymen for non-residence, 'whereby divine Service,
hospitality & relief of the poor have bin neglected & [are]
one occasion of the generall Non-conformity'.[1] No small part
of the Church legislation in Ireland in Swift's day was an
endeavour to correct this situation; and later Swift himself
took note of the difficulties frequently in his Church pamphlets. Tradition has long pointed to an oval house still
standing near the village of Kilroot as Swift's residence, but
no dependable evidence has been presented to support the
claim.[2] It is in fact impossible to say with any authority where
he lived. The only permissible inference is that he had no
manse house, and this is based upon the negative evidence of
the visitations of the seventeenth century: none mentions a
manse, and until the middle of the century none of the
parishes possessed a glebe. It is possible that by the time of
his incumbency one of his parishes had glebeland.[3]

With respect to Swift's three parish churches we are on
somewhat safer ground. They were typical of the majority of
Irish parish churches in the century—either neglected or in
ruins. It is almost certain that during Swift's incumbency
there was no church at Kilroot. It was reported in ruins in
1657 and again in 1679, and significantly Richard Dobbs
omits any mention of a church in his account of Kilroot (1683).
And even more significant—Kilroot was the only parish of
the three where Swift did not appear at the time of his
induction to read divine service.[4] Clearly the conclusion that
he never preached in Kilroot is warranted. At Ballynure and

[1] Rep. Church Body, Dublin, Libr/8, pp. 29–30.
[2] *Corresp.* i. 29 n. and the picture opposite p. 176.
[3] See above, p. 18, n. 3; *Corresp.* i. 25. Classon Porter ('Swift in Kilroot', in
Biographical Sketches, 2nd series, Belfast, 1884, pp. 13–14) writes that Swift resided
in the parsonage at Kilroot and that he had a glebe which he let to a farmer. Forster
(p. 82) mentions a glebe. I am inclined to believe that the allusion in *Corresp.* i. 25
is to a glebe, though it possibly refers to a tithe farmer.
[4] See above, p. 18, n. 4, and p. 15, n. 2.

Templecorran, however, parish churches were available and usable. It may be that Swift's parishioners in Kilroot attended his church at nearby Templecorran, which seemed to date from about 1622, when it was reported as having 'walls newly erected but not roofed as yet'. In 1657 it was said to be 'in repayre, & conveniently seated'; and in 1683 Dobbs refers to it as being in 'a small town or village, called Ballycarry', adding that 'there is a meeting house between the church and the village.[1] Swift read divine service and preached there in March 169$\frac{4}{5}$.[2] His own reference to a church without a roof could indicate either Templecorran or Ballynure. In the two extant mentions of the parish of Ballynure in seventeenth-century visitation returns the church is reported as 'decayed' and 'not in repayre' but in each instance the cure was being served, a fact which indicates that the church was at least in use whatever its condition.[3] In 1694 the three witnesses against Swift's predecessor made a particular point of his failure to serve the cure of Ballynure, to the detriment of the Anglican interest, thus permitting the inference that a church existed for an incumbent to make use of if he desired; and Swift is reported to have held service and preached there on 21 April 1695.[4] Swift had therefore two parish churches to serve, in what state of repair is not certain, and a handful of parishioners. It is not likely that he had a curate.[5] He may have preached alternately at his two cures—or even left one unserved, certainly not an uncommon practice.

[1] Reeves MS. I, p. 71 (for 1622); Rep. Church Body, Libr/26, pp. 26–27 (for 1657); Reeves MS. 16 reports the church as 'ruinous' (1679); Dobbs, 'Brief Description', p. 378. D. A. Chart reports, without evidence, that Templecorran church was destroyed in 1641 (see *Preliminary Survey of Ancient Monuments in Northern Ireland*, pp. 39–40), and never used thereafter, but his statement is confuted by the visitation return of 1657.

[2] See above, p. 15, n. 2.

[3] Reeves MS. I, p. 71; Rep. Church Body, Libr/26, p. 28.

[4] Bodleian, Rawlinson MS. c. 926, fols. 37–39; Reynell MS. II lists a curate for Ballynure as of 1693, thus suggesting the existence of a church. See above, p. 15, n. 2.

[5] J. B. Leslie informed me that he believes Swift made use of a curate, J. Calhoun (one of the witnesses to Swift's induction). Canon Leslie referred to his authority as a diocesan register 'not now extant'.

In the *Autobiographical Fragment* Swift disposes briefly of his career as prebendary of Kilroot by remarking that he grew weary of it in a few months, returned to England, and resigned in favour of a friend.[1] Although his incumbency covered a period of three years, from January 1695 to January 1698, his residence in his parishes was a bare year or less. He returned to the household of Sir William Temple in May 1696 under a licence of absence from his cure extendible if he desired; but he was expecting an appointment in England through the influence of Temple—another living in the Church, according to his sister.[2] It is not certain, however, that he actually expected a clerical appointment; Swift himself does not specify, though it appears that the Earl of Sunderland had been applied to. Unfortunately Sunderland's tenure in the government was even then insecure, and soon he left office —late in December 1697—without providing for Swift. This was a blow, but he was determined not to return to Kilroot. Ten days after Sunderland resigned office Swift relinquished his prebend and his parishes in the north, a step that he had actually been considering for some time. He was not without hope of aid from other sources, and in a letter to John Winder, his successor at Kilroot, he referred cryptically to efforts being made in his behalf.[3] These sources failed him too, and once again he became resident in the Temple household to await developments. The first phase of his clerical career, barren and inauspicious, had ended. It began with his departure from Temple and now closed with his return. It is not certain what his expectations were or what Temple would endeavour in his behalf. Whatever they were, they came to nothing. A year later Temple died, leaving Swift—in the words of his sister—'unprovided both of friend and living'.

[1] *Auto. Frag.* sec. xxv. For the discredited story of Swift's resignation resulting from attempted ravishment see Ricardo Quintana, *The Mind and Art of Jonathan Swift* (New York, 1936), pp. 370–1, where various references are given.

[2] *Corresp.* i. 24, 30.

[3] Ibid. i. 24.

II. LARACOR

In 1699, at the age of 32, Swift had still to seek his place in the Church; and he was again, as at the outset of his career, to meet with delays and broken promises. Once more he turned his hopes towards England—and to a royal prebend, 'upon the claim of a promise', he wrote in the *Autobiographical Fragment*, 'his Majesty [King William] had made to sir W. Temple, that he would give Mr. Swift a prebend of *Canterbury* or *Westminster*'.[1] Whether this is the promise dating back to 1692, made before Swift took Orders, or a more recent one made upon renewed solicitation by Temple to compensate Swift for resigning Kilroot, we have no way of knowing. In London, where he now pressed his claim, Swift depended upon the Earl of Romney to present his petition and remind the king of the promise. It was an unfortunate choice. Romney had 'professed much friendship' for him—so Swift declared later; and he was in a sense a logical choice to approach the king.[2] He had known William as Prince of Orange. It was Romney who carried over to the prince the secret invitation to take the throne; and he had gained William's confidence and friendship. After the Revolution he had served the Crown in various capacities. But in some respects he had proved himself notoriously incompetent, particularly as Lord Justice of Ireland, from which office he had been recalled. Nevertheless he reaped honours, was a court favourite, and was considered a good intermediary to reach the king. The 'professed friendship' for Swift doubtless grew out of the friendly relation between Temple and Romney, which existed from the reign of Charles II. There was, however, a fatal defect in Romney's character, his inability to apply himself to affairs. Even Bishop Burnet, who glosses over Romney's moral iniquities and characterizes him as 'of a sweet and caressing temper [with] no malice in his heart', admits what was widely known, that Romney did not 'follow business with a due application'.[3] If Swift is right, this was one of those instances

[1] Sec. xxvi.   [2] Ibid.
[3] For the Earl of Romney, see his *Diary of the Times of Charles the Second*, ed.

when Romney failed to 'follow business'. He said 'not a word to the King'. Swift's bitterness towards his professed friend was long lived: 'an old, vicious, illiterate rake, without any sense of truth or honour', he characterized him twenty-five years after the event.[1]

There is, however, another possible reason that Swift failed to receive a royal prebend. After the death of the queen, who had assumed responsibility for clerical appointments, William created an ecclesiastical commission to recommend candidates for all preferment. He instructed its members (the two archbishops and four bishops) to seek out only the worthiest clergymen for promotion. Although he was eager to be rid of place-seekers, probably such as Swift, whose claims had no very real foundation, William did not let the commission function unhindered: he made mandatory 'recommendations' and used preferment at times to win over opposition as well as to reward loyal supporters.[2] What did Swift possess of power or influence at this juncture, with Temple dead, which would impress the king to the point of making a recommendation to the commission? And if Swift's name were placed before the commission—a possibility that must at least be considered—what were his apparent merits or his services to the Church which would persuade the prelates of the commission to approve him for one of the valuable and sought after royal prebends? It is probable that Romney neglected to act, but it is even more probable that Swift's expectations were too high.

His resources in England failing him once again, Swift returned to Ireland in August 1699, in the minor but promising capacity of domestic chaplain to the Earl of Berkeley, who arrived to assume his duty as a Lord Justice. Swift could hardly find contentment in this new post for any length of time, yet it had certain temporary advantages. The

R. W. Blencowe, 1843; Burnet, *History of his Own Times* (London, 1818), ii. 397, iii. 5; *Poems*, i. 64–65.

[1] *Auto. Frag.* sec. xxvi; *Prose Works*, x. 358.
[2] See Edward Carpenter, *Thomas Tenison*, pp. 167 ff.

chaplains of the Lord Justices expected almost as a matter of course to be preferred when a place offered. Furthermore this position increased his opportunity for advancement through intercourse at Dublin Castle with people of power and position. The duties of domestic chaplain to Berkeley were not such as to make any unusual demands. Family prayers and perhaps an occasional sermon at Dublin Castle— little more was expected. There were no parochial duties, no vexatious dependence on tithes; and Swift was free for social intercourse, for reading, and for writing those amusing occasional poems which survive from this period—and to wait for preferment. It was not long in coming. The connexion with Berkeley brought him the benefice of Laracor (united with those of Agher and Rathbeggan) which he was to hold throughout his life. But more important, the sojourn in Dublin paved the way for his becoming a prebendary of St. Patrick's, in which capacity he served until his appointment as dean.

Swift's appointment to Laracor is another instance of those disappointed expectations which beset his endeavours for clerical preferment early and late. As he reports the circumstances in the *Autobiographical Fragment*, it is obvious that his sense of justice was outraged, and he makes charges which later biographers have accepted and even enlarged upon. The details deserve close scrutiny. A number of preferments in Ireland were in the gift of the Lord Justices, and there can be little doubt that Berkeley was committed, if not overtly, then tacitly, to provide something for Swift. The opportunity presented itself early in January 1700 on the death of Dean Ormsby of Derry. One of the most lucrative of the Irish deaneries, Derry was desirable in every respect. The manner in which it was disposed of is reported circumstantially by Swift:

In some months the deanery of *Derry* fell vacant, and it was the earl of Berkley's turn to dispose of it. Yet things were so ordered, that the secretary having received a bribe, the deanery was disposed of to another, and Mr. Swift was put off with some other church-livings not worth above a third part of that rich deanery; and at this present not a sixth. The excuse pretended was his being too young, although he were then 30 years old.[1]

It is instructive to observe the accretions to this story as it moves along in the stream of Swift biography. Orrery reported that Berkeley intended to appoint Swift to Derry but that William King, then bishop of the diocese, had interposed with a request that the deanery be given to a graver and older man who would be more effective in combating dissent. King is reported as saying that he knew Swift to be 'a sprightly ingenious young man' who would 'be eternally flying backwards and forwards to *London* . . .'.[2] Deane Swift, who had in his possession the *Autobiographical Fragment* in Swift's hand, embellished the account, he frankly admits, by hearsay and surmise: Berkeley's secretary, Arthur Bushe, is presumed to have received an offer of £1,000 for the deanery; he reserved action however until he gave Swift the refusal for a similar sum, an overture which Swift rejected 'with all imaginable disdain'. Deane Swift also repeats the tale of Bishop King's alleged intervention, but he garnishes it by suggesting that King's motive was fear of 'being eclipsed by the superior lustre of this young aspiring genius'.[3] Sheridan's embellishment is important: he indicates that Berkeley was complacently aware of Bushe's attempted simony.[4] Hawkesworth merely repeats in part what others have recorded, but Lyon's annotation of Hawkesworth supports, though rather cryptically, the story of the alleged simony.[5] In the nineteenth century, though Monck Mason absolves Bishop King, he, Craik, and Leslie Stephen appear to accept the story in its fundamentals as it appears in Swift's *Autobiographical Fragment*.[6] Not until F. Elrington Ball's edition of Swift's correspondence in the twentieth century do we get an unequi-

[1] *Auto. Frag.* sec. xxvii.   [2] *Remarks*, p. 35.

[3] *Essay*, pp. 112 ff.

[4] Thomas Sheridan, *Life of the Rev. Dr. Jonathan Swift*, 1784, pp. 29–30.

[5] Hawkesworth, *Life of Swift*, p. 29; Lyon, Hawkesworth, p. 29.

[6] Monck Mason, 240–1; Henry Craik, *Life of Jonathan Swift*, 1882, pp. 77–78; Leslie Stephen, *Swift*, p. 51.

vocal denial of the bribery alleged by Swift.[1] We are con-
fronted in this matter with a typical instance of how legend has
replaced fact with respect to Swift's clerical career—and important because typical. The circumstances deserve complete
examination, especially so since the source of the legend is
Swift himself in the *Autobiographical Fragment*, though there
is no reason to believe that he designedly misrepresented.
As the details unfold in the correspondence of Berkeley,
John Bolton, who received the appointment, Bishop King,
and others, they show conclusively that King did not inter-
vene against Swift, that Bushe did not receive a bribe from
Bolton, and that Berkeley should be rescued from his putative
role as villain in the piece.

When Dean Ormsby of Derry died on 29 January $\frac{1699}{1700}$,
William King immediately sent letters from Derry to two of
the Lord Justices, Berkeley and the Earl of Galway, as well
as to Narcissus Marsh, Archbishop of Dublin, requesting
that a new dean be appointed as expeditiously as possible.[2]
Dean Ormsby's long illness and his neglect of his duties had
brought deanery affairs into a sorry state; and King was thus
the more willing to address himself to Berkeley, with whom
he was not acquainted, as well as to Galway and Marsh, whom
he knew personally. It was his hope that Marsh would
approach the Lord Justices concerning the new dean, or at
least that he be consulted about eligible clergymen. In the
letters to Galway and Berkeley, King calls attention in general
terms to the qualities which the incoming dean should have
for this difficult dignity; and he specifically says to Galway
that the 'benefice is in your Excellency's gift', but assumes
also that Berkeley is to have a hand in the appointment. Thus
if by some agreement among the Lord Justices the gift of
the deanery was in Berkeley's power alone (as Swift reported),
King was not aware of it. To all three of his correspondents

---

[1] *Corresp.* i. 33 n.

[2] King Corresp. (tr. Fisher): see King to the Government, 29 Jan. $\frac{1699}{1700}$. One of
these is to Galway, one to Lord Berkeley; King to the Archbishop of Dublin, 29
Jan. $\frac{1699}{1700}$.

King pleaded that a man of prudence, piety, and learning be appointed to the post, which he declared to be unsurpassed in the north of Ireland for 'difficulty and consequence'. To the two Lord Justices he presents no names, remarking merely that a number of his diocesan clergy would be suitable. In the letter to Marsh, however, he mentions several Derry clergymen; but more significantly he adds: 'I suppose this will be given to some of the state chaplains, and I think Dr. Stearn of Trim, Dr. Singe, Dr. Bolton, Mr. Span and Mr. Perkinson . . . are all or have bin such, and I shall thank God if I get any of them.' 'I believe', he continues, 'your Grace's inclinations lead you to serve such men, and I pray use your interest on this occasion. . . .' It is important to observe that King does not name Swift and that he does name the two clergymen who played a role in the events which followed, John Bolton, then holding the benefice of Ratoath in the diocese of Meath and the prebend of Dunlavin in St. Patrick's Cathedral, and Dr. Synge of Cork.

At no point in the proceedings does King mention Swift. It is possible that he makes two erroneous references to Swift (in letters to Archbishop Marsh and an unknown correspondent) when he reports rumours: 'I know not who I shall have for Dean; some say Dr. Synge of Cork, some Dr. Bolton . . . and others talk of a relation of my Lord Berkeleys.'[1] The relative of Lord Berkeley, he told Marsh, is a clergyman: 'I wish it were worth his while to accept this benefice.' Confused rumour may have made Swift a relative of Berkeley; but rumour was right when it indicated that Synge and Bolton were receiving serious consideration. Swift appears not to have received very serious consideration, yet he was the only one of the three who actually desired the appointment. And he was the only one to whom it was not offered. Bishop King, it is quite clear, was in no way responsible for Swift's disappointment. There is nothing to indicate that he knew Swift at this time; and indeed Swift himself never charged him with

[1] King Corresp. (tr. Fisher), King to the Archbishop of Dublin, 9 Feb. $\frac{1699}{1700}$; King to ——, 13 Feb. $\frac{1699}{1700}$.

interfering in this affair. It is obvious that King, in residence at Derry and far from the scene, was ready to rely on Marsh and the Lord Justices. Swift's over-zealous biographers have simply enlarged upon the bare statement in the *Autobiographical Fragment* that the pretended excuse for his failure to receive the appointment was his youth.

The deanery was first offered to Bolton, significantly by the Earl of Galway, not by Berkeley. 'When the deanery fell,' Bolton wrote to King, 'discoursing accidentally with my Lord Galway, he of himself askd me whether I had any thoughts of it, I told him I was so well Settled that I did not intend to move for it, tho he gave further encouragment to doe it.'[1] There follows a passage which throws light on the part Berkeley played:

Soon after I receivd a message from Lord Berkeley (whose Chaplin I am) that he had heard a good Character of me, and that if I would give him an account of my Livings he would try to adjust matters and that the Deanry should be conferrd on me with an encouraging advantage, and this he likewise communicated to the Arch-bishop of Dublin.

Upon hearing from Berkeley that the Lord Justices were willing to bestow the deanery on Bolton, Archbishop Marsh urged Bolton to accept. Bolton, however, persisted in his refusal. He was then holding two livings which brought him a good income, and he felt no desire to give up his relative ease for the difficult position in the north. Thereupon the deanery was offered to Dr. Synge of Cork, also named by King as acceptable, who in his turn refused it. At this juncture one would expect that Swift's opportunity had arrived, but for reasons which do not appear he was ignored. Instead Bolton was asked to reconsider. As an inducement Archbishop Marsh offered to persuade the Lord Justices to permit Bolton to retain the valuable cure of Ratoath along with the deanery.[2] Pluralism was common enough, but pluralism involving two such widely separated benefices was frowned upon. That the conscientious Archbishop of Dublin

[1] King Corresp., Bolton to King, 12 Mar. $\frac{1699}{1700}$.
[2] Ibid. See also B.M. Add. MS. 28884, fol. 167; MS. 28885, fols. 244, 254.

should make this concession, at a time too when reform of such abuses was in the air—and when Swift was available without violation of a principle—indicates how ill founded Swift's hopes were. It is clear that he did not receive any determined support.

In the end Bolton, who was permitted to retain Ratoath, accepted the appointment to Derry. The arrangement affected Swift beyond the loss of Derry since he was given the benefices that Bolton vacated. It is likely that Ratoath as well, had it been vacated, would have gone to him, a living in itself almost equal in value to what he received. The negotiations had involved a fortnight, from the death of the incumbent dean on 29 January to 15 February, the day on which both Berkeley and Galway sent word to King that they had appointed Bolton, 'a person', wrote Berkeley, 'whose qualifications & character might answer your wishes'. 'I do not question,' he continued, 'but you'l think Doctor Bolton such, since I find by the Archbishop of Dublin, with whom I advisd on this occasion, that your Lordship namd this Gentleman, among some others that you judg'd worthy of that preferment.'[1] King replied to *both* Galway and Berkeley, expressing his sense of their 'kindness and goodness'.[2]

The foregoing account indicates that Swift's statements in the *Autobiographical Fragment* need correction or qualification. He declared that the gift of the deanery was in the hands of Berkeley, but it is clear that Galway was actively involved in the proceedings, perhaps even took the initiative. It was Galway who first offered the appointment to Bolton and encouraged him to accept. It is also clear that King and Marsh looked to Galway as well as to Berkeley. All the evidence creates a strong presumption, if not actual proof, that Galway divided the responsibility with Berkeley. Swift also declared that Arthur Bushe, Berkeley's secretary, had been bribed, as a result of which the deanery had been

---

[1] King Coresp. (tr. Fisher), Berkeley to King, 15 Feb. $\frac{1699}{1700}$.

[2] King Coresp. (tr. Fisher), King to Galway, 20 Feb. $\frac{1699}{1700}$; King to Berkeley, 20 Feb. $\frac{1699}{1700}$.

bestowed upon another. The facts do not support this charge. Certainly Bushe was not bribed by Bolton, who, far from seeking the deanery, accepted it only when unusual concessions were made. Bushe may well have used his influence (if he possessed any) in favour of Bolton and in opposition to Swift; but there appears to be no foundation for Swift's unequivocal charge that Bushe received a bribe. The particularity with which Swift's biographers have reported the details of the bribe—the amount involved, Berkeley's connivance—must be regarded as wholly imaginary; and Swift's forthright charge runs counter to the logic and the facts of the situation. Finally there is Swift's report that when he failed to receive the appointment 'the excuse pretended was his being too young'. Was it merely an excuse? Or was there honest doubt about his inexperience? If he had had determined support, his age and inexperience would probably have mattered little with Berkeley, and even less with Galway. Archbishop Marsh is another matter. His strong influence in the proceedings is obvious at every point; and it is worth observing that Swift's career as a churchman up to this point would hardly serve to bring him into favour with so conscientious a man as Marsh. Unless the archbishop had some special reasons, he would obviously favour a tried and sober clergyman (Bolton had been in Orders for twenty-three years) over one who must have seemed a place-seeker and who had resigned his first benefice after a brief residence. The deanery of Derry, as King had written to Marsh, demanded a man of prudence and piety, and the willingness to serve a cure of consequence and difficulty in a state of neglect. The sober facts of Swift's clerical career at this point would convince no one that he was the appropriate person. Marsh's importance in the disposition of the deanery and his part in the negotiations have hitherto escaped notice; and Swift himself may not have been aware of it. The man of whom he wrote that no one 'will be either glad or sorry at his death, except his successor'[1] played, the evidence indicates, a significant part at this critical juncture in

[1] *Prose Works*, xi. 190.

Swift's clerical career. In extenuation of Berkeley, whatever one's sympathies for Swift, it should be recalled that Bolton was also his chaplain. If Swift had some claim on this basis, so had Bolton, whose clerical career objectively considered made him far more eligible for this particular preferment. Swift's continued good relations with Berkeley would suggest that he did not feel at the time the bitterness implied in the comment set down twenty-five years later in the *Autobiographical Fragment*. Commentators have professed to see in the poem *The Discovery* Swift's satiric revenge on Berkeley and Bushe; but they have exaggerated its bitterness. It is exceedingly mild, and may in fact have been written before Swift's hopes for the deanery of Derry were disappointed.[1]

Swift tells us that he was put off with some other church livings not worth a third part of 'that rich deanery'.[2] These livings consisted of a union of three parishes in the diocese of Meath—the rectory of Agher and the vicarages of Laracor and Rathbeggan, resigned by Bolton. It may well be that Swift's disappointment was aggravated by his accession to only a portion of Bolton's holdings—and the less valuable portion at that. Seven months later Archbishop Marsh made him prebendary of Dunlavin in St. Patrick's Cathedral, possibly to compensate him for his failure to receive the valuable living of Ratoath, which Bolton insisted on retaining.

The diocese of Meath, into which Swift now entered, bore some striking contrasts and parallels to that of Down and Connor, where his career had begun.[3] Meath had its beginnings in the twelfth century when several small bishoprics were united, and it retained the peculiar constitution of the old deambulatory sees. It had no cathedral, no dean, no chapter. Swift's only obligation was to be present at the visitations of the Bishop of Meath, who by tradition was the

[1] *Poems*, i. 61 n.

[2] *Auto. Frag.* sec. xxvii.

[3] See Rowley Lascelles, *Liber munerum publicorum Hiberniae*, 1852, ii, pt. v. 184; John Erck, *An Account of the Ecclesiastical Establishment subsisting in Ireland* (Dublin, 1830), p. 17; Walter Harris, *The Whole Works of Sir James Ware concerning Ireland, revised and improved* (Dublin, 1739), i. 138.

ranking bishop of the Church of Ireland. At the time of
Swift's appointment to Laracor the diocesan was Richard
Tennison, whose translation from Clogher to Meath paved
the way for St. George Ashe to become Bishop of Clogher.
With Tennison he appears not to have clashed, but with later
bishops of Meath, such Whig appointments as John Evans
and Ralph Lambert, he was at odds, as we shall see. General
conditions in Meath when Swift's incumbency began could
only have struck him as distressingly similar to those he
encountered in Down and Connor, with one important
difference. Whereas in the northern diocese the preponder-
ance of the population was Presbyterian, in Meath it was
Catholic. In both instances there were only a few members of
the Church of Ireland. The temporalities of the Church in
Meath matched those of Down and Connor in decay and
neglect. A few years before Swift appeared at Laracor,
Anthony Dopping, then Bishop of Meath, reported that the
diocese contained 197 parish churches, of which only 43 were
in repair. He listed the number of clergymen as 55, with 40
in residence.[1] Dopping's account revealed a familiar situation
—decaying churches and chancels, lack of glebes and manses,
non-residence, lay impropriation of tithes, neglect of cures
because of pluralities. Although these conditions were by no
means unique in Down and Connor and Meath, it was in
these two dioceses that Swift could best make his observations
on the state of the Church of Ireland. Meath gave him further
and of course a more considerable experience of the sorry
condition of church temporalities, experience which is reflected in his practical approach to his own parishes and in
his views on tithes, pluralities, non-residence, and related
matters in the later Church pamphlets.

Swift did not hasten to undertake his duties in the new
parishes. His patent to Laracor is dated 20 February and he

[1] Marsh's Library, MS. Z 3.1.4. (5), p. 142; this is *The State of the Diocese of
Meath as delivered to the Lords Justices by Anthony, Lord Bishop of Meath, 1693*,
transcribed by John Stearne in 1697. See also Codex Gibsoniana 929, I, fol. 60
(Lambeth Palace).

was instituted 22 March, yet he remained at his post as
domestic chaplain to Berkeley through a dispensation which
permitted him to delay reading of assent and consent at
Laracor and Rathbeggan until June.[1] Of the three parishes
which constituted the union, little is heard of Agher and
Rathbeggan. It is with Laracor that Swift's name is usually
associated, and properly, because this is the parish which
figured prominently in his life. Located in the Barony of
Moyfenragh, Laracor consisted of thirteen townlands covering an area of 4,175 acres, mainly arable and pasture. Before
the Reformation Laracor was a rectory with tithes appropriate
to the monastery of St. Thomas, Dublin; but in Swift's day
it was a vicarage, the rectory having been united with the
vicarage in 1636, at which time the rectorial tithes were
granted to the incumbent vicar in consideration of a Crown
rent of £20 per annum.[2] Thus Swift received all the tithes of
his largest parish, which, as Irish parishes went in the period,
made him a substantial return. In the extant account books
he enters his income from Laracor and Agher jointly and in
such a way that separation is difficult; but it may safely be said
that Laracor brought him at least £100 per annum, and very
likely more, a sum reduced of course by the Crown rent, payment to his curate, and uncollected tithes.[3]

---

[1] Lyon, Hawkesworth, p. 30.

[2] Marsh's Library, MS. Z 3.1.4. (1), p. 43; MS. Z 3.1.4. (5), p. 147; *Visitation
of Meath about 1723*, transcript in Rep. Church Body, Dublin, Libr/10 (see no. 76,
'Laracor'). See also *Civil Survey A.D. 1654–1656: Vol. V, Meath*, ed. R. C.
Simington (Irish Manuscript Commission) (Dublin, 1940), pp. 173–6; Down Survey
Barony Maps (Moyfenragh, no. 27), published at the Ordnance Survey Office,
Southampton, 1908.

[3] When he purchased additional glebe in 1717, Swift valued Laracor at £126 (see
below, p. 40, n. 3); see the various Account Books in the Forster Collection,
South Kensington. The Account Book for 1702–3, for example, shows tithes of
Laracor and Agher set for £160 (Forster Collection 505, 48 D. 34/1). The Account
Book for Nov. 1703–Nov. 1704, now in the possession of Lord Rothschild, shows
Laracor and Agher set for £132. 8s. 0d. Lyon notes that the three parishes in
Swift's union were reckoned in his Account Books as about £230 (Hawkesworth,
p. 29). The sum varied somewhat from year to year. The Account Books reveal that
the Crown rent paid on Laracor and Agher was £7. 11s. 8d. each term, but see
Marsh's Library, MS. Z 3.1.4. (1), pp. 25, 43. See also *Corresp.* ii. 346.

The parish church of Laracor, located in the townland of Laracor, was the mother church of the union. Unlike Kilroot it appears to have no special claim to distinction in Irish Church history. The earliest records of its vicars date from 1408, Swift being the twenty-third to hold the benefice.[1] As in most seventeenth-century Irish parishes, the church had been in alternate states of repair and neglect. A visitation of 1615 reported the church and chancel in repair, but seven years later they were reported as ruined.[2] The ruinous state lasted throughout the Commonwealth and well beyond the Restoration. In 1682 church and chancel were still 'out of repayr', with the sixteen protestant families of the parish dependent on the chapel at nearby Sumerhill.[3] Under Swift's predecessor, however, Laracor fared better. The church was repaired in 1694 and services were held every Sunday. Bolton resided eight miles away at Ratoath, which he probably preferred; even if he had wished to reside at Laracor, there was no manse on the glebe.[4] The undeveloped state of Laracor gave Swift his opportunity. It was an outlet for his passion for improvement; indeed his attitude toward his little acre of ground was more that of the gentleman bent on improving his estate than that of a priest concerned with the cure of souls. Although his correspondence touching Laracor contains references to parochial matters, these are far less frequent than the mention of his willows, his fruits, the canal, and the river walk, all in a tone of evident satisfaction such as later was manifest in his remarks concerning Naboth's vineyard, his garden near the deanery. In the course of time Swift built a parsonage, a modest structure referred to in a visitation report of 1723 as 'a neat cabin'.[5] Despite his fondness for

[1] J. B. Leslie, *Biographical Succession Lists of the Clergy of the Meath Diocese*, vol. ii (see 'Laracor'). Unpublished compilation in Rep. Church Body, Dublin.
[2] Royal Irish Academy, MS. 23. F. 1, fol. 285; Trinity College, Dublin, MS. E. 3.6, fols. 80–81.
[3] Marsh's Library, MS. Z 1.2.31, fol. 81.
[4] Marsh's Library, MS. Z 3.1.4. (5), p. 147.
[5] *Visitation of Meath about 1723*, pp. 46–47. See also *Corresp.* i. 33; ii. 53, 240; iii. 10, 158.

Laracor it is true, as Orrery remarked, that 'a strict residence at *Laracor*, was not in the least suitable to his disposition'.[1] Primarily it was a place of retirement where he could find relief from the vexed problems he faced elsewhere. From the beginning it was clear that Swift would not serve the cure. Soon after reading assent in his parishes (which he delayed for three months or more) he returned to Dublin Castle and attendance on Berkeley, with whom he went to England in April 1701.

Swift's biographers early and late have been vague and brief concerning the clerical phase of his life at Laracor, contenting themselves in the main with relating that he conscientiously augmented the Sunday service by prayers on Wednesday and Friday and with recounting the well-known 'Dearly beloved Roger' incident.[2] Any implication that he was the regular incumbent should be discounted. His presence was intermittent; and Sir Walter Scott's unqualified statement that 'Swift's life at Laracor was regular and clerical' is not in accord with the facts.[3] That he preached there from time to time we know from an occasional reference, as in his letter to Stearne in 1710: 'I am this minute very busy, being to preach to-day before an audience of at least fifteen people, most of them gentle, and all simple.'[4] He performed other priestly duties occasionally when he visited Laracor, from being 'regular and clerical' his service to the merely incidental and casual. The regular duties were hands of curates. The first of these was a 'Mr. Smith', who received payments in 1702–3 for sermons and of whose relationship to Swift nothing is known beyond the unrevealing entries in the account book of those years.[5] Two of Swift's curates, however, figure prominently in his correspondence, Thomas Warburton and Stafford Lightburne. Warburton became curate at an undetermined date, at least as early as

---

[1] Orrery, *Remarks*, p. 34.

[2] Ibid. p. 32; *Works*, ed. Sir W. Scott, 1814 ed., i. 67–68.

[3] *Works*, i. 67; Lyon says Swift 'resided there but a short Time' (Hawkesworth, p. 156).

[4] *Corresp.* i. 180; ii. 305.   [5] Forster Collection 505, MS. 48. D. 34/1.

1709, and served in that capacity until 1717, when he was preferred to a living in the diocese of Armagh. Swift, who thought
highly of him—'a gentleman of very good learning and sense'
—worked for his advancement.[1] Swift's sincere concern to
see his parish served by competent and conscientious curates
is revealed by the care with which he chose and supervised
them. At Warburton's resignation he had difficulty in finding
a suitable person. He received an application from Lightburne, who had some claim to consideration since he was
married to a relative, Hannah Swift. At this time Lightburne
did not stand high in Swift's estimation, and despite the inconvenience he preferred to wait until he could be better
provided. Later, however, he revised his opinion of Lightburne, who served as curate from 1722 to 1733.[2] The same
conscientious spirit is observable in the care of Laracor
Church, which in the long period of Swift's incumbency
contrasts sharply with the neglect of the preceding century.
In the visitation of 1723 it was reported as a 'handsome well
built Church in very decent repair [and] Church & Chancel
ceiled and flagged & furnished with all conveniences except
a Surplice & carpet'. Of the glebe the report says it 'is exceedingly well enclosed; there is a good garden and a neat cabin
value £60 situated near the Church'.[3]

the course of his long incumbency Swift took two addi-
steps to increase the value of Laracor. The first of these
augmentation of the glebe. The need for larger glebes
to supplement the low income of the parochial clergy was
widely recognized. In Swift's own diocese of Meath the
situation was typical of Ireland as a whole, where a number of
causes had operated to deprive the clergy of their glebes or to

---

[1] Account Book, 1708–9, Forster Collection 506, MS. 48. D. 34/2; *Corresp.* ii.
56, 366. For Swift's difficulty with Bishop Evans over the appointment of a
successor to Warburton see *Corresp.* iii. 37.

[2] *Corresp.* ii. 370 and *passim*; J. B. Leslie, *Biographical Succession Lists of the
Clergy of the Meath Diocese*, ii. 446. In the list of names Swift compiled and desig-
nated as ungrateful, grateful, or indifferent, Warburton is marked indifferent and
Lightburne ungrateful (see Lyon, Hawkesworth, preliminary notes).

[3] *Visitation of Meath about 1723*, pp. 46–47.

reduce them in size—alienation by lay proprietors, seizure
in times of war and revolution, and general neglect, to mention
three which Swift himself refers to on occasions. Attempts to
remedy the situation, such as a clause in the Act of Settlement
apportioning 10 acres contiguous to every parish church as
glebe, proved ineffectual; and it is not surprising that Bishop
Dopping in reporting on the state of Meath in 1693 should
give some prominence to this dire situation.[1] Swift's recognition of the problem is indicated by the clause he inserted in
the First Fruits Memorial (1710) to be presented to Queen
Anne. 'Hardly one Parish in ten', he wrote, 'hath any Glebe,
and the rest, very small ones, and scattered, except very few;
and even these have seldom any Houses; For want of which,
the Clergy are forced to take Farms at Rack-rents in their
own or some neighboring Parish.'[2]

To increase the sadly deficient glebe at Laracor—a single
acre—he opened negotiations in the summer of 1716 with
his neighbour, John Percival, who held lands at Neal's Town
in the parish of Trim but located near to Laracor glebe.[3] The
transaction had a dual aspect, purchase and rental, involving
a total of 43 acres. Swift proposed the outright transfer of 20
acres for the sum of £200, the money to come from the First
Fruits fund designed for such purposes. In addition he was to
lease at his own expense 23 acres at a perpetual annual rental
of £14 and a fine of £55, a lease which he intended to devise
to his successors in the living. It was part of the agreement
that he should improve and build on the 23 acres; and he
estimated that the total expense to himself would amount to

---

[1] Gibson Papers, Codex 929, I, fol. 60 (Lambeth Palace).

[2] *Journal to Stella*, ii. 679.

[3] For the details of Swift's purchase of additional glebe see *Corresp.* ii. 336, 345,
and *passim*. See also Registry of Deeds, King's Inn, Dublin, Percival to Swift,
9 Feb. 1716–17, Memorial no. 8629. In the Treasurer's Accounts of the First
Fruits Fund, under date of 18 Dec. 1716, is entered an item concerning 'the
Purchase-Money for the Glebe of Laracorr—200: 0: 0'. (See appendix, p. 51, in
Edward Synge, *A Brief Account of the Laws now in force in . . . Ireland . . . for
erecting English Schools*, Dublin, 1723.) The Account Book for 1717–18 shows that
Swift spent a considerable sum—£190—on his new glebe soon after the purchase
(Forster Collection 510, MS. 48. D. 34/6).

approximately £50.[1] Rathbeggan Church suffered the usual dilapidations in the course of the seventeenth century.[2] Early in the century it was in good repair, with a manse and glebe, and the incumbent was resident; but like many other parish churches it fell into neglect during the Commonwealth. In 1682 it was reported as unroofed; the vicar was not resident, and no cure was performed. This apparently made little difference since by that date the parish had no Protestants, nor were there any in 1693. It is doubtful whether there was any material change for the better during Swift's incumbency. In 1723 the visitation which showed Laracor to be flourishing returned Rathbeggan Church as 'ruinous' and without manse; and a decade later a census revealed no Protestants.[3] To Swift Rathbeggan could have meant little more than a source of income, without any troublesome parochial problems. It had one aspect of significance that would deepen his impression of the unfortunate state of the Irish Church: its rectorial tithes were in the hands of a layman and the incumbent received only the vicarial tithes. The parish, which before the Reformation was appropriate to the Monastery of Colpe, was in Swift's time impropriate to Lord Drogheda, a member of a powerful family in Ireland which had played its part in the alienation of Church lands and tithes.[4]

[1] See the various Account Books in the Forster Collection.

[2] For Rathbeggan see Royal Irish Academy, MS. 23. F. 1, fol. 280; Trinity College, Dublin, MS. E. 3.6, fols. 66–67; Marsh's Library, MS. Z 1.2.31, fol. 39 and Z 1.3.4. (5), p. 145; *Visitation of Meath about 1723*, p. 43.

[3] 'A List of Protestant Families in the Various Parishes, 1733.' This is added to a visitation of Meath in 1818, in the Library of the Rep. Church Body, Dublin (a transcript). See also [David Bindon ?] *An Abstract of the Number of Protestant and Popish Families . . . of Ireland . . .* (Dublin, 1736), p. 4, for Meath as a whole.

[4] Marsh's Library, MS. Z 1.3.4. (5), p. 145. Orrery's own annotation of his *Remarks* (p. 31), where he states that Laracor and Rathbeggan were bestowed upon Swift, is of interest: 'These livings were given to *Dr Swift*, by the Earl of Drogheda . . . with a kind of tacit agreement that the livings should be given back to Lord Drogheda when *Dr Swift* was farther and more advantagiously preferred in the Church. *Ld Drogheda*, as soon as *Swift* was made Dean of St Patrick's, sent to put him in mind of the Agreement, and desired him to give up the livings. *Swift* returned in answer, "That [when] he saw *Lord Drogheda*, give up any one thing of which he was in possession, He was resolved to follow his lordship's example, and

From the foregoing account of his parishes it is clear that
Swift was never in any very active sense a parochial priest. His
occasional preaching or performance of other offices at
Laracor was merely coincidental with his visits. That he
carefully supervised his parishes is certainly true. He chose
his curates conscientiously and kept himself informed in
parish affairs, particularly concerning Laracor, the only
parish of his three that presented any problems—or indeed
had a church and parishioners. And even here there were 'but
few Protestant families in the Parish'—so the Visitation of
Meath in 1723 reports. It adds the important fact—'but
some are very wealthy'.[1]

III. PREBENDARY OF ST. PATRICK'S

Swift's appointment to the prebend of Dunlavin in St.
Patrick's Cathedral in September 1700 was in the light of
subsequent developments the most significant single event
in his early clerical career. It was the beginning of his long
connexion—forty-five years—with that cathedral; but more
important it was initially as a member of the cathedral
chapter that he conceived the idea and gained the opportunity
to solicit in England the First Fruits for the Church of Ireland,
the opportunity which led to his relationship to the Harley
Ministry and eventually to his appointment as dean. The
prebend of Dunlavin was in the gift of Archbishop Marsh,
who may have obstructed Swift's appointment to the important deanery of Derry but conceivably was quite willing to
give him the lesser place of prebendary in a large cathedral
chapter. Nevertheless, there is an obscure circumstance that
occasions some doubt of Marsh's attitude—an inexplicable

retain his two livings: because he possessed them" ' (Harvard College Library, MS.
Eng. 218.14). The story could conceivably apply to Rathbeggan, of which the
Earl of Drogheda was patron and impropriator, but not to Laracor and Agher, in
the gift of the Crown.

[1] *Visitation of Meath about 1723*, pp. 46–47. The visitation of 1682 reported
sixteen Protestant families in Laracor (Marsh's Library, MS. Z 1.2.31, fol. 81). See
also Wake Corresp. xiv, Evans to Wake, 3 Aug. 1722, reporting the few Protestants
in Meath.

delay in conferring the prebend on Swift. An interval of seven
months passed from the date of Bolton's appointment to Derry
and Swift's appointment to Bolton's vacated prebend. There
was no question of Bolton's retaining the prebend. His
other vacated livings, except Ratoath, which he was permitted
to retain, were conferred on Swift immediately. It is an
inference, but a reasonable one, that for some reason Marsh
did not hold Swift in high estimation or at least that he wished
to dispose of the prebend to another. The inference gains some
support from Swift's bitter *Character of P[rimate] M[ars]h*, in
which occurs this pointed remark: 'He hath found out the
secret of preferring men without deserving their thanks; and
where he dispenses his favours to persons of merit, they are
less obliged to him than to fortune.'[1] Though the matter
must remain obscure until further evidence, still a question
may be raised. With Bolton's retention of his most valuable
living, Ratoath, and Swift's receiving the relatively meagre
remainder, the failure to give him the prebend would seem
too pointed, in fact almost a rebuke. Did Berkeley therefore,
feeling his obligation to his disappointed chaplain, persuade
Marsh to give Swift his due?

Swift's instrument of collation is dated 28 September 1700,
and he was formally installed on 22 October.[2] The prebendal
stall of Dunlavin was not one of the original canonries endowed
at the foundation of the Church of St. Patrick in 1191; it
came into existence in 1227 when the number of prebends
was increased by five. Swift's prebend was of the diaconal
order, originally the third ranking one, it would appear, in
that category, being below the sacerdotal prebends in pre-
cedence and above the subdiaconal ones.[3] This distinction,
which had significance in the Middle Ages, had apparently
broken down after the Reformation, so that all the prebends
had equality of status in Swift's day. In the eighteenth

---

[1] *Prose Works*, xi. 189–90.
[2] Chap. Min. 1690–1719, fol. 96, formal entry of Swift's instruments and
installation.
[3] Monck Mason, pp. 48 ff.; Lawlor, *Fasti*, 29 ff.

century a great secular cathedral such as St. Patrick's made few demands of its canons. The prebendal stalls were sinecures in a literal sense and were nearly so in the wider sense of demanding few duties. To the parish of Dunlavin, whence the name of his stall, Swift had no obligations. This small parish, situated on the borders of Counties Dublin and Wicklow, endowed the prebend with tithes—but not very munificently, since Swift's annual return was only a few pounds.[1] The low income of the endowed stalls explains the long-standing practice of appointing the prebendaries to parochial cures which would provide a maintenance. This type of pluralism had established itself by long custom and no dispensation was required. With Swift relieved of parochial duties by a curate, he was personally responsible only to the cathedral. Here his chief duty was to preach in his turn. In his day the preaching was apportioned among all the canons, both dignitaries and prebendaries, who numbered more than twenty; thus his appearances in this capacity in the course of a year were few. In Swift's case even this limited duty was reduced by an unusual number of absences in the years before his deanship. Requirements concerning residence were explicitly stated in the canons of the Church, but the exceptions were many and faculties or dispensations for absence were easily obtained. Swift was not more culpable than others; many, if not most, of his absences were on occasions when he was doing some service to the Church, as soliciting the remission of the First Fruits. Yet the prolonged absence from 1710 to 1713, after his success in gaining the First Fruits grant, was wholly of a political nature. It may be argued that a churchman exercising political influence, as Swift did in the four years of the Harley Cabinet, was in the eighteenth-century view justifiably absent from his cathedral. Certainly there was an unusual latitude in this matter. Nevertheless,

[1] The Account Book for 1708 shows the tithes set for £14. 8s. 0d. (Forster Collection 506, MS. 48. D. 34/2). For Dunlavin see *The Civil Survey, A.D. 1654–56, Vol. VII, Co. Dublin*, pp. 296, 300; the notations for a history of Co. Dublin in the hand of John Lyon, National Library of Ireland (MS. no. 101, a. 37. 1348); John C. Erck, *An Account of the Ecclesiastical Establishment subsisting in Ireland*, p. 83.

Swift's absences leave an impression of a churchman remarkably free to come and go; and if that impression is of a person
not completely possessed by his clerical career, we cannot dispute its accuracy at the same time that we take into account
the age and the nature of the church. In certain lesser cathedral obligations, as attendance at the dean's visitations and at
chapter meetings, the impression is the same. In the decade
following 1702 he was present at the dean's annual visitation
only five times and at chapter meetings only thirteen.[1]

There is nothing to show that Swift's entry into the
cathedral chapter was in any respect auspicious or that he
impressed the dignitaries and his fellow canons as a promising
churchman. His recent connexion with Sir William Temple
and the immediate connexion with the Earl of Berkeley would
have indicated powerful influence and would perhaps be
taken as portents of future advancement. His departure from
Ireland with Berkeley in April 1701, barely six months
after his entry into the chapter, may well have been considered
a promise of non-residence. More hopeful, as an indication at
least of ambition, was his taking the degree of Doctor of
Divinity, 16 February 170½. There is little evidence in these
early prebendal years of his relationship to other members of
the cathedral chapter. Among the minor canons were John
and Robert Grattan, members of the distinguished Grattan
family, both later to serve as prebendaries during Swift's
deanship and to continue a friendship which originated in
the early days. From this time dates also the acquaintance
with John Worrall, whose tenure at St. Patrick's was to
last even longer than his own. A minor canon by 1690,
Worrall eventually came to serve Swift as dean's vicar.[2] The
intimacy between the two was apparently a later development; but not so the friendship with Thomas Walls, Archdeacon of Achonry and schoolmaster at St. Patrick's. He

[1] As given in Lyon's additions to the *Auto. Frag.*, Forster, p. 7. Lyon is not
always trustworthy.
[2] H. J. Lawlor, *Fasti*, for this and other members of the chapter contemporary
with Swift.

became a fast friend and intimate, one to whom Swift could unburden himself of his hopes and disappointments.

When Swift first entered the chapter, the dean was Jerome Ryves, whose death in 1705 reveals for the first time Swift actively participating in chapter affairs in something more than mere routine. In the course of its eventful history St. Patrick's Cathedral had known disputes between chapter and Crown over the right of presentation to the deanery. This controversial subject had been canvassed as recently as 1693, and the respective rights of chapter and Crown presumably clarified.[1] Nevertheless, on the death of Dean Ryves the chapter, fearing circumvention of its prerogatives, convened in haste to elect its own choice. Swift and two others were ordered to present a petition to the Lord Lieutenant requesting that the chapter's right to elect a dean should not be prejudiced. For a period of over two months the chapter was busily engaged in defence of its rights and in applying itself to the necessary legalities and procedures contingent on the situation. Swift played an important part. In the election which followed, John Stearne, then chancellor of the cathedral, was selected, with Swift—so he later wrote to Stearne—'the most busy of all your solicitors'.[2] The friendship between these two was to last for many years despite strains and lapses. While Swift gave himself some of the honour for Stearne's election to the deanery, he was freely given credit by Archbishop King as the instrument of Stearne's elevation to the episcopal bench in 1713. Dr. Stearne, King wrote to Archbishop Wake in 1716, 'was remov'd from the Deanry of St. Patricks . . . to Dromore, in the late Time; But was told, this was not for any Merit in him, but to make Room for Dr Swift'.[3] The statement is partially true, but omits to mention Swift's sincere belief that Stearne would make an able bishop. He could therefore conscientiously press Stearne's claims—

---

[1] Monck Mason, pp. 213–14.

[2] *Corresp.* v. 16; Chap. Register, 1698–1713, fols. 177 ff.; Chap. Min. 1690–1719, fols. 134 f.; *Corresp.* i. 53–54; Monck Mason, pp. 218–20.

[3] Gilbert Collection, MS. 28, King to Wake, 8 May 1716.

claims so strongly opposed that Swift reported to Stella from London, 'they say here tis much to my Reputation, that I have made a Bp in spight of all the Wor[l]d, to get the best Deanry in Ireld'.[1] Yet it is true that in serving Stearne, Swift was also serving himself. Stearne will appear later in another connexion; for present purposes the circumstances surrounding his election as dean indicate that by 1705 Swift had become a forceful member of the cathedral chapter. He was also gaining that invaluable experience, not only in internal affairs of the cathedral but in ecclesiastical precedents and prerogatives, which was to serve him well when he became the dean.

The other dignitaries of St. Patrick's from this early period are less important in Swift's career. The precentor, next in rank to the dean, was Samuel Synge, who was aware of Swift's merit and who was to sponsor his appearance in the Lower House of Convocation in 1707.[2] The chancellor was Edward Synge, later a Whig appointee to the sees of Raphoe and Tuam. He was Stearne's rival for the deanery in the election of 1705, but Swift's opposition to him appears not to have disturbed their relation which, if not cordial, reveals no special friction.[3] Other than Stearne, the dignitary for whom he had regard was the treasurer, Jeremiah Marsh, the son of Francis Marsh, Archbishop of Dublin from 1682 to 1693. Swift and Jeremiah Marsh had been contemporaries at Trinity College, Dublin, but whether they were friends at the time is not known. Swift held him in affectionate esteem—'one I always loved', he remarked in 1713, when he strove to secure preferment for Marsh.[4] One other person may be mentioned in passing, Enoch Reader, Dean of Emly and Archdeacon of Dublin, with whom Swift acted officially in 1705 in defence of the chapter's right to elect a dean. Reader was Chancellor of Connor during Swift's incumbency at Kilroot and was thus a link

---

[1] *Journal to Stella*, ii. 666; see also ii. 655. [2] *Corresp.* ii. 76.
[3] But see below, p. 89.
[4] *Corresp.* ii. 103.

between Swift's first benefice and his prebendal status in St. Patrick's.[1]

If the events of 1705 indicate that Swift had arrived at a respected position in the internal affairs of the chapter, the year 1707 was even more important. Two events took him beyond the confines of his cathedral. In July he was elected proctor to represent St. Patrick's Cathedral in the Lower House of Convocation, elected, so he maintained, at the instigation of Samuel Synge, who was then Prolocutor of the Lower House. Swift served a period of three months, from 22 July to the prorogation of Convocation on 30 October, during which time he heard the Lower House urge the Upper to lay plans for securing remission of the First Fruits and Twentieth Parts.[2] He also participated in a factional controversy which engaged both Houses of Convocation as well as the Irish House of Lords. Swift does not himself refer to this controversy, but it is mentioned briefly by John Lyon and by later biographers, all of whom leave Swift's part obscure. 'He was active in the Irish Convocation in 1707', Lyon wrote, 'as appears by his Protest 30 Oct 1707 signd singly by himself in the presence of Tho. Trotter N.P.'.[3] The wrangle was of the kind, perennial among churchmen, for which Swift showed some aptitude and zest. It grew out of the intention of the Primate Narcissus Marsh to establish a public benefaction—a library in connexion with St. Sepulchre, the episcopal palace of the Archbishop of Dublin. Hitherto it has not been known that Swift played a part, however small, in the founding of Marsh's Library, which on later occasions he used and which contains some of his books. A Bill for the establishment of the library was approved by the English Privy Council, and at the time of Convocation was pending in the Irish House of Lords, where it eventually received

---

[1] *Corresp.* i. 53–54; Lawlor, *Fasti*, p. 80. There were some minor canons with whom, possibly, Swift had close relations, for example, Thomas Leigh (see *Corresp.* i. 43; *Journal to Stella*, i. pp. 9 ff. and *passim*) and John Jones (see *Corresp.* i. 45).

[2] *Corresp.* ii. 76; Armagh Public Library, Reeves MSS. Box III (Irish Convocations), Diurni Superioris Domus Convocationis, I, fols. 393, 411, 431.

[3] Lyon, Hawkesworth, p. 37.

final passage. But in the Lower House of Convocation there were strong misgivings, particularly because the Bill annexed the position of librarian to a dignity of St. Patrick's Cathedral (either the treasurer or the precentor) in a fashion that smacked of simony and sacrilege. Resolutions were introduced protesting, among other things, that laymen, who might compose a majority of the governing board, were thus given undue power over a cathedral dignity— 'a New Law upon the Church contrary to all the Ecclesiastical Laws of the Land, the Common-Law, & the Law of God'. Another resolution protested that the Bill altered and lessened the jurisdiction of the dean and chapter of St. Patrick's Cathedral. After violent debate the principal resolutions were approved. In the meantime the House of Lords had passed Marsh's Bill, and the resolutions of the inferior clergy could have no practical effect. To reaffirm its opposition, however, a majority of the Lower House of Convocation voted to keep the resolutions in the records of Convocation as a permanent protest. To this action Swift dissented, and entered into the records a notarized statement of his protest. His position was that the resolutions were already recorded in the journal of the Lower House and that the final action to keep them there was wholly unnecessary.[1] It should be observed that his protest was merely a technicality concerned with procedure for permanently preserving the records; he was in agreement with the majority of the lower clergy in fearing that the Bill as drawn was potentially dangerous. This controversy is of more than passing interest for the view of Swift acting in a larger and more public capacity. But it is also of interest because it reveals him early in two roles he assumed with frequency in later years: as a guardian of the rights of churchmen, sensitive to encroachments by laymen, and as a lower clergyman in set opposition to the higher clergy. The latter of these grew out of the disputes over the Bill, during which Archbishop King, by violently criticizing the lower clergy for presumptuous

---

[1] For the controversy and Swift's part in it, see Bodleian, Ballard MS. 8, fols. 124–5; Ballard MS. 36, fols. 45–51.

opposition, had made the issue one between the Lower and Upper Houses of Convocation.

The prorogation of Convocation at the end of October left Swift free to engage in a project of profound significance for his career. He now began his endeavours to gain for the Irish Establishment remission by the Crown of the First Fruits and Twentieth Parts. His undertaking of this responsibility had eventually a momentous result: it brought about the realignment of his political position and friendships, and this in turn led to his appointment as dean. In the brief span of six years, from the time he first turned his thoughts to this bounty in 1704 to the day when the solicitation was granted, he rose from a relatively obscure churchman to one who seemed destined for a bishopric. The merit of originating the plea for remission does not, of course, belong to Swift. The matter had been agitated earlier in both England and Ireland. In February 1704 Anne promised the English clergy that she would grant them remission of the First Fruits. Thereupon the Irish clergy began to think seriously of obtaining the same benefit for themselves. In the Convocation of 1703–4—the first to be held in thirty-seven years—the two Irish Houses explored the possibilities; and in the course of the year 1704 the Bishop of Cloyne laid a petition before the queen on behalf of the Irish clergy, to which she returned 'a Gracious Answer'.[1]

At this juncture Swift revealed his interest. He had been in London when Anne announced her bounty to the Church of England; and it appears from his confident tone in a letter to Archbishop King that he had received assurances from influential personages that Ireland might be similarly favoured. It is quite possible, since at the time he was on friendly terms with such figures as Halifax, Somers, Burnet, and Peterborough. The letter to King came at the end of 1704, when Swift had returned to Ireland and King was in England. He reminded the archbishop that the queen had

---

[1] Armagh Public Library, Reeves MSS., Diurni Superioris Domus Convocationis, I, fol. 176; W. A. Phillips, *History of the Church of Ireland*, iii. 178–9; *Corresp.* i. 50.

given a favourable answer to the Bishop of Cloyne, and he suggested that King now use his credit to bring the solicitation to a successful conclusion. He added a point of special importance which would mean more for the welfare of the Irish Church than the First Fruits—that King should seek as well remission of the Crown rents on clerical holdings. 'And I am confident, with some reason', he wrote, 'that it would be easily granted. . . .'[1] The actual sum of money involved was inconsiderable, yet in the impoverished state of the Irish Church these annual levies were a hardship on the lower clergy. The First Fruits constituted a tax which before the Reformation went to the Popes. It was nominally a sum amounting to the annual value of the ecclesiastical benefice, required of every incumbent as he assumed his benefice. After the Reformation the levy was annexed to the Crown. Similarly the twentieth parts, nominally a sum, as the term implies, amounting to one-twentieth of the annual income of a benefice, was after the Reformation annexed to the Crown. But these imposts were no longer computed annually; instead they were based on a fixed valuation of each benefice. Thus the flow of money from the Irish benefices was a more or less constant sum, a figure which Swift estimated as approximately £1,000 annually.[2]

The Crown rents, which Swift refers to as 'a greater Burthen' than the other levies, had historically a different status, dating only from the Reformation. For the imposition of this burden on churchmen, Swift and other Anglican clerics held Henry VIII responsible.[3] This impost was a reservation to the Crown of certain rentals from Church and monastery lands and possessions seized at the Reformation. It remained in effect even when the seizures were granted away, whether to laymen or to the Church. In the course of time many of the lands were restored to the Church, but the Crown continued

---

[1] *Corresp.* i. 50.

[2] *Journal to Stella*, ii. 680; a table showing the revenue gained from the First Fruits and Twentieth Parts 1682 to 1702 may be found in the Reeves MS. (fol. 179) cited on p. 50, n. 2, above.

[3] See below, pp. 161 ff., for the attitude to Henry VIII.

to receive an annual rental. Thus many parishes were in effect impropriate to the Crown. The levy bore hard on some of the poor Irish livings, amounting generally—so Swift declared —'to the third Part of the reall Value of the Living; and often, a full half'.[1] Swift's desire to gain this additional favour from the queen is an instance of his alert concern for the inferior clergy, on whom the tax weighed most heavily. The Irish Convocation had actually considered the feasibility of asking for remission of the Crown rents but judged it more discreet to confine its petition to the same grant Anne had made to the English establishment. Later Swift was to take this matter into his own hands.[2]

He was well aware from the beginning that the project could be valuable to him personally as well as to the Church. There is no doubt that he derived great satisfaction from being the chief solicitor. He was glad of the opportunity; and he was justly proud of his final success in achieving the remission. For the Irish bishops, who failed to give him credit, he conceived a bitter resentment which affected his future relations with the episcopal bench. Swift's part in the enterprise falls into two periods: the first concerns his failure to achieve his purpose with the Whigs during the years 1707 to 1710; the second, his ultimate success with the Tories in 1711.

The Irish clergy had hoped much from the Duke of Ormond, who was Lord Lieutenant at the time the first petition was presented in 1704; but for reasons not apparent (Swift hints at negligence by Ormond) nothing was done.[3] Three years later the Lower House of Convocation, of which Swift was a member, urged the Upper House to make a further effort toward attaining remission. To this the Upper

---

[1] *Journal to Stella*, ii. 680; *Corresp.* i. 50, 52. For an explanation of the origin and nature of the Crown rents, and their importance in the eyes of Irish churchmen contemporary with Swift, see Wake Corresp. xiii, John Evans to Wake, 10 [Oct.] 1718 (in which Swift is interestingly mentioned); Gilbert Collection, MS. 28, King to Wake, 15 Nov. 1720; P.R.O., S.P. 63 (Ireland), 388. Swift says they amounted to 'about Two Thousand Pounds' yearly; King says £1,400.

[2] See below, p. 62.

[3] *Corresp.* i. 50, 220.

House replied that a speedy application would be made to the government.[1] At this juncture Swift began his activity as the solicitor in England, warranted to do so by the Irish bishops. He had by now consolidated his acquaintance with several powerful Whigs: Halifax; Pembroke, who succeeded Ormond as Lord Lieutenant of Ireland in April 1707; Somers, to whom Swift had dedicated *A Tale of a Tub* and who was shortly to be Lord President of the Council; and Sunderland, one of the Secretaries of State, whom Swift had met in the Moor Park days.[2] In view of such friendships Swift's usefulness was obvious, although some members of the episcopal bench were never wholly reconciled to his part in the negotiations. Archbishop King, however, had no misgivings; and he and Swift laid the plan of procedure—and with King Swift kept in constant touch. When, near the end of 1707, Pembroke crossed from Ireland to England, Swift went in the same packet. He had been commissioned, so Pembroke was informed by the archbishop, to 'put his Excellency in mind of the business of the first fruits and twentieth parts'; and Pembroke had 'desired that it might be so'.[3] This restrained statement should not conceal the fact that the entire matter was in Swift's hands, to be pursued with caution and diplomacy so as not to imperil success which, it was felt, depended in large measure upon Pembroke. There was some fear that any endeavour to enlist the aid of other statesmen might displease Pembroke. In London Swift was eager to make use of Somers and Sunderland, who he thought would be particularly serviceable; but he was warned that 'all the danger is of shocking my Lord Lieutenant'.[4] After an irksome delay of almost three months Swift received a representation concerning the First Fruits, signed by certain of the archbishops and bishops of Ireland, to be presented to Pembroke.[5] By April of 1708 there had been no progress,

---

[1] Armagh Public Library, Reeves MSS., Diurni Superioris Domus Convocationis, I, fols. 411, 431.

[2] *Prose Works*, v. 379–80; *Corresp.* i. 61.

[3] Ibid. i. 64.   [4] Ibid. i. 65.

[5] Ibid. i. 64, 72, 77. At the same time he was charged with another affair of

and Swift appealed to Somers for advice, who counselled him to go directly to Earl Godolphin, the Lord Treasurer. With the aid of Sunderland, who agreed that this was the best way to press the claims of the Irish Church, an interview was arranged between Swift and the Treasurer.[1]

The interview, which took place in June 1708, was a turning point in Swift's relations with the Whigs. It was a moment of decision, in which he had to choose whether he should retain the principles he believed beneficial to the Church of Ireland or whether he should make a sacrifice to political expediency. Godolphin brought him face to face with political realities by indicating that his ministry would support the plea for remission only if 'due acknowledgments' were received, a cryptic remark but interpreted correctly by Swift as a demand that the Irish clergy acquiesce in the intention of the ministry to remove the Test Act in Ireland as a gesture to the dissenters.[2] In fact, he had learned soon after his arrival in London that the grant of the First Fruits might depend upon this *quid pro quo*. The Sacramental Test dated in Ireland only from 1704 (2 Anne, c. 6), as compared with the English Act of 1673, yet its exclusion of all except Anglican communicants from public offices had already become a subject of bitter controversy. The chief effort of the Irish Presbyterians was directed to removing the Test clause and securing full legal toleration. The policy of the Godolphin Ministry to comfort the dissenters, which had been hinted at by Pembroke in Dublin, now began to crystallize. A month before his meeting with the Lord Treasurer Swift sent word to Ireland of the political manoeuvring. The way for removing the Sacramental Test was being prepared by addresses to the throne from dissenters in Ireland and by the Whig speaker of the Irish House of Commons, Alan Brodrick, who was in London at the moment pushing the cause. In anger

the Church: to use his endeavours to prevent action against forfeited tithes (see *Corresp.* i. 77–78, 81).

[1] *Corresp.* i. 88, 92.

[2] Ibid. i. 93. For the account which follows see ibid. i. 67, 83–86, 104, 117–18. See also J. C. Beckett, *Protestant Dissent in Ireland, 1687–1780*, pp. 46–47.

Swift wrote to Dean Stearne: 'Here has the Irish Speaker been soliciting to get the Test clause repealed by an Act here; for which I hope he will be impeached when your Parliament meets again. . . .' He expressed his belief that the Irish clergy should also prepare addresses to the throne, to make clear its opposition to any tampering with the Test; and he indicated his desire to present personally such a representation from the Dublin province. It was at this critical juncture too that he was approached by Lord Somers in a moment requiring tact since the conversation might affect not only the First Fruits but his chances for preferment in the Church. He 'desired my opinion upon it [the Test Act],' Swift wrote to Archbishop King, 'which I gave him truly, though with all the gentleness I could, because as I am inclined and obliged to value the friendship he professes for me, so he is a person whose favour I would manage in this affair of the first fruits.'[1]

The situation which Swift faced at the time of the meeting with Godolphin had a personal significance. At a compromise of his convictions he might have transmitted to Ireland, as emissary of the Irish clergy to win the First Fruits, a sympathetic view of the ministerial policy. Whatever the reception of his views in Ireland, his own acquiescence would certainly have eased his task and, it may be, led to his preferment—something seldom far from his thoughts at this period. He knew how to be circumspect. Reporting to King at one stage in the proceedings, he declared that he was 'unwilling to ruin myself in any man's favour, when I can do the public no good'.[2] But he held firm to his conviction that the Irish clergy should resist bartering its privileged position to gain the First Fruits; and in the following months he watched with irritation the delays, excuses, and tortuous evasions of the statesmen upon whom he depended to further the cause of the Irish Church. There was for a brief moment, early in November 1708, a prospect that his personal position would improve as a result of certain changes in the ministry incident on the death of Prince George, a possibility that he would act as

---

[1] *Corresp.* i. 86.   [2] Ibid. i. 105.

Queen's Secretary in the entourage of the Earl of Berkeley at Vienna. Fearing that such recognition would indicate compliance with ministerial views, he hastened to assure friends in Ireland that he would not fall in with any policy he deemed injurious to the Church. 'No prospect of making my fortune', he wrote to King, 'shall ever prevail on me to go against what becometh a man of conscience and truth, and an entire friend to the Established Church.'[1] The embassy to the Continent, however, did not materialize. But at last, near the end of November, Swift received word that the plea for remission of the First Fruits had been granted. Pembroke, who had now been succeeded by the Earl of Wharton as Lord Lieutenant of Ireland, sent notice that the grant had been made before he went out of the office. 'The thing is done', Swift wrote to Ireland; and he accepted congratulations from 'two great men in office' who assured him that he had been chiefly responsible.[2] His pleasure, however, was tempered. He had succeeded, so he thought, in the affairs of the Church but had failed dismally in his own: no preferment had been proffered, not even a chaplainship to the newly appointed Lord Lieutenant. His disillusionment about statesmen was deepened; and his uneasiness about the Church of Ireland persisted as the government continued in its policy of favouring the dissenters in Ireland. The letter to Archbishop King in which he announces the success of his mission is gloomy rather than cheerful, and filled with forebodings for the Church. 'I hope', he wrote ironically, 'you are prepared to take off the Sacramental Test, because that will be a means to have it taken off here among us; and that the clergy will be for it, in consideration of the Queen's bounty; and that men in employment will be so wise as to please the Court, and secure themselves. . . .'[3]

As it turned out, the news of the grant was, in the words of Archbishop King, 'a mouthful of moonshine'. Pembroke, it appears, had been premature in representing the matter as officially accomplished. Swift expressed his wonderment that 'a great Minister should make no difference between a grant

---

[1] *Corresp.* i. 117. [2] Ibid. i. 126 ff. [3] Ibid. i. 126-7.

and the promise of a grant'; and in March 170⅜ he received
instructions from Dublin to begin his solicitations anew with
the Earl of Wharton.[1] Swift now faced Whig leaders who were
even less willing to grant a favour to the Irish clergy without
a consideration. Pembroke, Somers, and Sunderland had not
been insistent on a concession, but the new Lord Lieutenant
stood with Godolphin in demanding 'due acknowledgments'.
Wharton's reception of Swift, which marked the beginning
of a bitter enmity, clearly indicated that the plea for remission was not to get speedy attention. Swift wrote later that
Wharton 'thought fit to receive the Motion as wholly new,
and what He could not consider (as He said) till He were
fixed in the Governmt, and till the same Application were
made to Him, as had been to his Predecessors'. This recital
of fact does not reveal that Swift felt he had been personally
affronted by Wharton. When he attempted to answer some of
Wharton's objections, the earl 'rose suddenly, turned off the
discourse, and seemed in haste; so I was forced to take my
leave'.[2] Recalling the event later, in 1714, Swift wrote that
Wharton had received him 'with sufficient coldness'. 'I
complained of this usage to Lord Somers', he adds, 'who
would needs bring us together to his house, and present me
to him; where he received me as dryly as before.'[3] Swift's
interpretation of this usage is that Wharton, committed to a
policy of removing the Test in Ireland, suspected him (quite
justly) to be the author of a tract written expressly to oppose
that policy—the anonymous *Letter concerning the Sacramental
Test* (1709).

Swift's active part in soliciting from the Whig government was now ended. He returned to Dublin early in July
1709, where the Irish clergy in Convocation had petitioned
Wharton to act upon their plea for remission of the First

---

[1] Ibid. i. 139; see also i. 149; *Journal to Stella*, ii. 679; Lewis A. Dralle, 'Kingdom in Reversion: the Irish Viceroyalty of the Earl of Wharton, 1708–1710',
Huntington Library Quarterly, xv (1952), 393–431.

[2] *Corresp.* i. 148.

[3] *Prose Works*, v. 381. Swift had his revenge for Wharton's ill usage (see *Prose
Works*, v. 7–28).

Fruits. In reporting later on Wharton's failure to heed the request, Swift refers to a quarrel between the Lower House of Convocation and Wharton's chaplain, as a result of which 'the Convocation was suddenly prorogued, and all further Thoughts about the First-fruits, let fall as desperate'.[1] That the chaplain involved was Ralph Lambert adds interest since at the time of Wharton's appointment as Lord Lieutenant, Swift himself had reasonable expectations of the chaplaincy. For Lambert it was a stepping-stone first to a deanery and then to a bishopric, by which he became Swift's diocesan. When Swift arrived in Dublin, the clergy were quarrelling over Lambert's alleged attack on the rights and powers of Convocation, published in a tract entitled *Partiality Detected* (1708). As the controversy grew warmer Wharton, already at odds with the clergy because of his endeavours against the Test Act, tried to prevent a censure of his chaplain by offering to support remission of the First Fruits.[2] His tactics split the clergy, some of whom, including Archbishop King and Dr. Peter Browne, the Provost of Trinity College, Dublin, were eager to stop the proceedings against Lambert in the Lower House of Convocation in order to gain the friendly offices of the Lord Lieutenant. When certain members of the lower clergy showed themselves determined to censure Lambert, Wharton decided to prorogue Convocation. Although he was not a member of Convocation, Swift was present in Dublin during July and August when the quarrel reached its climax; and it is not to be doubted that he watched with close attention the events which once again left the matter of the First Fruits pending.[3] A year later he was to continue in his role as solicitor.

Swift returned to England in September 1710, authorized by the bishops of Ireland to solicit the First Fruits in conjunction with the bishops of Ossory and Killaloe, who were

---

[1] *Journal to Stella*, ii. 679.

[2] Bodleian, Ballard MS. 8, fols. 17, 53, 75, 78, 99; Ballard MS. 36, fols. 55, 57. See also *Corresp*. i. 202.

[3] *Journal to Stella*, i. 127; ii. 596.

already in England for the purpose. He discovered on his arrival that the two bishops had departed and he was left alone—very likely to his gratification—to seek remission. He sought out Godolphin only to find him as before, intractable: he 'gave me a reception very unexpected, and altogether different from what I ever received from any great man in my life; altogether short, dry, and morose . . .'. So Swift wrote to Archbishop King.[1] To Stella he added one touch: '[he] received me with a great deal of coldness, which has enraged me so, I am almost vowing revenge'.[2] The Godolphin Ministry was breaking up. Changes had been made; others were momentarily expected, and Swift was counselled to suspend his activities: 'Things are in such a combustion here, that I am advised not to meddle yet in the affair I am upon. . . .'[3] It is noteworthy that he turned to Godolphin, who had already been dismissed by the queen (7 August), as had the more sympathetic Sunderland (13 June). Swift had learned that Harley was likely to be the new Lord Treasurer, but at the moment he still relied on the Whigs both for the Church and for himself. Harley, whose plan called for a coalition, a moderate government, had no wish to force the entire Whig party into opposition; and there was an expectation that Somers and Halifax among Swift's friends, as well as such other Whigs as Cowper and Newcastle, might retain power in a reconstituted government. Rumours were so thick that Swift hardly knew what to believe. In any case he appears to have had no misgivings that the changes would in the end affect his mission adversely; and he came to watch with indifference, if not with a certain satisfaction, the fall of those who had failed him previously. Late in September, in a letter to Dean Stearne, he revealed his state of mind—'I am weary of the caresses of great men out of place'—a letter which in retrospect shows that he was ready for his great change in allegiance from Whig to Tory.[4]

---

[1] *Corresp.* i. 191 ff.   [2] *Journal to Stella,* i. 6.
[3] Ibid. i. 26–27; cf. i. 15, and *passim.*
[4] *Corresp.* i. 200.

'They tell me all affairs in the Treasury are governed by Mr. Harley, and that he is the person usually applied to. . . .'[1] Swift penned these words early in September. A month later, in two interviews, Harley received him 'with the greatest marks of kindness and esteem', and immediately offered his support to the plea for remission of the First Fruits. 'In order, if possible, to have it done in this interregnum', Harley declared his willingness to present a memorial to the queen.[2] The memorial which Swift drew up for Harley, dated 7 October, is of interest for a number of its clauses. These will be discussed later; for the moment only one need be mentioned. Assuming discretionary power, he went beyond his authorized commission to solicit the First Fruits and Twentieth Parts and included also a request for the Crown rents, this with Harley's acquiescence.[3] He felt a special satisfaction that on his own initiative he might make possible a remission to the Irish Church of greater value than the combined sum of the other two imposts. Harley acted quickly, and on 21 October Swift wrote in confidence to Stella that the queen had granted the First Fruits and Twentieth Parts. The Crown rents he thought might 'follow in time'. The matter was to be kept quiet until the queen was ready to send official notice to the bishops in Ireland.[4] It was not until 4 November that Swift wrote to inform Archbishop King of his success. He was still unable to say anything of the Crown rents. 'All I know yet is, that the Bishops are to be made a corporation for the disposal of the first fruits, and that the twentieth parts are to be remitted.'[5]

Once again in a moment of successful endeavour Swift's personal satisfaction was diminished, this time by the behaviour of the Irish bishops. As we have seen, he had gone to England with only a limited commission, to act in conjunction with the two Irish bishops already engaged in the affair. Their absence had left him the sole emissary, but still with

---

[1] *Corresp.* i. 193.   [2] Ibid. i. 205.
[3] Ibid. i. 206 n., 220; *Prose Works*, v. 383.
[4] *Journal to Stella*, i. 66.   [5] *Corresp.* i. 212.

limited authorization—a point which so irked him that he
wrote a strong hint to Archbishop King that he desired more
ample powers: '. . . and I have since wondered what scruple
a number of Bishops could have of empowering a clergyman
to do the Church and them a service, without any prospect or
imagination of interest for himself . . .'. Ironically he received
these powers several days after Harley had assured him that
the grant was approved.[1] But the extension of his warrant
was followed a week later by a circumstance at which he took
umbrage: his fitness was questioned and he was in effect
ordered to begin application for remission anew in another
quarter. Unaware of the queen's approval, because Swift was
not permitted to report it sooner, the Irish bishops had
tactfully decided that the plea should be channelled through
the new Lord Lieutenant, the Duke of Ormond, who had
replaced Wharton on 19 October. Even worse, Swift was
informed that though he was still empowered to act, some of
the bishops feared that his effectiveness had been greatly
reduced by his association with the fallen Whigs. 'I am not to
conceal from you', Archbishop King wrote to him, 'that some
expressed a little jealousy that you would not be acceptable
to the present courtiers, intimating that you were under the
reputation of being a favourite of the late party in power.'[2]
Before this letter from King, written 2 November, reached
London Swift had sent one to Dublin recounting his success.
The two letters crossed in transit and the injury, so far as
Swift was concerned, was done. '. . . if my Lords the Bishops
doubt whether I have any credit with the present Ministry,
I will, if they please, undo this matter in as little time as I have
done it.' So he wrote angrily to King.[3] To Stella he expressed
his resentment more fully, a resentment that was deep and
long-lived.[4] The incident made a profound impression on
him, and if that frank contempt for bishops which later
manifested itself frequently did not have its inception at this
point, it was at least strongly reinforced. To understand his

---

[1] Ibid. i. 206, 210–11.　　　　[2] Ibid. i. 211.
[3] Ibid. i. 216–17.　　　　[4] *Journal to Stella*, i. 102–3.

reaction one must recognize the importance of his role as he himself conceived it and his pride in the fact that he had been the chief, if not the sole reason, for the success of the plea. This was a project he had nursed carefully over a period of six years, one bound up with his personal fortunes and ambitions as well as with the welfare of the Irish clergy. When the queen finally agreed to grant the bounty, Swift wrote to Stella with unmistakable gratification that 'the queen designs to signify it to the bishops in Ireland in form, and to take notice, That it was done upon a memorial from me . . .'. 'I believe', he adds, 'never any thing was compassed so soon, and purely done by my personal credit with Mr. Harley . . . When this thing is made known, tell me impartially whether they give any of the merit to me, or no. . . .'[1] He wrote to King that he was indifferent to receiving personal credit, and to Stella that he despised 'the credit of it, out of an excess of pride'; but these disclaimers may be rejected.[2] In his many subsequent references to the affair he reveals his anger and his sense of injury that he had not received his due.

The Irish House of Lords and the Convocation in formal addresses returned thanks to the queen, to Ormond, and to Harley, without any mention of Swift's part.[3] It was a particularly sore point with him that Ormond should receive credit in an affair 'wherein [he] had no more share than a cat'. On every possible occasion he insisted that the grant had been made before Ormond became Lord Lieutenant.[4] It is not wholly clear why Swift was slighted; it is only clear that the slight was deliberate. Almost certainly party differences played their part, as Archbishop King insisted, with 'the

---

[1] *Journal to Stella*, i. 66–67.

[2] *Corresp.* i. 217; *Journal to Stella*, i. 103.

[3] P.R.O., S.P. 63 (Ireland), 367; see also *Corresp.* i. 275; Armagh Public Library, Reeves MSS., Diurni Superioris Domus Convocationis, II, fol. 129, where Ormond informs the bishops of the grant on 1 Aug. 1711. The sums remitted are given as Twentieth Parts 'not above £563' and First Fruits as 'seldom amounting to above £450'. Ormond is thanked as being 'in a great measure responsible' for the grant (fol. 118). Cf. *Corresp.* i. 269–70.

[4] *Journal to Stella*, i. 334; see also i. 307, 332 f., 336, 347, 368; ii. 387–8; *Corresp.* i. 217, 275, and *passim*.

highest Tories' showing most distrust, an ironical fact in the light of Swift's new alignment with Harley. Although relations with King were subsequently to be marred, on this occasion the archbishop was one of his strongest supporters and gave him constant encouragement. In fact, his alliance with King worked to his disadvantage. The archbishop's enemies, out of a determination to thwart him, refused to do Swift justice—so King told Swift.[1] Welbore Ellis, Bishop of Kildare, was, it appears, a strong antagonist. If the word of John Evans, later Bishop of Meath, can be accepted, when Swift's friends among the bishops moved that he be thanked for his services to the Church Ellis 'oppos'd it & Spoil'd the Fine Complement much expected by yt...'.[2] The ungenerous behaviour of the bishops made Swift all the more eager to get justification and support from Harley, who promised to reply to the bishops' address of thanks and to mention Swift's part. Thus the bishops were to receive an implied rebuke for the slight. Harley, Swift wrote to Stella, was to make it known that the merit lay with him and the queen, and that the grant had been made before Ormond was appointed Lord Lieutenant.[3] For a period of two months thereafter Swift regularly mentions Harley's prospective letter to the bishops; and then, without indicating that it had been sent, he refers to it no more, either at this juncture or later. Clearly the letter was never sent. As late as 1716 the slight still rankled. In an application to the Trustees of the First-Fruits Board for funds to purchase the additional glebe land for Laracor, Swift asked that a clause in the deed refer to his instrumen-

---

[1] *Corresp.* i. 222–3, 270, 284; ii. 117–18, 339.

[2] Wake Corresp. xiii, Evans to Wake, 10 [Oct.] 1718: Queen Anne's memory, Evans wrote, is 'very Dear among many of the clergy [for remitting the First Fruits] & if Jonathan Swift is to be believ'd, all this was owing to his Zeal & interest among the Great ones with you & the Port-Corn had been added to the rest If a Strife had not arose between the then Treasurer, & (the late) D: of Ormond. The one would not allow the other to claim the merit of so good an act, For which reason it Fell to the ground—Swift's Friends (att our Board) mov'd for thanks to him for those his good Services to this Church, but our Bro: Kildare oppos'd it & Spoil'd the Fine Complement much expected by yt' &c. Cf. *Corresp.* i. 210.

[3] *Journal to Stella,* i. 336, 347–8, 368; ii. 388.

tality in securing the remission; but even this belated justice was not accorded him. Writing to Archbishop King at this date, he refers to sums of money paid to the bishops of Ossory and Killaloe for their efforts to secure remission, though both had failed. 'It seems more reasonable', he declared bitterly, 'to give Bishops money for doing nothing, than a private gentleman thanks for succeeding where Bishops have failed. I am only sorry I was not a Bishop, that I might at least have got money.'[1] By this time it was the staunch Whigs who would refuse him the accolade.

Doubtless Swift magnified 'the baseness of those bishops'. 'I remit them', he wrote to Stella, 'their First-Fruits of Ingratitude'; but he went on to see that the queen's promise was officially embodied in a warrant and to press for the remission of the Crown rents. Of this last Harley gave him hopes, but indicated that it could not be done at once. Later Swift maintained that Anne had promised to remit the Crown rents but that the untimely intervention of the bishops had prevented him from achieving this favour.[2] He may well have believed that left to his own devices he would have succeeded; but he does not mention—if indeed he was aware of it—a complication fatal to this part of his negotiations: a rivalry developed between Harley and Ormond over the Crown rents and the honour of remitting them.[3] In the end what Swift gained for the Irish Church was not an impressive sum, though the gesture from the throne was much prized.[4] The lower clergy, however, did receive certain clear benefits. They were no longer subjected to the levy of the Twentieth Parts; and the First Fruits were henceforth to be used for the purchase of glebes, manses, and impropriations. For Swift's personal fortunes the undertaking cannot be overestimated in its significance. It led to his alignment with the Tories and started the train of events which made him Dean of St. Patrick's.

[1] *Corresp.* ii. 336–7.
[2] *Journal to Stella*, i. 66, 106; ii. 387, 647; *Prose Works*, v. 383.
[3] See above, p. 65, n. 2, and Wake Corresp. xii, Evans to Wake, 10 Oct. [1716].
[4] See above, p. 53, n. 2, and p. 64, n. 3.

The memorial which Swift prepared for Harley as a basis for the plea to the queen deserves a brief comment.[1] It reveals Swift's awareness of the decayed temporalities of the Church of Ireland, such as existed in his early parishes in the north and in Meath. These temporal difficulties, though by no means limited to Ireland, made the lot of the Irish clergyman harder than that of his English counterpart. He calls attention to the many impropriations in Ireland, to the small value of most of the benefices, a prime cause of pluralism, to the churches in disrepair, to the lack of glebes and manses. He remarks also on another significant aspect of the Irish economy which greatly concerned the Church, the increase in lands devoted to grazing rather than tillage; from the standpoint of the Church this meant lands converted to a usage which greatly decreased the income from tithes. All of these were matters of concern to Swift as a parish priest, directly affecting his own welfare. They are matters as well which preoccupied him later as a dean and as a writer of Church pamphlets.

[1] Reprinted in the *Journal to Stella*, ii. 679–80.

II. *The Dean and his Chapter*

'I am Lord Mayor of one hundred and twenty houses, I am absolute lord of the greatest Cathedral in the kingdom, am at peace with the neighbouring Princes, the Lord Mayor of the city and the Archbishop of Dublin; only the latter, like the King of France, sometimes attempts encroachments on my dominions. . . .'[1] Thus Swift humorously described to Pope his jurisdiction over the Liberty of St. Patrick's, a 'realm', as he says, of one hundred and twenty houses, extending to an area of approximately $5\frac{1}{2}$ acres surrounding the cathedral.[2] He omits to mention that many of his powers he held only in conjunction with his chapter. From the founder of the cathedral and from later patrons the dean and the chapter received certain rights, confirmed by Acts of Parliament and by Letters Patent, which exempted them from the jurisdiction of the secular authorities and, perhaps even more important, from any significant jurisdiction of the archbishop. The possibilities of conflict between the Dean of St. Patrick's and the Archbishop of Dublin were increased by the fact that the Liberty of St. Patrick's was an *imperium in imperio*: it was geographically within the archbishop's Liberty of St. Sepulchre, yet it was essentially free of the archbishop's jurisdiction. Although deans before Swift had

---

[1] *Corresp.* v. 4. For jurisdictional conflict between the Liberties of the Archbishop of Dublin and the Dean of St. Patrick's, see Herbert S. Wood, ed., *The Court Book of the Liberty of St. Sepulchre* (Dublin, 1930), 'Preface'. See also Monck Mason, pp. 18 ff.

[2] *Corresp.* v. 406. See also J. H. Bernard, *The Cathedral Church of St. Patrick* (Dublin, 1940), p. 21; Monck Mason, p. 11; John C. Erck, *An Account of the Ecclesiastical Establishment subsisting in Ireland*, pp. xvi f.

clashed with their metropolitans over temporal powers in their respective liberties, he had little difficulty with King on this particular score.[1] With King's successor, John Hoadly, there was one incident which revealed Swift's determination to permit no encroachment in the Liberty of St. Patrick's. To the Seneschal of Archbishop Hoadly he penned a letter (for some reason never sent) accusing him of 'encroaching upon the Liberties of the Dean and Chapter of St. Patrick's, in a most arbitrary and unprecedented manner'. 'I resent this so highly,' he added, 'that knowing I am in the right, by having the opinion for many years of several able lawyers, I will resist by force any of your people who dare to enter our Liberty, as having any power here.'[2] The occasion was late in his career (1737) and the incident probably minor, but it is worth mentioning because it reveals the characteristic defiance, early and late, with which he met such challenges.

'Dr. Swift', wrote John Lyon, 'knew the rights and jurisdiction of his place very well . . . and would not suffer any encroachments thereupon by any person whatsoever.'[3] As dean of a great cathedral Swift had responsibilities both temporal and spiritual (realms not always easily distinguishable) which he accepted with the utmost seriousness. Certain aspects of his decanal career, hitherto either little known or misunderstood, become clearer if we have some awareness of his conception of the dignity of the dean and of the rights and powers that he possessed by precedent and custom or by charter. These are matters that preoccupied him to an unusual degree and determined how he met certain vexatious problems posed by his relationship to his chapter and to his metropolitan. On occasions he had to defend himself against the circumvention of his privileges; and if his career as dean seems to exist in an atmosphere of bickering and litigiousness, we must recognize that the very fact of controversy was a heritage from the cathedrals of the middle ages, in which the respective jurisdictions of bishops, deans, canons, and

---

[1] See below, p. 92.   [2] *Corresp.* vi. 9–10.
[3] *A Supplement to Dr. Swift's Works*, ed. John Nichols, 1779, i. xliv (small 8vo).

ministri inferiores were ill defined. Jurisdictional authority
was a matter of slow, casual development, often left un-
recorded or recorded ambiguously. The historians of secular
cathedrals present an impressive picture of clashes between
dignities, deans asserting themselves against bishops, other
dignities rebelling against deans, and an equally impressive
picture of the lesser cathedral clergy, such as vicars choral
or chantry chaplains, in prolonged dispute within their
chapters. 'A modern reader', writes a recent historian, 'might
form the impression that medieval cathedral clergy spent most
of their time in bickering.'[1] Similarly in the eighteenth
century cathedral government was often confused, uncertain,
and disputatious because of the undefined rights of its dignitaries, the dubious nature of chapter registers, the doubtful
authority of chapter acts, and the undetermined validity of
custom or precedent. The history of St. Patrick's Cathedral
reveals that it is no exception. Knowing this, we may put the
disputes during Swift's tenure as dean in historical perspec-
tive and thus avoid exaggerating their importance or attribut-
ing them entirely to his peculiar temperament.

The opportunity to clarify and defend his privileges came
early in his deanship, in 1716, in a momentous clash with his
chapter, which had challenged one of his cherished rights.
This conflict elicited from him a statement of what he called
the dean's 'great prerogatives'.[2] Though the argument cen-
tred in a single issue, it involved in actuality the exact relationship of the dean to the chapter, in substance whether he was
only *primus inter pares*, president of the chapter *ex officio*, or
whether his rights were more extensive. We are not concerned
here with the validity of Swift's claims but merely with his
conception of his privileged position. In the statement of
his rights he refers first of all to his power of visitation.[3]

---

[1] Kathleen Edwards, *English Secular Cathedrals in the Middle Ages* (Manchester,
1949), pp. viii, 26, and *passim*. See also A. Hamilton Thompson, *The English Clergy
and their Organization in the Later Middle Ages* (Oxford, 1947), ch. iii.

[2] See below, pp. 84 ff.

[3] For this and the following prerogatives, see *Corresp.* ii. 311. See also Monck
Mason, pp. 201–2.

The dean, he declared, 'visits the chapter as ordinary, and the Archbishop only visits by the dean'. This privilege was probably listed first because he conceived it to be a symbol of his jurisdiction over his chapter; and he added a reference to the archbishop's limited power of visitation in St. Patrick's because this was a symbol of his privileged exemption as dean from any superior, including his metropolitan. He next lists his power to suspend any member of the chapter, sequester the fruits of the offender's benefice, and to punish all crimes except heresy and one or two others reserved to the archbishop. The right to suspend and deprive was a drastic one which Swift exercised at least once and which he threatened against the whole body of his vicars choral soon after he became dean.[1] To these various powers he adds the sole right to call and dissolve chapter meetings, the appointment of petty canons and vicars choral, the appointment of a sub-dean in his absence (with powers limited as the dean sees fit), and a more general power which would seem to subsume a larger jurisdiction—the requirement that the other dignitaries of the chapter swear canonical obedience to him. There follow several prerogatives perhaps more strictly temporal, or at least extra-cathedral, as his right to hold court-leet, his exemption from the authority of the Lord Mayor, and a right he valued highly and used to protect the cathedral economy, his negative in the leases of Church lands and properties.

These are prerogatives of large scope, and Swift was sensitive to any assault on them and firm in his defence, not out of arrogance or a lust for power but out of respect, as he would have insisted, for order and decorum constitutionally and immemorially established. It is conceivable that he was occasionally over-zealous as a guardian of his rights, particularly at the beginning of his deanship. The independent temper which characterized his guidance of cathedral affairs manifested itself at the very outset. The incident, in which Swift was supported by his chapter, constituted an assertion of the corporate independence of the dean and canons of

[1] See below, pp. 75 f., 94.

St. Patrick's from any obligation, however slight, to the dean and canons of Christ Church, the sister cathedral in Dublin. From the time of Queen Elizabeth the members of the chapter of St. Patrick's had taken their turns in preaching at Christ Church, an irksome duty but one with the sanction of long custom and generally heeded. There had been, however, rebellion from time to time. In 1702, soon after Swift became a prebendary of St. Patrick's, the usage was reaffirmed and penalties annexed to violations.[1] Swift was himself an old offender, who had been subjected to a fine on at least one occasion,[2] a fact which perhaps influenced his decision, soon after his installation as dean, to endeavour to end the practice; but doubtless a chief reason was that in the jealous relationship between the two cathedrals the canons of St. Patrick's viewed the obligation as a form of subservience. When Swift returned to England in the autumn of 1713, he failed to provide a substitute for himself or to make provision for the chapter to continue its turns. Welbore Ellis, who as Bishop of Kildare held the deanery of Christ Church *in commendam*, wrote to England that 'the new dean of St. Patricks is bringing a new broil upon us:—There has been an ancient usage ever since Queen Elizabeths time & before for the Dean & Prebendaries of St. Patricks to take their turns of preaching at Christ church . . . the Dean [has] given out he will break this usage'.[3] To Swift he wrote a temperate protest; but this did not prevent Swift and his chapter from notifying Ellis in the following year that they proposed to make 'null and void the act for members to preach at Christ Church'.[4] In this instance Swift would seem to be culpable

---

[1] *Corresp.* ii. 74; Chap. Min. 1690–1719, 17 Mar. 170$\frac{1}{2}$.

[2] Chap. Min. 1690–1719, 22 Dec. 1702; Monck Mason, 291–2 n.

[3] B.M. Add. MS. 28935, fol. 30, to John Ellis, 20 Aug. 1713. See also B.M. Add. MS. 28935, fol. 34.

[4] *Corresp.* ii. 74; Chap. Min. 1690–1719, 10 and 17 Dec. 1714. In the meeting of 17 Dec. the chapter suspended penalties for the neglect of preaching at Christ Church until the next visitation of the dean. See also the Chapter Book of Christ Church Cathedral, p. 77, 17 Dec. 1714, in the Registry of the Archbishop of Dublin, Dublin.

in his readiness to violate that 'constant immemorial custom' which later he found useful in defending one of his own important rights.[1] The controversy came at a time when he was ready to show his contempt for the Irish bishops who had slighted him in the First Fruits endeavour. Bishop Ellis had particularly angered him, and in the circumstances he may have been all the more willing to oppose Ellis in his capacity as Dean of Christ Church. Swift's manner of breaking off the traditional practice, without giving Ellis the courtesy of a warning, suggests that a personal affront was intended.[2] This, however, was a minor conflict, of less interest than the clashes within the cathedral chapter itself.

Swift's relations with his chapter have been explored in only the most cursory fashion. Unquestionably it was expected in some quarters that he would find not only his chapter but indeed the body of the Irish clergy hostile. The currency of this viewpoint is indicated by a letter to Dr. Arthur Charlett, Master of University College, Oxford, written soon after Swift's appointment as dean was publicly announced. Charlett's correspondent wrote:

> You are not a Stranger to the Character of . . . Dr Swift, & I am perswaded that Hoadly wou'd have been a more acceptable man to the Clergy of Ireland, because he is in the point of Episcopacy more ortho- dox than the other. The Clergy of that Kingdom Detest Dr Swift because they think him an Enemy to the Order, when he liv'd among them he was a vehement Whig, even in Bad times a Whig Clergyman was there thought a Monstrous Composition, & Abhorred by the rest of the Body, & even the Station Dr Swift is now Preferr'd to, will gain him very little respect from them.[3]

Charlett, known as a great gossip—he was called The Gazetteer or the Oxford Intelligencer—carried on a wide- spread correspondence and could be expected to spread this view. But Swift's biographers early and late do little more than mention that on entering his duties as dean he

---

[1] See below, p. 86.
[2] *Corresp.* i. 219; B.M. Add. MS. 28935, fol. 30.
[3] Bodleian, Ballard MS. 36, fol. 111, Ezekiel Hamilton to Charlett, 30 Apr. 1713.

encountered opposition, which he was soon able to overcome. 'The chapter of St. *Patrick's*, like the rest of the kingdom, received him with great reluctance'—so wrote Orrery. 'They thwarted him in every point that he proposed. He was avoided as a pestilence.' This is gross exaggeration, as is Orrery's remark that Swift speedily reduced the chapter to 'reason and obedience' so that 'in a short time after his arrival, not one member of that body offered to contradict him, even in trifles'. Then, with a flourish, Orrery depicts Swift as sitting in the chapter house 'like Jupiter in the Synod of the Gods'.[1] Delany corrects Orrery by asserting that Swift was received with respect, but admits that 'the Archbishop of *Dublin*, and some of his old friends in the chapter, gave some check to that plenitude of power, which they saw plainly, he intended to assert there'. Here is more than a suggestion that Swift proposed to rule with firmness. Like Orrery, Delany sees the opposition as soon melting away. By his integrity, his public spirit, his care of the cathedral and the deanery, Swift 'soon convinced them, that he had no views beyond those of his duty'.[2] Swift did, he adds, meet with 'little obstructions in personal promotions'. To these general statements John Lyon adds one fact of worth: the opposition to Swift came from Archbishop King and King's friends in the chapter, particularly from King's nephew, Robert Dougatt, who was successively prebendary of Swords, Archdeacon of Dublin, and Precentor of St. Patrick's. Lyon too observes that Swift overcame the resistance—by steadily 'maintaining his rights'.[3] In the light of these uninformative comments, it is worth while to examine in some detail what actually occurred.

Swift was installed dean on 13 June 1713,[4] and soon after left 'party-mad' Dublin for Laracor, to recover his health and, if possible, his spirits. By the end of August, however, he had departed once again for England where the Harley

[1] *Remarks*, pp. 50–51.   [2] *Observations*, p. 88.
[3] Lyon, Hawkesworth, p. 67.
[4] Chap. Min. 1690–1719, 13 June 1713.

cabinet was 'running headlong into the greatest confusion imaginable' and where he was counted upon to help prevent disaster. In the brief sojourn in Dublin he had not closed his eyes to the realities and could read the portents of the hundred visits made to him, 'all to the Dean and none to the Doctor'.[1] And in London word soon reached him that he could expect difficulties with Archbishop King;[2] but any major differences with his canons were in the future since he was absent for a year—until the death of the queen.

The vicars choral of St. Patrick's, however, erupted immediately; and from London, in the midst of political embroilments and the dissolution of the Harley Cabinet, Swift faced the first challenge to his jurisdiction. The College of the Vicars Choral was a corporation endowed with lands and, it was presumed, the power to make leases. In December 1713 the vicars choral had under consideration a lease to the Earl of Abercorn, which they proposed to negotiate without the consent of the dean and the chapter as a test of their right of independent leasing. When word reached Swift of this contumacious action, he wrote a peremptory letter to John Worral, who as dean's vicar was the head of the vicars choral, indicating that he would have no trifling with precedent or transgression of his rights. 'I desire you will let the Vicars know that I shall to the utmost resent their presuming to make any lease without the consent of the Dean and Chapter. . . .' 'Let them know further', he added, 'that I will immediately deprive every man of them who consents to any lease without the approbation aforesaid, and shall think the Church well rid of such men who to gratify their unreasonable avarice would starve their successors.'[3] It is possible to impute an ulterior motive to Swift in this instance, to see in his resistance to the lease a desire to thwart Lord Abercorn, formerly a friend of his Whig days with whom he had had differences;[4] but there are two considerations which

[1] *Corresp.* ii. 52.   [2] Ibid. ii. 81.
[3] Ibid. ii. 113–14; see also ii. 149.
[4] *Journal to Stella*, ii. 593, 607; *Corresp.* ii. 121, 242 n.

make such suspicions unjust. He thought that the lease was disadvantageous to the Church, a factor that always weighed heavily with him; and he was determined that his rights should be respected. The latter was the crux of the matter: the vicars choral were attempting to seize unwarranted power. 'I am well instructed in my own power . . .' Swift told the vicars, a probable reference to the new charter granted the vicars choral by Charles I, in which the corporation was prohibited from making any lease of more than a year's duration without the consent of the dean and chapter.[1] Swift's legal position was sound; and it was reinforced by a cathedral statute in 1692 reaffirming that clause in the original charter which governed leases.[2]

Nevertheless the vicars choral were not deterred, nor was the conflict settled finally until Swift's return. His sub-dean, Edward Synge, kept him informed of the progress of the controversy, and Swift remained determined: '. . . I am fully resolved to call the Vicars to account to the utmost I am able'.[3] Back in Dublin in September 1714, he and the chapter took action: '. . . we have consulted a lawyer, who, as it is usual, makes ours a very good case; my desires . . . are very moderate, only to break the lease, and turn out nine singing men'.[4] The controversy dragged on.[5] In April 1715 the dean and chapter ordered a petition to be laid before the government. Six months later they refused to receive a petition from the vicars until that body acknowledged the right of the dean and chapter to confirm leases; and as late as November the dean and chapter were still waiting for a 'final answer' from the vicars. In the end the vicars capitulated. The prerogatives of the dignitaries were maintained against the assault of the 'singing men'.

When Swift returned in September 1714, trouble was in the offing. His friend Chetwode warned him in December:

[1] *Corresp.* ii. 113; Monck Mason, appendix xix, p. xliv.
[2] Monck Mason, p. 93 n.   [3] *Corresp.* ii. 149.
[4] Ibid. ii. 242.
[5] For the controversy as revealed in the Chap. Min. 1690–1719, see fols. 253–4, 259–60, 267–8 (Mar. 1715–July 1716).

'I hear you will meet with great difficulty with your Chapter.'[1]
To this Swift replied optimistically early in January, as he
laid plans for his first visitation: 'I design great things at
my visitation, and I believe my Chapter will join with me.
I hear they think me a smart Dean; and that I am for doing
good.'[2] Soon afterward he was better able to gauge the temper
of his canons. Swift himself maintained that his difficulties
with his chapter resulted from political antagonisms. The
fall of the Harley Ministry, the rise of the Whigs to power,
the tensions created by the Jacobites, his intense personal
disappointments, the seizure of his correspondence, and the
possibility that he might be taken to England to be prosecuted
or to give testimony—all these left him with a more than usual
sensitivity to opposition if it came from persons of Whiggish
persuasion; and it is likely that he mistook at times in the
following years an honest difference of opinion for politically
inspired opposition. He blamed Archbishop King for unwarranted interference in chapter affairs and for fomenting
trouble. Three years after he had assumed the deanship, Swift
wrote to King frankly accusing him of unfriendly actions.[3]
To this protest the archbishop returned a soft answer, insisting that he had an 'earnest desire and intention to live in
all good understanding with you'; but it was a letter which
at the same time indicated that he would not make concessions
or yield in his convictions.[4] The quarrel between the dean and
the archbishop was in part the result of their similar tempera-
ments, both forceful assertors of their prerogatives and not
disposed to compromise. King, whose career was filled with
litigation, was an even more jealous guardian of his rights
than Swift; and the very nature of their relationship made for
certain conflicts. As metropolitan, King had influence as
well as some restricted jurisdiction in St. Patrick's. He
possessed certain powers of appointment in the cathedral,
and he and Swift had several interrelated rights which they
collaboratively exercised. A struggle for power or advantage

[1] *Corresp*. ii. 262.　　　　　　　[2] Ibid. ii. 265.
[3] Ibid. ii. 318–21.　　　　　　　[4] Ibid. ii. 324–5.

between a dean of St. Patrick's and an archbishop of Dublin (for which there was ample precedent) was inherently present. Nor have deans and their chapters always lived in that amity befitting their vocations. But in the instance of Swift, King, and the canons of St. Patrick's it is abundantly evident that not only jealous maintenance of prerogatives but political antagonisms as well played a strong part, aggravated from time to time by the eruption of personal ambitions.

The chief bone of contention was preferment. As a staunch Whig, King sought the appointment and preferment of Whig clergymen. Swift knew, of course, that the archbishop would do everything possible to keep down Tory influences in the cathedral. With the accession of George I and a Whig ministry, King was appointed a Lord Justice of Ireland and was thus better able to make his influence felt. Sunderland's tenure as Lord Lieutenant in October 1714 opened the way for favouring 'dependable' clerics. King immediately urged that Theophilus Bolton, then prebendary of Stagonil in St. Patrick's, be nominated for the vacant chancellorship of the cathedral, 'a person', King wrote to Sunderland, 'for Learning, piety & prudence superior . . . to any in my Diocese and a most excellent preacher besides'. In addition to possessing these qualifications, Bolton's elevation to this dignity was urged for another cogent reason: 'Besides,' King tells Sunderland, 'I believe your Excellency knows Dr. Swift the Dean of my Cathedral and what I am to expect from him, and except I have such a person as Dr. Bolton in a Station in the Chapter, I am afraid my Affairs there will not go very well.'[1] The archbishop's plea was heeded; and Bolton as chancellor was consistently in opposition to Swift until his translation to the bishopric of Clonfert in 1722. On this later occasion Swift wrote to his friend Robert Cope, who was also a friend of Bolton, that the chancellor 'was born to be my

---

[1] King Corresp. (tr. Fisher), 29 Oct. 1714. See also King's letter to Addison urging Bolton's appointment, 16 Nov. 1714. To Stearne King wrote, 10 Sept. 1714: 'I have none of my clergy that I can depend on but Dr. Synge.' Bolton was installed as chancellor, 6 Dec. 1714 (see Chap. Min. 1690–1719, fol. 245).

tormentor; he ever opposed me as my subject'.[1] Earlier, in 1717, Swift had made some gesture of conciliation, but he complained to Cope that his advances had 'signified nothing; for he [Bolton] has taken every opportunity of opposing me, in the most unkind and unnecessary manner, and I have done with him'.[2] As a matter of fact, Swift was not 'done with him'; after Bolton's departure from St. Patrick's their relationship became more agreeable, nourished to a certain extent by Bolton's espousal of the Irish as opposed to the English interest.[3] But in the chapter Bolton was troublesome, where his knowledge of canon law—'the best canonist in Ireland, skilled in common law', so King described him—was useful to the archbishop's faction in the legalistic embroilments with the dean.[4]

The elevation of Bolton to the dignity of chancellor was followed immediately by a contest over a vacated benefice, with King and his supporters ranging themselves against Swift in a trial of strength that persisted for almost two years. The cure of St. Nicholas Without was then vacant, and both the archbishop and the dean had their candidates. Swift wished the benefice to go to Thomas Walls, Archdeacon of Achonry and master in the cathedral school, a friend of long standing whom he was eager to prefer. King desired the place for Philip Chamberlain, a canon of St. Patrick's who held the prebend of St. Audoen—'a good man and an excellent preacher', King wrote to Addison, then serving as Chief Secretary to the Lord Lieutenant; and the archbishop added significantly, one who 'has bin little encouraged of late by reason of his not runing in with the late Managers'.[5] Swift's opinion of Chamberlain was different. He described him as 'a man of very low parts and understanding, with a very high conceit of himself and party-mad into the bargain'.[6] The situation was complicated by conflict with the Crown, which

[1] *Corresp.* iii. 138. [2] Ibid. ii. 392–3.
[3] See below, pp. 179–80.
[4] Gilbert Collection, MS. 28, King to Wake, 13 Jan. 172½; *Corresp.* v. 157.
[5] King Corresp. (tr. Fisher), King to Addison, 18 Dec. 1714.
[6] *Corresp.* ii. 322; but see also iv. 230–1.

claimed the right of presentation, though the Dean and
Chapter of St. Patrick's maintained that the right of nomination was theirs, as in practice it actually was. With a Tory
dean at the head of the chapter, Archbishop King realized
that he could more readily win the place for his follower if
the right of the Crown were upheld, and he accordingly
urged the government to make a test of its right, this despite
the fact that he had previously accepted, at least tacitly, the
right of the chapter.[1] Nevertheless the matter was finally
determined without interference by the government. There
was, however, a long impasse. Swift was able to do nothing
for Walls without support from King, and King was unable
to proceed without support from Swift. After six months of
futile delay, Swift wrote encouragingly to Walls that the
archbishop, Bolton, and Chamberlain 'shall be deceived as
far as all my power reaches, and they shall not find me altogether so great a cully as they would willingly make me'.[2]
But a year later Walls had resigned himself to the acceptance
of another benefice if it could be obtained, and Swift was
ready to accept the compromise provided Chamberlain were
similarly given a lesser benefice.[3]

In the midst of these protracted negotiations and involved
moves Swift wrote a letter to the archbishop, protesting that
Walls (whose merit King himself recognized) should be
obstructed merely because of his friendship with a person
out of favour.

... those who are most in your confidence make it no manner of secret,
that several clergymen have lost your Grace's favour by their civilities
to me. ... And I cannot but think it hard, that I must upon all occasions
be made uneasy in my station ... and this openly acknowledged by those
who say they act under your Grace's direction. ... I regard not the
consequences as far as they are intended to affect myself, yet your
Grace may live to lament those which from thence may happen to the
Church.[4]

---

[1] King Corresp. (tr. Fisher), King to Addison, 18 Dec. 1714.
[2] *Corresp.* ii. 279.   [3] Ibid. ii. 315.
[4] Ibid. ii. 319 ff. King had earlier been willing that Walls should have St.

This letter, written in June 1716, transcends the single affair of Walls and reviews the deterioration in the relations between Swift and King. Swift wrote with dignity and restraint, asserting that he could not be effective in his station in the Church if he was to be constantly thwarted by the archbishop and his friends in the chapter. He indicated clearly his awareness that party differences were at the root of the opposition, and by implication he made a plea for friendlier relations that the interest of the Church might be served. In a letter to Walls at the same time Swift disclaimed any personal malice against Chamberlain, who was to him, quite obviously, a symbol of the archbishop's bid for power in the chapter. 'My ends', he told Walls, 'were to make as good a bargain for you as I could, and to have some regard to my own credit.' At the same time he remarked, 'in my conscience, I think Mr. Chamberlain doth not deserve such a living nor is equal to such a cure.'[1]

Archbishop King's answer to Swift was unyielding with respect to the point at issue but friendly and conciliatory in tone. He regretted that some persons had been 'very industrious to sow dissension between you and me', and he expressed his earnest desire 'to live in all good understanding with you, as being sensible it is necessary for our common quiet and good'.[2] Like Swift, King was a man of strong convictions who believed his actions best calculated to serve the Church. Their mutual protestations on this occasion cleared the atmosphere at least briefly—and outwardly. Both saw the need for a *modus vivendi*, yet in the end it was Swift who made the concessions. The matter was settled to the satisfaction of the archbishop and his supporters by the appointment of Chamberlain to the cure he coveted; Walls was consoled with a minor rectory. It is clear that Swift saw the futility of fighting further in this instance, and

Nicholas Without and Chamberlain, St. Luke's; but he gave way, so he told Swift, to Chamberlain's insistence on having St. Nicholas Without. Nevertheless the political motive seems to have been decisive (see King Corresp., tr. Fisher, King to Addison, 18 Dec. 1714; *Corresp.* ii. 319, 323, 324).

[1] Ibid. ii. 322 f.   [2] Ibid. ii. 324–5.

soon afterward he wrote to King, then in England, in a friendly spirit, referring to Chamberlain's election to St. Nicholas Without. King's reply was equally friendly, expressing his gratefulness to Swift for yielding in the matter and his wish that the two might work in harmony. Yet neither man was quite able to master his political passions. Swift ended his otherwise cordial letter with a barbed thrust at another of the archbishop's supporters in the chapter, and King, apparently in retaliation, closed his reply with a political insinuation which ruffled Swift and to which he made a forceful reply.[1] The clergyman to whom Swift alluded was Charles Whittingham, who had recently come into the chapter as prebendary of Mulhuddart, to the disappointment of Swift. He had sought this prebend for his friend Walls, only to see it filled by one who would strengthen the opposition.[2] The archbishop, who saw enough merit in Whittingham to appoint him Archdeacon of Dublin in 1720, had described the new prebendary to the Archbishop of Canterbury as a deserving man 'who had managed with such Prudence, good Sense and Courage, that has contributed to keep the whole Country firm in his Majesty's Interest in the Worst of Times'.[3] Other Whig members of the episcopal bench, similarly aware of Whittingham's dependability, joined King in praising him to the Archbishop of Canterbury.[4]

Whittingham's appointment appears to have been part of a concerted attempt to nullify any possible Tory influence in cathedral affairs. In the previous year Swift had written lightly to Pope that one of his amusements was 'defending my small dominions against the Archbishop';[5] but he was

[1] *Corresp.* ii. 336, 338, 340, 343, 348–9. But King seemed to be genuinely grateful to Swift for yielding (see Armagh Public Library, MS. h. II. 19, King to Bolton, 18 Aug. 1716).

[2] *Corresp.* ii. 319.

[3] Gilbert Collection, MS. 28, King to Wake, 8 May 1716.

[4] Ibid. Synge to Wake, 9 Oct. 1716. See also Wake Corresp. xii, Evans to Wake, 31 Mar. 1717: '. . . a Person of very good Learning & Sence, Honest, Bold, & Active att all times . . . besides he is an Englishman, which (without a jest) is a very serious thing'.

[5] *Corresp.* ii. 288.

increasingly perturbed at King's effectiveness in filling the prebends of St. Patrick's with men who would do his bidding. The archbishop had not missed a single opportunity. Shortly before Whittingham's appointment King took another step which increased his power in chapter affairs. He revived the prebend of Tymothan which had been dormant from the time of Queen Elizabeth.[1] The prebend was in his gift, and he was wholly within his rights in restoring it, yet he could not have been indifferent to the advantage gained from an additional vote in a chapter that was at the moment evenly divided. Swift and his supporters protested, but to no avail; and after the fact Swift could do nothing more than frankly accuse the archbishop of reviving the dormant prebend 'on purpose to oppose me'.[2]

Robert Dougatt, the nephew of King, is the person usually named by the biographers as the leading opponent of Swift in chapter affairs and ready to challenge his jurisdiction.[3] When Swift was made dean, Dougatt was prebendary of Swords, having been appointed to that stall in 1709; but in 1715 he was preferred to a more important station through the offices of the archbishop.[4] He became the Archdeacon of Dublin, a dignity which made him a diocesan officer and a member of both Christ Church Cathedral and St. Patrick's. Four years later he was elevated even higher, to Precentor of St. Patrick's, the dignity next in order to the dean. Swift apparently had some respect for Dougatt—at least at the beginning. He appointed him subdean in February 171$\frac{5}{8}$; and his only extant reference to Dougatt in a period when the chapter was being stubborn and exasperating is less bitter than sorrowful.[5] Nevertheless in the chapter meetings of the years 1715 and immediately following Dougatt, in collaboration with Bolton, was troublesome, and these two at times prevailed in the chapter. Late in 1715 Dougatt proposed

[1] Lawlor, *Fasti*, p. 178.
[2] *Corresp.* ii. 320, 322; Chap. Min. 1690–1719, 2 June 1716.
[3] Lyon, Hawkesworth, p. 67. [4] See Lawlor, *Fasti*, pp. 58, 80, 160.
[5] Chap. Min. 1690–1719, 23 Feb. 1715; *Corresp.* ii. 323.

Bolton as proctor to represent the chapter in Convocation, and Bolton was duly elected.[1] With significant regularity these two served on chapter committees or were appointed to make investigations into chapter affairs. The pattern which internal cathedral affairs followed is revealed by a few events of the year 1716. In March Swift proposed a member of the chapter as proctor for the ensuing year, but his choice was voted down by a count of eight to six.[2] He then proposed himself, only to be rejected by the same count.[3] The presence of only fourteen canons at this meeting leaves a false impression of the division within the chapter. Actually Swift could muster more votes, as was evidenced at the next meeting when a second person he proposed was elected by a vote of ten to nine.[4] Nevertheless, only the fact that Swift's nominee voted for himself carried the proposal. It is perhaps not a matter of mere coincidence that Archbishop King decided about this time to revive the dormant prebend of Tymothan. With the division in the chapter so even, a single additional vote could be decisive. These trials of strength were mingled with other activities which doubtless Swift viewed as deliberate attempts to oppose his jurisdiction, as, for example, Bolton's protest against the form of citation and summons by which Swift ordered members of the cathedral to appear at the chapter house.[5] Bolton, who was well versed in these matters, may have innocently desired to abide by precedent; but his strict legalistic attitude was open to another interpretation.

It was also in 1716 that members of the chapter made their most serious threat to Swift's jurisdiction. This challenge inspired two important letters to Francis Atterbury, with whom he had become friendly in the days of the Harley Ministry. This particular controversy was instigated, Swift declared, by Edward Synge, formerly Chancellor of St. Patrick's, whom Swift had opposed for the deanery when

---

[1] Chap. Min. 1690–1719, 10 Nov. 1715.
[3] Ibid.
[5] Ibid. 26 July 1716.

[2] Ibid. 17 Mar. 171$\frac{5}{6}$.
[4] Ibid. 24 Mar. 171$\frac{5}{6}$.

Stearne was elected by the chapter in 1705.[1] Synge, a recent Whig appointment to the archbishopric of Tuam, incited King, who in turn influenced a member of the chapter to challenge the power of the dean's veto. To Swift the incident seemed clearly to have risen out of political partisanship.

I am here [he wrote to Atterbury] at the head of three and twenty dignitaries and prebendaries, whereof the major part, differing from me in principles, have taken a fancy to oppose me upon all occasions in the Chapter-house; and a ringleader among them has presumed to debate my power of proposing, or my negative, though it is what the deans of this Cathedral have possessed for time immemorial, and what has never been once disputed.[2]

Atterbury, at this time the Bishop of Rochester and Dean of Westminster, was a person of extensive experience in capitular conflict. Particularly he could view the controversy from the vantage of a dean, having been earlier Dean of Carlisle and of Christ Church, Oxford. Swift appealed also to John Younger, Dean of Salisbury, because he believed that the constitution of St. Patrick's was derived from that of Sarum.[3] The two deans cautioned him against pressing his powers too far even though he had the support of statutes or custom. They informed him that a dean of Sarum possessed no extraordinary power or privilege beyond that of the other canons or residentaries—he was the first of the chapter, it is true, but his presence was 'not necessary toward the dispatch of any one capitular act'. Swift had expected, or at least hoped, to hear that the constitution of Sarum held a dean's consent requisite before an act of the chapter could be formally ratified, or, in other words, that he possessed a power of negative. Atterbury gave him no encouragement: '. . . a nice search into the peculiar rights of the dean of Sarum will be needless, if not mischievous to you'.[4]

The debates in the chapter and possibly Atterbury's

---

[1] *Corresp.* iii. 71.   [2] Ibid. ii. 306–7.

[3] Swift's correspondence with Younger is lost, but he mentions writing to Younger and receiving a reply (see *Corresp.* ii. 307; iii. 72).

[4] *Corresp.* ii. 308 ff.; iii. 72.

answer spurred Swift on to a closer investigation of the constitution of St. Patrick's and the rights and privileges of the dean. In acknowledging Atterbury's letter he introduced a new factor which he believed gave a firmer support to his right of negative. The constitution of St. Patrick's, he told Atterbury, was indeed modelled on that of Sarum, but the prerogatives of the dean had been defined and enlarged by 'several subsequent grants, from Popes, Kings, Archbishops, and Acts of Parliament'. He then listed these prerogatives as evidence that a dean of St. Patrick's has an unusual range of rights and privileges beyond other members of the chapter. These he conceived to be later enactments, and to be so extensive in their nature as to comprise the dean's right to propose and to negative, a right which he defends also as being based on 'constant immemorial custom'. Nevertheless Swift does not state that the subsequent grants of power to the dean specifically name the right of proposal and negative. His contention, it appears, is that such a right is an implied one. He was not so convinced of his position that he was ready to risk litigation or any final determination of the point if that could be avoided; and he heeded the admonition of Atterbury: 'I shall, as your Lordship directs me,' he wrote to the latter, 'do my utmost to divert this controversy as much as I can.'[1] Nor did his opponents in the chapter feel that they were on more secure grounds, since they too dropped the discussion without pressing for a final answer. In fact, they had never directly challenged the dean's right of negative as an ordinary procedure. They had approached the matter obliquely by 'arguing the ill consequences which might follow if it [the dean's negative] had no exceptions'.[2] As time passed, Swift came to feel strongly convinced that his view was right. In 1721, when the Dean of Ossory, engaged in a similar conflict, appealed to him for advice and encouragement, he replied confidently: 'It is an infallible maxim, that not one thing here is done without the dean's consent.' He counselled the Dean of Ossory to argue that his constitution was

[1] *Corresp.* ii. 311.   [2] Ibid. iii. 71.

modelled on St. Patrick's, '... if they allow that, I will provide
you with power and privilege enough'.[1]

In 1717, after Swift had been dean for four years, the
chapter lines were clearly drawn and the alignment against
him had increased in strength. In July of that year he wrote
again to Atterbury, complaining that opposition 'in everything relating to my station, is made a merit in my Chapter'.[2]
Still, he was now facing the situation more philosophically,
and even with a wry sense of humour. Shortly before, he had
written to Archbishop King concerning the preferment of
one of the prebendaries then under consideration: '[I] shall
be glad to proceed with your Grace's approbation, which is a
less compliment, because I believe my Chapter are of opinion
I can hardly proceed without it.'[3] The clergyman referred to
was Robert Howard, who held the stall of Maynooth in St.
Patrick's and was now seeking the cure of St. Bride's Church,
which was in the gift of the dean and chapter of St. Patrick's.
Howard also was vicar of St. Anne's Church, Dublin, which
he proposed to vacate for St. Bride's. An eighteenth-century
clergyman as a matter of course kept a watchful eye on the
health of any of his brethren whose benefices were worth
coveting; and, as the incumbent of St. Bride's lay dying, the
potential successors and those empowered to dispose of the
benefice, Swift included, began to lay plans. 'It is a tedious
thing to wait for Dead mens Shoes; Mr. Duncan [the incum-
bent] I hear is better than he has been this many Years'—so
Archbishop King, then in England, wrote to a hopeful clergyman in April 1717.[4] But soon afterward Robert Howard was
able to inform King that 'Mr. Duncan has at last left us'; and
Swift himself, although absent from Dublin, took note of
Duncan's death, and reported that he had had 'a great increase
of disinterested correspondents ever since'.[5] The involved
negotiations which now began for the filling of this benefice
are a further revelation of Swift's relationship to his chapter

[1] Ibid. iii. 72.   [2] Ibid. ii. 397.   [3] Ibid. ii. 383.
[4] King Corresp. King to Samuel Molyneux, 1 Apr. 1717.
[5] Ibid. Howard to King, 13 Apr. 1717; *Corresp.* ii. 383.

and the extent to which the Whig bishops injected themselves into chapter affairs. In this instance the Archbishop of Tuam, as well as Archbishop King, made his influence felt.

Earlier Swift's opinion of Robert Howard had been highly favourable. In 1715 he had occasion to recommend him to Bolingbroke as 'a Senior Fellow of our College & more than all, one of my Prebendaryes . . . worthy to be recommended even to you'.[1] Two years later, however, he regarded Howard with less favour as a result of the latter's joining with King's supporters in the chapter. The prebendary of Maynooth had not taken the lead in opposing Swift. He had been cautious in his policy of restrained opposition, as he himself explained to the archbishop: '. . . tho I was never a favourite [with the dean], I have always been upon good terms with him; I know some would choose to give him unnecessary Opposition; but I think that if wee are steady in pursuing our point, I think the fairer we carry it the better'.[2] On Swift's return to Dublin Howard requested his support for the vacancy. Although not enthusiastic, Swift was willing to consent, on the principle, he wrote to King, that since he was unable to prevail with the chapter to appoint anyone he proposed, he must choose from among those he least disliked one whom the chapter would approve.[3] But he attached a condition to his support. He himself must be permitted to name a successor to the vacated cure of St. Anne's.[4] This insistence was designed to oblige Swift's friend Samuel Dopping, a convinced Tory for whom he had great esteem, by appointing his brother, the Reverend Anthony Dopping, to that cure; or, failing that, Swift wished to secure St. Anne's for the Reverend Thomas Forbes, rector of Dunboyne, who formerly through Swift's influence had been a chaplain to the Duke of Shrewsbury when the duke was Lord Lieutenant of Ireland in 1713. In the meantime working busily and effectively Howard had secured the more

[1] An unpublished letter in the possession of Lord Rothschild, 1 Mar. 171⅘; see also *Corresp.* ii. 267–8.

[2] King Corresp. Howard to King, 4 June 1717; cf. Howard to King, 9 May 1717.

[3] *Corresp.* ii. 374–5.

[4] King Corresp. Howard to King, 18 June, 4 July 1717; *Corresp.* ii. 316, 374.

valuable support of Archbishop King, but not until he had addressed to the absent prelate several letters strongly affirming his deep devotion to Whig principles, his personal loyalty to King, and—as added bait—a willingness to present to the benefice of St. Anne's anyone the archbishop named (the incumbent had the right of presentation in this instance).[1] The complete homage to himself and his principles won the archbishop; in addition, it meant that he could ensure the appointment of a dependable Whig to St. Anne's. From England, King indicated to Dougatt that Howard should be supported for St. Bride's.[2] Similarly, Howard was to receive support from another influential quarter, the Archbishop of Tuam, whose son was a prebendary of St. Patrick's and was eligible for the cure of St. Anne's. It is not clear to what extent the Archbishop of Tuam was influenced by the possibility that his son would succeed to St. Anne's if Howard received St. Bride's. Howard had suggested this possibility to King, who in turn is presumed to have influenced the Archbishop of Tuam. In any event, this prelate was active. 'The Archbishop of Tuam', Howard wrote to King, 'has very kindly assisted me to the utmost in my Application to the Chapter, he thinks the Matter sure from the Disposition he finds amongst the Members, and says the Dean will make no unnecessary Opposition.'[3]

Swift, of course, was unaware of Howard's obsequious courting of the archbishops. He was wholly ignorant that the right of presentation to St. Anne's had been bargained away. When he mentioned to Howard that he wished, in return for his support, to name the successor to St. Anne's, that cleric shrewdly returned no answer.[4] In the midst of

---

[1] King Corresp. Howard to King, 3, 9 May 1717. At first, King had been willing that Anthony Dopping should be appointed (see King Corresp. King to Howard, 2 Mar. 171$\frac{6}{7}$; King to Samuel Molyneux, 1 Apr. 1717; *Corresp.* ii. 373, 378).

[2] King Corresp. Howard to King, 3, 9 May 1717.

[3] Ibid. Howard to King, 9 May 1717. See also Howard to King, 2 Feb. 171$\frac{6}{7}$, 13 Apr., 4 July, 1717.

[4] Ibid. Howard to King, 4 July 1717.

the negotiations Swift turned recalcitrant for a moment. To Archdeacon Walls he wrote:

I have had abundance of letters about St. Bride's, and now Dr. Howard gravely writes to me that the Archbishop of Dublin has declared for him, and hopes I will consent. Nothing could put me more against him than the Archbishop's declaring, and I am now resolved to oppose it as long as I can.[1]

Nevertheless he realized that it was to his advantage to support Howard, and he added: 'Not but that next to a friend it is most to my interest that Howard should have it, because he hath something to give up which I may bestow [on] a friend; I mean the advowson of a town living. . . .' In the end it was Swift himself who proposed to his chapter the appointment of Howard to St. Bride's, and the proposal was duly carried.[2] Yet curiously Howard continued to hold St. Anne's for another three years, and even then neither of Swift's choices was appointed.[3] It is not clear why he yielded. Apparently there was a compromise; but one can hardly doubt that in the final arrangements he gained some kind of *quid pro quo* which does not appear.

If further proof is needed of the validity of Swift's assertions and complaints concerning the alignment within his chapter and the unabashed political manœuvring, the situation with respect to St. Bride's offers indubitable evidence. In his letters to King, Howard relied chiefly on his political reliability for winning that prelate over: he would be valuable, he promised, in keeping 'all things steady for the present Interest, for which I have struggled to the utmost of my power'.[4] 'It was your Grace's Measures and Principles that I always thought right. . . .'[5] But he also urged the importance of enlarging 'the Numbers of your Grace's friends in the

---

[1] *Corresp.* ii. 386.   [2] Chap. Min. 1690–1719, 26 Nov. 1717.
[3] See 'Precentors of Christ Church' in *Fasti of Christ Church*, compiled by J. B. Leslie, typescript in Rep. Church Body, Dublin. See also 'John Madden', in J. B. Leslie's *Dublin Clergy Succession List*, in Rep. Church Body. Swift was not so determined that he would avoid a compromise (see *Corresp.* ii. 386).
[4] King Corresp. Howard to King, 2 Feb. 171$\frac{6}{7}$.
[5] Ibid. 9 May 1717.

Parishes of the Citty', and of adding to his Grace's majority in the Cathedral.[1] In fact, King hardly needed additional supporters, as Swift wryly observed, and as Howard clearly confirmed. 'Your favour', he wrote to the archbishop, 'will give me an indisputable Majority in the Chapter, and I know the Dean will not struggle with such a Difficulty; Your Grace's friends in the Chapter reserve themselves till they know your pleasure . . .'.[2] The extent of King's dominance is revealed by Howard's assertion that 'your friends are near two thirds'.[3]

Since the Whigs remained in power during Swift's tenure as dean, he continued to be an irritated spectator of political intrigue and preferment as various members of his chapter ascended to the episcopal bench; and to the end he regularly complained that he could not get preferment for worthy clergymen among his canons because of party. Quite obviously those biographers who report that he soon reduced his chapter to obedience or that he was able to overcome the political conflicts within the cathedral have overstated the case. It is true that Swift was always restive in the face of opposition; and it may be that after 1720 certain of his complaints have less justification. Nevertheless, in any consideration of his relationship to his chapter his outbreaks of impatience and anger have significance. There was, for example, 'an ugly depending Chapter business' (to use his phrase) in 1723, touching his endeavour to get the cure of St. Bride's, soon to be vacated, for Robert Grattan, one of his prebendaries for whom he had great affection. To Archdeacon Walls he wrote:

There is a long difficulty, that concerns the Government, the Archbishop, the Chapter, the Dean, Dr. Howard, and Robin Grattan, and I know not whether it will be determined in a month. All my design is, to do a job for Robert Grattan, but the rest have their different schemes and politics, too deep and too contemptible for me to trouble myself about them.[4]

[1] Ibid. 3 May 1717.
[3] Ibid. 3 May 1717.
[2] Ibid. 13 Apr. 1717.
[4] *Corresp.* iii. 157–8.

This 'ugly business' concerned the vacancies to be filled by reason of the translation of Bolton from St. Patrick's to the bishopric of Clonfert. The usual Whig and Tory manœuvring took place within the chapter, this time with better results for Swift. The chancellorship vacated by Bolton went to Robert Howard, now a favourite of the government. This was no improvement in Swift's eyes, but in the succession of removals he succeeded in obtaining St. Bride's, left vacant by Howard, for Grattan and the prebend of Maynooth for Samuel Holt, of whom he thought well.[1] Six of the archbishop's faction entered their dissent to the appointment of Grattan; and Robert Dougatt, now precentor through King's influence, and Whittingham made formal protests against Swift's assuming to himself alone the right to nominate in all elections, a violation, they maintained, of his oath and his privilege.[2]

An era of better feeling between Archbishop King and Swift set in after the controversy over Wood's coinage in 1724. The two were firmly united on this issue and on another matter of great importance to both, their opposition to the government's policy of filling Irish benefices with clergymen from England instead of preferring those born and educated in Ireland.[3] King found Swift an increasingly satisfactory neighbour and churchman for whom on occasions he could find words of praise. In 1727 their agreeable relationship was endangered momentarily by a brief quarrel over their respective rights when King at his visitation of St. Patrick's demanded a proxy for Swift's absence—'a thing wholly new and unheard of', Swift wrote to King from England, 'let the consequences be what they will, I shall never comply with it'. He prepared for legal defence, declaring that he would 'spend a hundred or two pounds, rather than be enslaved, or betray a right which I do not value threepence, but my successors

---

[1] P.R.O. Ireland, British Departmental Corresp., vol. ii, the Duke of Grafton to the Lord Justices, 29 Nov. 1722; *Corresp*. iii. 138, 157-8; see also *Corresp*. ii. 316, 386; King Corresp. Whittingham to King, 28 Aug. 1722; King to Edward Hopkins, 1 Oct. 1722.

[2] Chap. Min. 1720-63, 12 Mar. 172$\frac{2}{3}$.   [3] See below, pp. 169 ff.

may'.[1] But the matter was dropped. The archbishop's kindlier attitude may in part account for the reduced friction within the chapter. At the same time the number of his loyal supporters had been reduced by translation to deaneries and bishoprics. Nevertheless, in 1727, he could still rely, among others, on three dignitaries of the cathedral—Dougatt, Whittingham, and Edward Synge, the last of whom became chancellor at his recommendation early in that year.[2] The atmosphere was by no means wholly serene. In 1728 Swift wrote to Pope that 'There might be a Lutrin writ upon the tricks used by my Chapter to tease me.'[3] By 1729 he had not much reason to complain. There were, indeed, minor matters. A slight difference with Synge and Whittingham in May[4] was followed in July by another attack on his rights. In his absence, John Wynne, Dougatt, and Whittingham ordered a committee to investigate 'a Right in the Dean which the Chapter have always denied'—his privilege of proposing candidates for benefices in the gift of the dean.[5]

After 1730 Swift is strangely quiet concerning his chapter. King's death in 1729 brought John Hoadly to the archbishopric of Dublin, and with him Swift appears to have had no unusual friction after an initial clash.[6] Bolton's elevation to the see of Clonfert in 1722, Howard's to Killala in 1727, and Synge's to Clonfert in 1730, were followed by the death of Dougatt in 1730. This removed a majority of the more forceful spirits among his opponents in the chapter. Although Wynne and Whittingham succeeded respectively to the precentorship and the archdeaconry of Dublin, Swift's relations with Wynne greatly improved in the following years, and his friend and future biographer, Patrick Delany, replaced Synge as chancellor. In the course of the years younger

---

[1] *Corresp.* iii. 390–2, 393, 400.
[2] King Corresp. King to Carteret, 12 July 1726; Lawlor, *Fasti*, p. 65.
[3] *Corresp.* iv. 34.   [4] Chap. Min. 1720–63, 23 May 1729.
[5] Ibid. 30 July 1729. Swift, who apparently read the chapter minutes on his return, drew a finger pointing to the entry and wrote in the margin: 'Mem[d] The Dean then abs[t].'
[6] *Corresp.* v. 71 n. See also *Corresp.* iv. 175; v. 4. See below, Ch. IV, p. 185.

men, as James King, Robert and John Grattan, John Towers, and Francis Wilson, moved into the prebends, to become his friends or supporters. In 1731 Swift proposed himself as proctor for the ensuing year. It will be recalled that he had proposed himself in 1716 and had been rejected. This time he was elected by unanimous consent.[1] Later in the year his proposal of John Grattan for the cure of St. Nicholas Without carried easily, in sharp contrast to his long and futile struggle in 1715–16 to obtain that benefice for Archdeacon Walls.[2] Relatively peaceful years followed within the chapter, with only occasional friction. The vicars choral gave a little trouble individually and in their corporate capacity. They had to be cautioned again in 1731, as at the very beginning of Swift's tenure, against giving leases or taking fines without the consent of the dean and chapter.[3] He found it necessary to deprive three of them in 1732 for contumacious behaviour.[4] One of these was restored later after 'declareing his Sorrow and repentance for the neglect of his Duty and for setting up an illegall Claim and rebelliously defending a Law suite against the Dean and promising Obedience to all the Dean's lawfull Commands for the future'.[5] Probably Swift's last official act as dean concerned the fractious vicars choral, appropriately since they had been the first to challenge his decanal jurisdiction. In January 174$\frac{1}{2}$, only a few months before the inquiry into his sanity, he ordered his chapter 'to preserve the dignity of my station, and the honour of my Chapter' by forbidding the vicars to appear in public musicals. He denied the report that he had given a licence to 'certain vicars to assist at a club of fiddlers in Fishamble Street'; and in characteristic phraseology he required his subdean and chapter 'to punish such vicars as shall ever appear there, as songsters, fiddlers, pipers, trumpeters, drummers, drummajors, or in any sonal quality, according to the flagitious

---

[1] Chap. Min. 1720–63, 17 Mar 173$\frac{0}{1}$. [2] Ibid. 20 May 1731.
[3] Ibid. 20 Nov. 1731.
[4] Ibid. 28 Nov. 1732 and following meetings.
[5] Ibid. 30 Jan. 173$\frac{4}{5}$.

aggravations of their respective disobedience, rebellion, per-
fidy, and ingratitude'.[1]

For practical purposes Swift ceased to be dean in 1739.
In July of that year he appointed John Wynne subdean, 'being
oftentimes as we now are not able by Reason of sickness
to be present and personally to preside in the Chapter'.[2]
It was in this year that the chapter at its own expense ordered
his portrait to be painted by Bindon and hung in the deanery.[3]
On occasions in the years 1739 to 1741 the chapter meetings
were transferred from the chapter house to the deanery in
order that Swift might preside or at least be officially present.
The last such occasion was 17 March 174$\frac{1}{2}$. The date is not
without significance. It is the festival day of St. Patrick, patron
saint of the cathedral; and in better times Swift used to entertain the chapter at the deanery. His last reference to this
entertainment was on 17 March 17$\frac{39}{40}$, when he penned a
not uncharacteristic comment: 'A Patrick's Day: our annual
feast when I shall be overloaded with my Chapter, but without
any expense.'[4] At the chapter meeting of 17 March 174$\frac{1}{2}$,
Swift did not preside; and the state of his health was such that
he may well have been insensible to the date or the occasion—
and if not insensible, quite indifferent.[5] The members of the
chapter apparently concluded that this was an appropriate
time to end even the pretence that he could share in their
proceedings. Thenceforth they met in their chapter house
without their dean.

[1] *Corresp.* vi. 220–1.
[2] Chap. Min. 1720–63, 18 July 1739. The original instrument with Swift's
signature and seal, dated 30 April 1739, is in the Pierpont Morgan Library.
[3] Chap. Min. 1720–63, 17 Mar. 173$\frac{8}{9}$.
[4] *Corresp.* vi. 154.
[5] Swift presided for the last time on 11 Dec. 1741.

III. *Temporalities*

An ecclesiastical corporation has its existence in two worlds, the spiritual and the temporal. However widely separated these may be in theory, they constantly interact and impinge one upon the other. As F. W. Maitland remarked, 'the attempt to draw an unwavering line between "spiritual" and "temporal" affairs is hopeless'.[1] To an eighteenth-century clergyman their interdependence was a matter of course. Church temporalities in the form of lands and tithes were his constant concern; and no small part of his time and energy was devoted to guarding these possessions because he conceived that upon ecclesiastical possessions depended not merely the physical welfare of the individual clergyman but the spiritual functioning of the Church as a whole. The poverty of the Church of Ireland, the deplorable state of its temporalities—this was often cited as the reason for its spiritual failure, particularly for the flourishing of Catholicism and the encroachments of dissent. It is hardly surprising that the correspondence of the clergy, as well as much of their published writing, leaves an impression that they were more concerned with profitable leases and the collection of tithes than with the saving of souls. Swift's awareness of such matters, as we have already observed, came early in his career from the bleak temporal aspects of his first benefice in the north of Ireland. We have seen too his endeavours to improve the financial structure of the Church of Ireland by securing remission of the First Fruits; and as ordinary of a

[1] F. W. Maitland, *Roman Canon Law in the Church of England* (London, 1898), p. 56.

cathedral worth, by his own estimate, 'in preferments and real estates above ten thousand pounds a year', he displayed a remarkable determination to maintain and improve the temporal welfare of his foundation.[1] He believed that the clergy, as makers of leases and as landlords, played a vital part in the economic life of the nation, that a Church temporally strong nourished the economy of Ireland. Thus we find him spending an incalculable amount of time on 'ecclesiastical economics'. This aspect of his career is best revealed in a series of tracts and poems, written between 1723 and 1736, concerning bishops' leases, tithes, clerical residence, and related matters. These works were mainly topical, written in part to attack pending legislation in the Irish parliament: '. . . some effects of anger on public grievances here, which would be insignificant out of this kingdom'—so Swift described certain of them to Pope.[2] Yet they should not be undervalued. They are, in the first instance, valuable for an understanding of Swift's role as a vigorous polemicist in the interest of the Church and, so he felt, Christianity. At the same time they touch perennial problems affecting the Church as a temporal organization, as well as conflicts deep rooted in Irish life.

I. THE CLERICAL LANDLORD

The first of Swift's tracts to present a significant treatment of Church temporalities was *Some Arguments against enlarging the Power of Bishops in Letting of Leases, with Remarks on some Queries lately published*, written in 1723. Ironically this tract reveals him in an unaccustomed guise as a defender of the episcopal bench. It is doubtful that he would have come to the aid of the individual Whig bishops, but the issue in this instance transcended, he believed, particular clergymen and threatened the inheritances of the Church as a whole. The conflict that inspired his pamphlet was economic primarily, between the churchmen on one side and the landlords (i.e.

---

[1] *Corresp.* iv. 113; cf. iv. 143.   [2] Ibid. iv. 307.

landowners) and their representatives in the Irish House of
Commons on the other. Conflict between laity and clergy
was, of course, nothing new in Ireland. As the Bishop of
Elphin wrote to the Archbishop of Canterbury: the gentry
are 'perpetually nibbling at our constitution';[1] but about 1720
the Irish bishops perceived in the House of Commons an
increased hostility to their interest. Swift himself took note of
this at the time, in a scathing reference to the greed of 'our
Country Landlords' and of their endeavours to undermine the
value of episcopal leases when they themselves were '*screwing*
and *racking* their Tenants all over the Kingdom'.[2] Churchmen
watched with great concern the resentful and jealous spirit
of the gentry in Parliament. A Bill introduced in 1720 to
provide clergymen with glebes was attacked and defeated on
the grounds that it might make churchmen freeholders and
thus influential in parliamentary elections. 'The true reason
[it] did not pass the house of Commons', the Archbishop of
Tuam reported to Wake at Canterbury, 'was because many,
even Church-men, are of the opinion that the Clergy have
too much already.'[3] A year later, after the defeat of another
Church Bill, the Bishop of Kilmore similarly complained to
Canterbury that the 'H. of Commons will not suffer any
Church bill to pass that may do us good'.[4] These comments—
and they could easily be multiplied—serve to clarify the
atmosphere which gave rise to the Bill of 1723 in a Commons
dominated by the landed gentry.

In the autumn of that year the Irish House of Commons
was engaged in debating 'An Act for the Preservation of the
Inheritance, Rights, and Profits of Lands belonging to the
Church and Persons Ecclesiastical'.[5] Despite its misleading
title the Bill was immediately recognized by the clergy as a
dangerous attack upon the possessions of the Church. The

---

[1] Wake Corresp. xiv, Henry Downes to Wake, 4 Feb. 172¾.

[2] *Prose Works*, Davis, ix. 21.

[3] Wake Corresp. xiii, Edward Synge to Wake, 15 Aug. 1720. See also Synge to
Wake, 6 Mar. 1720; Henry Downes to Wake, 15 Oct. 1720.

[4] Ibid. Timothy Goodwin to Wake, 23 Dec. 1721.

[5] *Journal of the House of Commons of Ireland* (Dublin, 1796) iii. 358.

episcopal bench was aroused; and though there was some division among the bishops as to the most effective method of combating the peril, they were agreed that vigorous action was necessary. Within a fortnight of the introduction of the Bill, assistance came from a quarter where the bishops least expected it—the Dean of St. Patrick's. Swift's tract appeared anonymously, but he was at once known as the author. The reaction among the Whig bishops is indicated by the comment of William Nicolson, Bishop of Derry, who hitherto had found nothing to praise in Swift: to Canterbury he reported that the dean's tract 'is allow'd to atone for a multitude of bypast Transgressions'.[1] Similarly the Bishop of Elphin, who appealed to the English primate to come to the aid of the Irish Church, sent a copy to Wake, praising it as 'well wrote' and 'an Antidote against several Pamphlets [designed] to invade the Inheritance of the Church'.[2] In this tract which so won the favour of those least disposed to favour him, Swift addressed himself to the members of the Established Church of Ireland who desired its 'Continuance and Transmission . . . to Posterity, at least, in as good a Condition as it is at present'.[3] His discourse, he declared, is not directed to the dissenters or to those members of the Establishment who oppress the inferior clergy and perpetually quarrel with the income of the bishops. It is, in fact, this latter group who were the object of his attack, since they were the sponsors of the pending legislation.

To understand Swift's position it is necessary to realize the great importance churchmen attached to their property rights and to grasp their deep-rooted, constant fear of an invasion of these rights by a rapacious laity. Certain statutes existed to safeguard Church possessions, one of the most

---

[1] Wake Corresp. xiv, Nicolson to Wake, 26 Oct. 1723.

[2] Ibid. xiv, Henry Downes to Wake, 26 Oct. 1723. Swift scholars, perhaps misled by the title, have misinterpreted the tract. They point out that the bishops were acting rapaciously to improve their personal fortunes and that Swift opposed them (see *Prose Works*, iii. [219–20]; Quintana, *Mind and Art of Jonathan Swift*, p. 259; Monck Mason, p. 392).

[3] *Prose Works*, Davis, ix. [45].

important in the eyes of Irish churchmen being an act passed in the reign of Charles I (10 and 11 Charles I, c. 3) to prevent alienation of Church lands, especially lands attached to sees. The proposed legislation of 1723, as Swift recognized, was clearly an attempt to weaken or undermine this important safeguard, and he endeavoured to show in his tract that passage of the Bill would destroy the temporal welfare of the Church. The statute of Charles I—the 'great Magna Charta for our Church Revenues', as Swift's enemy, Bishop Evans of Meath, called it—contained two valuable clauses.[1] One of these prevented bishops and ecclesiastical corporations from giving leases for a period longer than twenty-one years. Its intention was to prevent a greedy prelate from injuring a successor by a long lease extending beyond his own incumbency. There was a great temptation to let lands at a low annual rent in return for a large and unjustifiable fine. In such a transaction the incumbent bishop, who received the fine, naturally profited; but if the lease extended into the incumbency of a successor that successor suffered, being saddled with a lease of low annual return. A series of such leases in a particular see meant its eventual impoverishment; the consequence was in effect an alienation of Church lands. Yet this practice, Swift pointed out, was common among 'Popish Bishops' at the Reformation and was continued by Protestant bishops, who could plead that it was not a violation of common law.[2] Thus, to avoid such 'sacrilegious alienations' of Church lands, the statute of Charles I imposed a limit of not more than twenty-one years to the duration of a lease. The second clause of the statute, designed also to protect Church revenues, provided that see lands be leased at not less than one-half of their real value at the time the lease is made; otherwise the lease was voidable. This provision was assurance to an incumbent, because he could thus legally resist any tenant in a position to bargain; and it made for a continuance from incumbent to incumbent of a fair return from the see

[1] Wake Corresp. xiv, Evans to Wake, 5 Dec. 1723.
[2] Prose Works, Davis, ix. [45].

lands. More important, it meant that the Church as owner of lands always participated in the rise in value of those lands. If it could be shown at the renewal of a lease that the lands had risen in value, whatever the cause, the churchman was entitled to renewal at a higher rent, to yield not less than half the new value. Even though the law was evaded, it was in the statutes as a comfort to clerical landlords.

The landed gentry who introduced into the Commons the Bill to amend the Act of Charles I, 10 & 11, argued, of course, that its purpose was to ease certain difficulties arising out of that statute, but the bishops saw that this was pretence and self-interest. They pointed to two pernicious clauses in the proposed Bill.[1] The first of these permitted a bishop to let see land at a rental as high as any paid within the twenty preceding years, the effect of which was to repeal that vital safeguard in the original statute whereby the lowest legal rent was half the *present* value. Under such a provision a tenant whose land had risen sharply in value could not be forced legally to renew at a higher rental. A second clause in the pending Bill, equally disturbing, proposed the removal of the twenty-one year limit on leases of see lands and allowed bishops to let at fee-farm or for lives. It was obvious that the landed gentry were making an appeal to the cupidity of the present bishops by offering them the opportunity which earlier bishops had seized, of pocketing large fines in return for low annual rental of see lands and long leases. The bishops did not rise to the bait. They were too well aware, from many historical instances, of the pitfalls involved in long-term leases made by predecessors, whose dead hand thereby determined the income of succeeding bishops, some of them perhaps unborn when the leases were made. In the many urgent letters sent from Ireland to Canterbury the bishops showed that they understood the immediate advantage to themselves, but they were agreed that these clauses constituted a deliberate attack on their strongest bulwark against alienation

[1] See, for example, Wake Corresp. xiv, Timothy Goodwin to Wake, 26 Nov. 1723; Josiah Hort to Wake, 29 Nov. 1723.

of Church lands—'wicked Designs on our Ecclesiastical Revenues', Nicolson of Derry described it to Wake.[1] John Evans declared that the legislation was a specious pretence 'to alter the Tenure of our Lands'. It would 'turn to the advantage of the present Bishops,' he added, 'but If we consent to it, I think we justly incur (I will not say the Curses) but the very ill report of those that come after . . . [it] may hereafter bring all the Church Lands into Laymen's hands'.[2] Similar sentiments of high-mindedness and concern for his successors came from Bishop Downes of Elphin: he characterized the Bill as a 'Pretence of Kindness to the Present Possessors of [Church lands] but I hope we shall always act as becomes those who are in Truth Trustees for our Successors, & not by any act of our own prejudice their Rights out of a Prospect of any immediate advantage to ourselves'.[3] Like the bishops, Swift too exposes the strategy of the landowners in appealing to the immediate advantage of an incumbent bishop. 'The present Bishops', he writes, 'will, indeed, be no Sufferers'; and he uses their very phraseology in his insistence that they will not be 'excuseable before God or Man' if they fail to oppose a Bill which must result in 'the Ruin of the Church, and of their own Order in this Kingdom'.[4] There can be no doubt, as he penned his tract, that Swift knew and approved of the bishops' attitude. Nothing else can explain his kindly reference to several members of the episcopal bench and the absence of any suggestion that the bishops were ready to serve their own interest. If they had been in any respect culpable in his eyes, he would have seized his opportunity.

Although concerned primarily with bishops' lands and incomes, Swift's tract is actually a discussion of the problems facing all Irish churchmen who held lands—the ecclesiastical landlords. This group, of whom he was one, unceasingly

---

[1] Wake Corresp. xiv, Nicolson to Wake, [Dec. ?] 1723.
[2] Ibid. Evans to Wake, 24 Oct. 1723.
[3] Ibid. Downes to Wake, 26 Oct. 1723.
[4] *Prose Works*, Davis, ix. 51–52.

complained of being subjected to discrimination in their rents and leases. From his own experience Swift knew that Church lands were usually leased at substantially lower terms than their real value. It was a subject of his bitter comment. 'A reasonable Man will wonder . . . that an *Ecclesiastical* Landlord should expect a moderate, or third Part Value in Rent for his Lands, when his Title is, *at least*, as ancient and as legal as that of a Lay-man; who is yet but seldom guilty of giving such beneficial Bargains.'[1] The bishops complained, and Swift echoed their plaint, that lay juries, regularly antagonistic to the clergy, very seldom enforced in the courts the statutory guarantee that Church lands be set at not less than half the real value. It is not therefore surprising, Swift declares, that a bishop and ecclesiastical bodies as a matter of course accept less than half value in their leases rather than engage in suits.[2] The situation was aggravated in that churchmen often leased to the gentry, who then themselves turned landlords by subleasing profitably to tenants. The subleasing was frequently carried farther, to an extent that the person who actually worked the soil was several removes from the Church landlord, and his tenure so impermanent that he was indifferent to making improvements, or could not improve if he wished, his rent 'being screwed up to the last penny'.[3] Thus Church lands failed to get the improvements which would tend to raise them in value. In effect Swift's plea is not that discrimination against clerical landlords be eliminated—of this he saw little possibility—but that the prevalent discrimination be not intensified. He pleaded for recognition of the churchman's role in the economy of the nation. '. . . there can be no Disadvantage to the Publick, in a

[1] Ibid. p. 57. Cf. *Corresp.* v. 430.

[2] *Prose Works*, Davis, ix. 53. Josiah Hort wrote to Wake: 'All Jureys in trying Bishops Leases have been partial without any kind of modesty, and will ever be so in this kingdom, and indeed the Gentlemen do not stick to glory in it' (Wake Corresp. xiv, 29 Nov. 1723; see also Goodwin to Wake, 26 Nov. 1723; Gilbert Collection, MS. 27, Nicolson to Wake, 2 Nov. 1723).

[3] *Prose Works*, Davis, ix. 54 f.; Wake Corresp. xiv, Goodwin to Wake, 26 Nov. 1723.

Protestant Country,' he wrote, 'that a Man should hold Lands as a *Bishop*, any more than if he were a *Temporal* Person.' 'I was never able to imagine what Inconvenience could accrue to the Publick, by one or two Thousand Pounds a Year, in the Hands of a Protestant Bishop, any more than of a Lay Person.' Internal trade received its stimulus from the circulation of money, whether it came from clerical or lay sources. 'Ecclesiastical Beneficence' was too valuable to be sacrificed. The extensive see lands played no inconsiderable part in the prosperity of 'lords and great 'Squires' who leased them; and Swift resented that this class, 'who, in Reason, were never designed to be Tenants', should receive from these lands more than the clerical landlords.[1] All the circumstances surrounding Church leases struck him as unfavourable to the churchman as well as to the actual farmer, and favourable only to the holders of the leases, the landlords and squires. On these two, whom he tended to equate, Swift used some of his most forceful invective. In his scathing *Character of an Irish Squire* he declared that 'Every Squire, almost to a man, is an oppressor of the clergy, a racker of his tenants, a jobber of all public works, very proud and generally illiterate', and he concluded with a remark on the 'detestable tyranny and oppression' of squires as landlords.[2]

Any Irish churchman of the eighteenth century would recognize immediately the danger in the landed gentry's endeavour to lengthen leases beyond twenty-one years. He had before his eyes the example of see lands in England under long-term leases which were favourable enough when originally made but whose present return was wholly inadequate because of the increased value of land or of the lower purchasing power of money. He needed, in fact, to look no farther than certain of the Church of Ireland's fixed endowments and perpetual pensions to observe how sums adequate a century earlier had shrunk in the light of changed conditions to woeful inadequacy. A lease for ever or even for

---

[1] *Prose Works*, Davis, ix. 54–55.
[2] *Prose Works*, xi. 193–4. See also *Prose Works*, Davis, ix. 21; *Corresp.* iv. 118–19.

lives was subject to these contingencies; and the pending
legislation in the Commons would pave the way for such
extended leases by removing the limiting clause in the Act
of Charles I, 10 & 11. Swift reports Bishop Burnet (with
whom he could agree at least on this point) as believing 'that
the Liberty which Bishops in *England* have of letting Leases
for Lives, would ... be one Day the Ruin of Episcopacy there'.
The Irish Church, Burnet thought, was 'happy by the
Limitation Act'.[1] Thus the attempt to repeal the limiting
clause brought apprehension, and Swift argued eloquently in
his tract for its retention, the crux of his argument being '*the
perpetual Decrease of the Value of Gold and Silver*', that is,
monetary inflation. On this point he appears to have made
use of a book in his library by Bishop William Fleetwood,
entitled *Chronicon Preciosum* (1707).[2] This work, as Fleetwood describes it, is an historical account of money in order
'to determine what Proportion, a *Pound*, a *Mark*, a *Shilling*,
or a *Penny*, now bears to the same Denomination many Years
ago'.[3] The investigation is in terms of the relative cost of
commodities: '. . . to find out how much Meat, Drink, or
Cloth might be purchased in H[enry] VI reign with V£ and
then to find out, how much of the money now current will
be required to purchase the same quantity of Meat, Drink,
and Cloth.'[4] Fleetwood's concern is with Church revenues
derived from fixed endowments, perpetual pensions, and long
leases with fixed rents, precisely the problem that faced Swift
and the Irish clergy. A change in the value of money (i.e.

---

[1] *Prose Works*, Davis, ix. 52. The problem of limited leases to avoid the harmful
results of inflation was of course not merely a churchman's concern. For an interesting discussion of it in its lay and clerical aspects, see Edward Laurence, *A Dissertation
on Estates upon Lives and Years, whether in Lay or Church-Hands*, London, 1730.
Laurence was a land surveyor with experience in Ireland.

[2] Harold Williams, *Dean Swift's Library*, Cambridge, 1932. See the 'Sale
Catalogue'.

[3] [William Fleetwood], *Chronicon Preciosum : or, An Account of English Money,
the Price of Corn, and other Commodities for the last 600 Years* (London, 1707), p. 18.

[4] Ibid. pp. 60–61. See also [Bishop Brown of Chichester], *The Value of Church
and College Leases Consider'd*, 2nd ed. (London, 1722), pp. 12–13 and *passim*, for
the impact of monetary inflation on clerical leases.

purchasing power) must be taken into account, Fleetwood argued, if Church revenues are to remain adequate. Since money is of no use except for the things it will purchase, if £120 is needed at present to purchase what £5 purchased in the reign of Henry VI, it is evident to what extent money had sunk. Swift, making use of historical facts of the kind supplied by Fleetwood, similarly traced the history of money to show that it had decreased in value, that in the last 100 years alone its value had dropped one-half. '. . . a Barrel of Corn', he remarked, 'is of a real intrinsick Value, which Gold and Silver are not'—a fact which must be taken into account by any person or corporation, whether ecclesiastical or lay, whose revenues are to be protected over a long period of time.[1] He drew an analogy between the lay and the clerical landlord to enforce his point. A gentleman's estate leased for ever at its highest value in the reign of Charles II would now in terms of purchasing power be reduced to one-half of its original worth, £1,000 now buying only half of what it would then buy. Suppose see lands to have been leased under the same circumstances, or, even more enlightening, two or three hundred years ago, at a rent adequate at that time for the bishop's performance of works of hospitality and charity. As money sank in value, each succeeding bishop in this particular see would find his rent purchasing fewer and fewer commodities, until the income eventually would be equal to no more than that of a 'small chiefry'. 'If the Fortune of a private Person', Swift wrote, 'be diminished by the Weakness, or Inadvertency of his Ancestors, in letting Leases for ever at low Rents, the World lies open to his Industry for purchasing of more; but the Church is barred by a *dead Hand*. . . .'[2] Thus he argued against repealing the statutory limitation of leases

---

[1] *Prose Works*, Davis, ix. 51. Cf. White Kennet, *Parochial Antiquities attempted in the History of Ambrosden, Burcester, and other adjacent Parts in the Counties of Oxford and Bucks* (Oxford, 1695), pp. 604–5.

[2] *Prose Works*, Davis, ix. 52 f. For a similar parallel of lay and clerical landlords in an anonymous tract siding with the clergy, see *A Letter to a Member of the Honourable House of Commons, on Occasion of a Proposal for a Law to be made setting Church Lands at the Present Yearly Rent* [Dublin, 1723].

to twenty-one years, since leases of excessive length constitute in effect an alienation or near alienation of Church
lands, the power of the clerical landlord to profit by frequent
renewals being gone.

Swift and his fellow churchmen viewed the Bill introduced
into the Commons as the action of a self-interested group
seeking economic advantage. The anonymous author, possibly one of the bishops, of another tract which appeared
shortly before Swift's, described the legislation as a design
'to secure much greater bargains to the tenants of church
lands than what the law now permits or the tenants ought to
have'.[1] The gentry's side was contained in *The Case of the
Laity, with some Queries* (1723), a tract which Swift answers
in the final part of his own. The author refers to the many
laws passed 'for aggrandizing the clergy' and to the wealth
and power annexed 'to an Office *purely Spiritual*'.[2] By way
of reply Swift charged the tract with being 'full of the
strongest Malice against the Clergy' and the gentry as being
'Enemies to the Church'.[3] This, of course, was not true in
the religious sense, however much the gentry and clergy
found themselves in economic conflict. As Archbishop King
had written a few years earlier, 'the bulk of the common
people in Ireland are either Papists or dissenters, equally
enemies to the Established Church; but the gentry are
generally conformable, and the Church interest lies in them.'[4]
In fact, it can be effectively argued that the strength and
security of the Church of Ireland in Swift's time, its privileged
position, lay in its alliance with the landlords.[5] That Swift
realized this made him all the more bitter against the landed
group when, seeking their own economic advantage, they

---

[1] In the tract cited above, p. 106, n. 2.
[2] *The History of the Popish Clergy, or The Case of the Laity, with Some Queries*
(Dublin, 1723), pp. 9, 12.
[3] *Prose Works*, Davis, ix. 56.
[4] Quoted by Richard Mant, *History of the Church of Ireland*, ii. 293.
[5] See J. C. Beckett, 'The Government and the Church of Ireland under William
III and Anne', *Irish Historical Studies*, ii (1941), 280–302, where this view is
convincingly presented.

weakened the temporal position of the Establishment. If this powerful and prosperous group proved undependable or unrestrained in its short-sighted self-interest, he felt that the Church was doomed. Thus it is that he tried to set his arguments in an historical context, appropriate to a Church which 'is supposed to last for ever, both in its Discipline and Doctrine', and made his appeal to the 'true Lovers of the Church [who] would be glad it should continue in a tolerable Degree of Prosperity to the End of the World'.[1] In the outcome the views of Swift and the bishops prevailed, though there is no way of assessing Swift's influence. He did not persuade the Commons, where the Bill carried. It was, however, dropped in the Irish Privy Council.[2]

Although all of the bishops were fully alive to the dangerous implications of this thinly disguised attack on temporalities, they differed, as already indicated, over the method of combating it. The division was between the bishops of the English interest, that is, the prelates born and educated in England, who had been translated from the Church of England, and the bishops of the Irish interest, who were born and educated in Ireland. Swift's sympathies and alignment were usually with the latter. He had only contempt for the 'worthless bishops' sent from England; but in this momentous instance he found himself in agreement with such despised prelates as his diocesan, Bishop Evans of Meath. The Irish bishops, led by the Archbishop of Tuam and Archbishop King, believed that the turbulent gentry must be pacified by minor concessions since certain pending Church Bills in the Commons would otherwise suffer defeat. They therefore introduced 'a sort of Antibill' in the House of Lords to counteract the violent Bill in the Commons.[3]

---

[1] *Prose Works*, Davis, ix. 50.

[2] See the *Journal of the House of Commons in Ireland*, iii. 364; Wake Corresp. xiv, Edward Synge to Wake, 13 Dec. 1723; Evans to Wake, 17 Dec. 1723; Josiah Hort to Wake, 14 Dec. 1723.

[3] Gilbert Collection, MS. 28, King to Wake, 17 Dec. 1723; Wake Corresp. xiv, Josiah Hort to Wake, 26 Oct. 1723; Edward Synge to Wake, 13 Dec. 1723; King Corresp. (tr. Fisher), King to Annesly, 1 Nov. 1723. The 'Antibill' was passed in

To this compromise measure the English bishops reacted with suspicion; in fact, it confirmed suspicions already formed, that the Irish interest was willing, perhaps eager, for a diminution of episcopal incomes to prevent the invasion of Irish bishoprics by English clerics. One of the English bishops, Timothy Goodwin of Kilmore, wrote to Canterbury:

> Perhaps the Gentlemen of this Country may be griev'd that so many of us have lately been promoted from England. *Hinc illae lacrymae* and are afraid if our Sees should increase in their Rents more would be incourag'd to come over. A view of this kind I am afraid some of our order have had in so feebly opposing those Bills. The great man at St. Sep[ulchre, i.e. Archbishop King] has been heard to say, that *He would not increase his Rents because he expected an English Man would probably succeed him.*[1]

The Bishop of Ferns likewise reported to Canterbury that the bishops had divided, that a '*National Policy*' prevails among 'our Irish prelates of the first rank ... not to encrease the Rent Roll, because this would be a means to Invite English Clergymen and Bishops to come over'.[2] Swift, in fact, confirms that this strategy had an appeal for some members of the Irish interest: 'I know indeed, some Persons who offer, as an Argument for repealing the limiting Bill, that it may in future Ages prevent the Practice of providing this Kingdom with Bishops from *England*, when the only Temptation will be removed'.[3] Antagonistic as he was to the English invasion of Irish sees and benefices, he rejected this argument, which probably was not advanced in complete seriousness in the first instance. He agreed with the English interest that there must be no compromise with the landlords. This Church tract of 1723 was very likely among those he lightly dismissed to Pope as 'effects of anger on public grievances here, which would be insignificant out of this

the House of Lords but killed in the English Privy Council (see P.R.O., S.P. 63 [Ireland], 381–2, and P.C. 1. 4, Bundle 20; Henry Maul to Wake, 21 Feb. 172¾; Downes to Wake, 4 Feb. 172¾).

[1] Wake Corresp. xiv, Goodwin to Wake, 26 Nov. 1723.

[2] Ibid. Hort to Wake, 29 Nov. 1723; see also Henry Downes to Wake, 30 Nov. 1723; Evans to Wake, 10 Dec. 1723.   [3] *Prose Works*, Davis, ix. 52.

kingdom', yet Swift was fully aware of larger implications and issues.[1] Particularly he faced the question of how the Anglican Establishment in Ireland was to endure, sound and flourishing, in a society increasingly secular in its ideas and acquisitive in its instincts. He may not have known that his tract was sent to England, but he would have understood its sympathetic reception by the English bishops, who watched apprehensively the proceedings in Ireland—'with the concern', the Bishop of Exeter wrote to Nicolson of Derry, 'which people naturally have when they see their neighbour's house on fire'.[2]

When Swift wrote his tract in defence of the bishops late in December 1723, Ireland was in the midst of the ferment over Wood's coinage, and he was soon to write his first Drapier's Letter. The events of 1724 absorbed most of his time, but he still let his mind dwell upon the subject of clerical and lay landlords, as is evident from his broadside entitled *An Excellent New Song upon his Grace Our Good Lord Archbishop of Dublin*.[3] Honest Jo, a farmer, the mouthpiece of the poem, reflects on the two types of landlords:

> Why, there's my Landlord now the *'Squire*, who all in Money wallows,
> He would not give a Groat to save his Father from the Gallows.
> A *Bishop* says the noble *'Squire*, I hate the very Name,
> To have two thousand Pounds a Year, O 'tis a burning Shame!

The following lines depict the easy lease under the bishop at 'scarce five Shillings in the Pound' and the indulgent attitude of the ecclesiastical landlord in hard times. Then Honest Jo turns again to the squire:

> And then I went to pay the *'Squire* and in the Way I found,
> His *Baily* Driving all my Cows into the Parish Pound.
> Why Sirrah said the Noble *'Squire*, how dare you see my Face,
> Your Rent is due almost a Week beside the Days of Grace.

[1] *Corresp.* iv. 307.
[2] *Letters on Various Subjects, Literary, Political, and Ecclesiastical, to and from William Nicolson*, ed. John Nichols (London, 1809), ii. 563.
[3] *Poems*, i. 342–3.

And Yet the Land I from him hold is set so on the Rack,
  That only for the *Bishop*'s Lease 'twould quickly break my Back.

This doggerel was Swift's final public utterance on the immediate controversy between the churchmen and the landlords. The topic of Church lands and leases, however, is one that never ceased to preoccupy him; and he took up the matter of the bishops' lands once more in a tract published in 1732, where he recommends ironically that these lands be sold to pay off the debt of the nation. He argues gravely that this would be a popular action. It would 'enrich an hundred gentlemen' and free them of dependence on the churchmen— '... for the immediate tenants to bishops, being some of them persons of quality, and good estates, and more of them grown up to be gentlemen by the profits of these very leases, under a succession of bishops, think it a disgrace to be subject both to rents and fines, at the pleasure of their landlords'.[1]

II. RESIDENCE

Nearly a decade later, in 1732, Swift again was engaged in a controversy over church temporalities. On this occasion the roles of the Irish House of Commons and the bishops were reversed. The bishops, Swift believed, were in 'an open avowed attempt ... to destroy the Church', and the Commons played the part of saviour.

  Our B[ishop]s puft up with Wealth and with Pride.
  To Hell on the Backs of the Clergy wou'd ride;
  They mounted, and labour'd with Whip and with Spur,
  In vain—for the Devil a Parson wou'd stir.
  So the *Commons* unhors'd them, and this was their Doom,
  On their Crosiers to ride, like a Witch on a Broom.[2]

The conflict in this instance was between the higher and the lower clergy, and these unrestrained lines from Swift's poem *On the Irish Bishops* (1732) reveal his bitterness toward the

[1] *Prose Works*, vii. 257: *A Proposal for an Act of Parliament to pay off the Debt of the Nation without Taxing the Subject.*
[2] *Poems*, iii. 804.

bishops for supporting two Bills in the Irish House of Lords inimical to the lower clergy. Over a year later, when the legislation had been effectually disposed of, his anger was undiminished, and he wrote to Bishop Stearne in unmeasured language of 'those two abominable Bills, for enslaving and beggaring the Clergy, which took their birth from hell':

... I call God to witness, that I did then, and do now, and shall for ever, firmly believe that every Bishop, who gave his vote for either of these Bills, did it with no other view, bating farther promotion, than a premeditated design, from the spirit of ambition and love of arbitrary power, to make the whole body of the clergy their slaves and vassals, until the day of judgement, under the load of poverty and contempt.[1]

The first of these two Bills, which passed in the Lords and was supported by all except three of the spiritual peers, concerned clerical residence.[2] Its most objectionable clause gave a bishop the right to force any clergyman of his diocese holding a benefice of £100 annual value (£50 under some circumstances) to build a manse house on such part of the glebe as the bishop thought suitable. The other Bill, approved without dissent, permitted the division of any large parish into two or more parishes without the consent of the incumbent provided that the original one retained an annual value of £100. Both Bills were defeated in the Commons.[3]

From this bare account it may appear that Swift's indignation was out of all proportion to the threat posed by the legislation. His contempt for many of the bishops was such that he had no compunction in ascribing to them the worst of motives; but even if his indictment is not wholly free from personal animus, his views are no different from those of other members of the lower clergy, who petitioned both Houses of Parliament against the passage of these Bills and appeared

[1] *Corresp.* v. 17.
[2] *Journal of the House of Lords of Ireland,* iii. 182–91. 'A Bill more effectually to enable the Clergy having Cure of Souls to reside on their Respective Benefices and to Build on their Respective Glebe Lands' passed 21 Feb. 173½. The Bill of Division passed 24 Feb. 173½.
[3] *Journal of the House of Commons of Ireland,* iv. pt. 1, 54, 26 Feb. 173½.

in numbers to witness the debates.[1] It is possible that he aided
in drawing up the petition; certainly there is a close parallel
between the language of the petition and the arguments in his
tracts written to combat the legislation. Swift is only one of
several who endeavoured on this occasion to sway opinion,
as one controversialist remarked, by 'pamphlets and libels'.[2]
The animosities raised were so great that even after the Bills
were defeated each side was still intent on proving the validity
of its cause. An anonymous pamphleteer, probably one of
the bishops, set out to show that all the 'Clamour and Noise
against the Bishops ... is groundless and unjust'; and in his
defence of the bishops he inserted some criticism of Swift's
attack.[3] He in turn was answered by 'A Commoner of Ireland',
who was then followed by a 'Reconciler', a person so much
disturbed at the spectacle of bishops and lower clergy pursuing 'each other with the greatest Heat and Animosity' that
he felt compelled to endeavour a reconciliation of the views of
Swift and the author who had attacked him.[4]

Swift's contribution in prose to the controversy consists
of three pamphlets. The first of these, *On the Bill for the
Clergy's residing on their Livings*, is little more than a preliminary sketch, left incomplete. It was written near the end of
January 173½,[5] well in advance of the final vote in Parliament;
but it appears not to have been published at the time, being
replaced by a second pamphlet in which a more complete
and informed treatment of the two Bills is found. The first
pamphlet is not without interest. It sets forth Swift's conception of the historic despoliation of the Church of Ireland,

---

[1] Ibid. See also *The Reconciler, or, Some Remarks upon Two Pamphlets lately
publish'd* . . . (Dublin, 1732), pp. 3–4.

[2] *An Answer to a Letter from a Lord to a Commoner concerning the Two Church
Bills lately rejected*, by A Commoner of Ireland (Dublin, 1732), pp. 53–54.
(Advertised in the *Dublin Evening Post*, 11–15 July 1732).

[3] *A Letter from a Lord to a Commoner concerning the Two Church Bills lately
rejected* (Dublin, 1732), p. 4. (Advertised in Faulkner's *Dublin Journal*, April 8–11
1732.)

[4] *The Reconciler*, p. 3.

[5] Swift refers to the approaching anniversary (30 Jan.) of the martyrdom of
King Charles I (see *Prose Works*, iii. 254).

of the seizures and forfeitures of its lands, the destruction of
its churches, and its reduction in the course of time to its
present impoverished condition. He therefore maintained
that single parishes are usually too poor in glebe or tithes
to provide a competence for an incumbent, an argument
obviously intended to counter the proposal to divide the more
valuable parishes into units of reduced value. He apparently
felt that the bishops were moving in the wrong direction by
suggesting division of parishes, that in fact union of parishes
was dictated by the hard realities. As early as 1710 he had
complained of the impoverished clerical livings, insisting that
five or six united barely sufficed to give an incumbent £50 a
year.[1] Again in 1723, in his fight against the landed gentry,
he had made a similar assertion, which reflected a sharp
awareness of how the Irish Church had been despoiled in the
course of history:

> The Clergy having been stripped of the greatest Part of their
> Revenues, the *Glebes* being generally lost, the *Tythes* in the Hands of
> Laymen, the Churches demolished, and the Country depopulated; in
> order to preserve a Face of *Christianity*, it was necessary to unite small
> *Vicarages*, sufficient to make a tolerable Maintenance for a *Minister*.[2]

By contrast the English Establishment seemed to him in a
flourishing condition and the lower clergy more amply provided for. Here as elsewhere Swift's consciousness of the
difference between the two Churches deepens his pessimism
concerning the Irish Establishment;[3] and his dwelling on the
point in this tract may have been intended as an appeal to the
English Privy Council, which had to approve Irish legislation, not to ratify any Bill endangering the meagre livelihood
of the lower clergy in Ireland.

Swift's second pamphlet, *Considerations upon Two Bills . . .
relating to the Clergy of Ireland*, is dated 24 February 173½,
only two days before the Bills were defeated in the Commons.
Faulkner, Swift's publisher, reprinted the pamphlet in 1738,

---

[1] *Journal to Stella*, ii. 679.   [2] *Prose Works*, Davis, ix. 58.
[3] See *Prose Works*, iii. 251–2, 267, 280.

with an advertisement stating that the supposed author '*who hath always been the best Friend to the inferiour Clergy . . . opposed this pernicious Project with great Success*'; and Swift's commentators have tended to accept the view that his opposition, as Temple Scott remarked, 'largely influenced the Lower House in rejecting' the legislation.[1] His opposition was known and, it may be, had some influence, but the pamphlet itself was not published until a month after the Bills were defeated, and then apparently in England.[2] It thus belongs to the after phases of the controversy, when indeed it played a part. Nevertheless it is directed as a piece of persuasion to the Commons where the two Bills were under consideration; and Swift shrewdly utilizes certain appeals effective with the gentry and landed class in the Commons who could be depended upon to guard their own interest. He argued that the gentry would find the Bills inimical to their welfare, in the first instance by increasing the number of poor inferior clergymen who would bear hard on landlords and farmers in the payment of tithes, and secondly by creating more freeholders among the clergy, whose influence in parliamentary elections might become disproportionate. That Swift resorted to such arguments is a measure of his determination to combat the 'abominable bills'. He added another which came from his deeper convictions: '. . . my lords the bishops enjoy as ample a power, both spiritual and temporal, as will fully suffice to answer every branch of their office'. To a House of Commons in frequent conflict with a

---

[1] Swift, *Works*, 1738, vi. [139]; *Prose Works*, iii. [249–50].

[2] As the vote approached in the Commons Swift had insufficient time to get his tract into print. He therefore anticipated it by inserting in Faulkner's *Dublin Journal*, 22–26 Feb., 'Some Queries' which embodied his chief arguments, with a promise that the entire tract would be printed if the Bill depended long enough. On 26 Feb. the Bill was thrown out, and nothing is heard of the tract until the following notice appeared under a London date line in the *Dublin Journal* of 21–25 Mar.: 'The Clergy of this Nation, and all the young Gentlemen in our Universities, are wonderfully pleased with a Pamphlet lately transmitted from Dublin (which we are informed was prohibited being printed there). 'Tis Entitled, Considerations on Two Bills lately sent down from the R—— H—— the H—— of L—— to the H—— H—— of C——, relating to the C——y of *****. 'Tis said some Copies are sent to Ireland.'

House of Lords where the spiritual peers often dominated, this reference to the amplitude of episcopal power would have its appeal.[1]

The most disputed clause in the Bill for clerical residence gave the bishop the right to name the spot on which an incumbent must build his manse. This Swift believed to be an extraordinary grant of power. He painted a picture of the dire possibilities:

. . . if there be a single spot in the glebe more barren, more marshy, more expos'd to winds, more distant from the church, or skeleton of a church, or from any conveniency of building: the rector, or vicar may be obliged by the caprice, or pique of the bishop, to build, under pain of sequestration . . . upon whatever point his lordship shall command. . . .[2]

If this is extreme, it is nevertheless a reflection of the fear prevalent among the inferior clergy. An apologist for the bishops protested against this harsh interpretation, and maintained that the diocesan by virtue of his office and disinterestedness was the best judge of where a manse should be constructed.[3] But the *Reconciler* remarked that this was no answer to that part of the Bill 'which most of all disturbed the inferior clergy'. 'The dread and apprehension', he continued, 'of such an Arbitrary Power as this, to be lodged in the Hands of an Exasperated or Angry Bishop, would be apt to make deeper Impressions of Bitterness and Resentment, on the Minds both of Clergy and Laity, than any other Suspicion whatsoever.'[4]

There was another disturbing aspect of the legislation— the 'whole temporal support' of the inferior clergy was endangered. The Bill for the division of parishes meant more benefices for the bishops to fill with loyal dependents, a scheme, Swift called it, for 'multiplying beggarly clergymen through the whole kingdom'.[5] A valuable parish, already too

---

[1] *Prose Works*, iii. 265 ff.
[2] Ibid. iii. 264.
[3] *A Letter from a Lord to a Commoner . . .*, pp. 8–9.
[4] *The Reconciler*, p. 10.   [5] *Prose Works*, iii. 267.

rare in Ireland, could be divided and made to support two or even more clergymen. Whereas the income from the original parish might support its incumbent with a competency and enable him to live with the dignity befitting his profession, that same income split among two or more merely created a group of 'reduced divines', who would then be permitted to supplement their incomes by becoming 'lappers of linen, bailiffs of the manor', or 'they may let blood, or apply plasters' and their wives and daughters 'may make shirts for the neighbourhood. . . .' The eventual result, Swift maintained, would be to spread even more thinly among the increased number of clerics the tithes and other Church income insufficient for the present number, to the destruction of that decency, comfort, charity, and hospitality which presumably are the prerogatives of a clergyman. He feared the creation of a horde of lesser clergy—'twenty, thirty, forty, or fifty pounders'—ill equipped and living in poverty.[1] The *Commoner of Ireland* echoed Swift in this plaint. Men of superior attainments were likely to be 'discouraged from entering the study of divinity' if good parishes were not obtainable and if the quality of the clergy was low.[2] For Swift this is one of the more important considerations. If the younger sons of the gentry of Ireland are not tempted into the Church by the hope of a reasonable maintenance, if 'learned, pious, diligent, conversible' clergymen are not recruited for the lower clergy, then the Church will suffer further from a type already bringing it into contempt—the 'little, hedge, contemptible, illiterate vicar from twenty to fifty pounds a-year, the son of a weaver, pedlar, tailor, or miller'.[3] The apologist for the bishops refused to grant the validity of this attitude: he argued that the sons of meaner families were no less pious, diligent, and learned than the sons of gentlemen and that their poverty gave them an incentive to excel. They were particularly suited, he thought,

---

[1] Ibid. iii. 268 ff.

[2] *An Answer to a Letter from a Lord to a Commoner*, pp. 30 ff.

[3] *Prose Works*, iii. 264–5.

for the country parishes.[1] The *Reconciler* in this instance supported Swift's insistence that the Church would gain from attracting the sons of the gentry.[2] It is clear that Swift himself recognized the importance of an alliance between the Church and the gentry, who could support the Establishment in its temporal and political aspects and thus eventually improve the social and intellectual level of the inferior clergy.

Perhaps the chief problem involved in this controversy was a recurrent one—the non-residence of the clergy, a problem no less vexing in the eighteenth century than earlier and no less disturbing to the Church of Ireland than to the Church of England. Sir Simon Degge's description of it as 'one of the three pests of the Church' is borne out by the constant concern with the subject in Swift's day in every quarter.[3] The canonical injunction to reside was easily evaded, and often justifiably when the physical circumstances made residence almost impossible. The bishops themselves frequently exercised great latitude in granting dispensations; and the many legislative attempts to enforce residence proved ineffectual, or at best provided only partial relief.[4] From 1710 there was increased agitation for more effective measures. Pressure was exerted from England. Wharton, then the Lord Lieutenant, received instructions from the English Privy Council to introduce a Bill in the Irish Privy Council for the more regular residence of the clergy.[5] The Irish Convocation of 1711 made representations that lack of glebes, churches, and manse houses makes 'the *Local Residence* of the Clergy in many Places impracticable'.[6] The bishops of the English interest sent frequent appeals to Canterbury for assistance. Shocked by the contrast between England and Ireland, they tended to blame the Irish clergy. Bishop Evans complained

---

[1] *A Letter from a Lord to a Commoner . . .*, pp. 20–21.
[2] *The Reconciler*, p. 18. See below, pp. 169 ff.
[3] Sir Simon Degge, *The Parson's Counsellor, with the Law of Tithes or Tithing* (London, 1676), pp. 19 ff.
[4] See below, p. 119, n. 4.
[5] P.R.O., S.P. 63 (Ireland), 366.
[6] *The Present State of Religion in Ireland* (London, [1712]), p. 17.

to Wake in 1717 of the 'many Churches (even where there are Protestants) being unserv'd for want of a competent maintenance, & the numbers of Non-Residents under the pretence of want of Glebes, & a Protestant Flock'.[1] This view was confirmed in the following year by William Nicolson of Derry, just arrived from England, who received his first impressions of Ireland by accompanying Evans on a visitation in Meath. 'The Churches', he wrote to Wake, 'are wholly demolish'd in many of their Parishes; which are therefore call'd *Non-Cures*: And several Clergymen have (each of 'em) four or five, Some Six or Seven of these. They commonly live in Dublin; leaving the Conduct of their Popish parishioners to Priests of their own Persuasion. . . .'[2] This, it should be recalled, is the diocese in which Swift held his country bene-fices. Three years later, when Nicolson's impressions were more fully formed, he wrote again to Wake: 'The Clergy of this Kingdom have so universally neglected their old palaces and Glebe-Houses that Canonical Residence is one of the greatest Rarities (or Miracles) in the Land. . . . An Irish Bishop (Rector or Vicar) chooses to live in a Cabine or hay-Farm sooner than upon any inheritance of his Church.'[3] The Irish bishops, despite Nicolson's strictures, were as eager to solve the problem as their English brothers of the bench. The Archbishop of Tuam published an extensive survey of the question in 1723, with a series of recommendations;[4] and the bishops collectively joined with Archbishop Boulter in several attempts from 1724 to 1732 to provide glebes, repair and build churches, and enforce the building of manse houses.[5]

The conflict of 1732 between higher and lower clergy in

[1] Wake Corresp. xii, Evans to Wake, 10 July 1717.
[2] Ibid. Nicolson to Wake, 17 June 1718.   [3] Ibid. xiii, 3 May 1720.
[4] Edward Synge, *A Brief Account of the Laws now in force in the Kingdom of Ireland, for encouraging the Residence of the Parochial Clergy, and Erecting of English Schools*, Dublin, 1723.
[5] Boulter, *Letters*, i. 5, 170, 262; *Dublin Weekly Journal*, 12 Mar. 172$\frac{5}{6}$; P.R.O., P.C. 1. 4, Bundles 23 and 25; S.P. 63 (Ireland), 395; Richard Mant, *History of the Church of Ireland*, ii. 478–82 and *passim*.

which Swift became so warmly involved grew out of one
of these earlier legislative attempts to induce the regular
residence of the parish clergy, the Act of 1 George I, c. 15,
which required an incumbent of a benefice valued at £150 to
build a manse after two years' possession where no fit residence
existed. The building was to be done at the bidding of the
bishop, who had the right of sequestration if his order was
disobeyed.[1] The two Bills of 1732 were intended to amend
and strengthen this earlier Act, already considered irksome
by the lower clergy, who objected to adding more power to
the already extensive power the bishops possessed.[2] Thus
Swift's violent reaction to the proposed legislation should be
viewed in a context of successive endeavours by the bishops,
striving for means to solve effectively the problem of non-
residence. This was no sudden umbrage so much as an
accumulated resentment of repeated attempts, as Swift
described it, to invade the 'liberty and property' of the lower
clergy who—as an added insult—were 'the only persons
concerned' and 'the sole persons not consulted'.[3] Nevertheless, in view of the widespread evidence concerning
non-residence, Swift's position was not wholly tenable. He
obviously believed that an incumbent must serve his cure, if
not in person then by a curate; and his own conscientiousness
in this respect has been indicated. When he argues that the
great majority of the parish clergy are too impoverished to
build, that most parishes have no glebes, that many glebes
where they exist are remote from the churches, he is supported
by general opinion. All recognized the difficulties facing a
clergyman who sincerely wished to reside. But in the heat of
the argument Swift tends to deny that non-residence is
widely prevalent. In 1723 he asserted: 'As to *Non-Residence*,
I believe there is no Christian Country upon Earth, where
the Clergy have less to answer for upon that *Article*.'[4] He

---

[1] *Statutes at Large, passed in the Parliaments of Ireland*, v. 255.
[2] See *An Answer to a Letter from a Lord to a Commoner*, pp. 14–15; *The Reconciler*,
p. 10.
[3] *Prose Works*, iii. 269.   [4] *Prose Works*, Davis, ix. 58.

repeated this view again in 1732, denying that 'the crying sin of the Clergy in this kingdom [is] non-residence'.[1] His denial, it is true, deserves an interpretation in the light of the objections which the lower clergy presented against the legislation. They maintained that residence among the parish clergy was frequently effectual if not canonical—a reference to the widely prevalent practice of incumbents who lacked manses or profitable glebes to reside at a distance, perhaps in an adjacent parish.[2] The practical effect of this, as the bishops pointed out, was the neglect of parochial duties.[3] An incumbent often appeared among his parishioners only once a week, and in inclement weather not at all. The proposed legislation was intended to correct this inadequate residence by requiring an incumbent to live near his church so as to function regularly in his parish. One of the controversialists complained that the Bill is not so much one 'to enable the clergy to reside, as *compelling* them to build'.[4] In a sense then this part of the controversy turned on what was meant by residence, though the crux was the resentment of the arbitrary power sought by the bishops. Swift was fully aware of the inadequacies the legislation set out to correct. He realized that the problem was urgent, but he believed it unreasonable to put the onus on the lower clergy. The bishops themselves, as all knew, were often guilty of non-residence or of encouraging it, choosing frequently to spend long periods in Dublin and failing to build manse houses on benefices they held *in commendam*. Thus Swift remarks with bitter irony on the logic that 'bishops build no houses, because they are so rich; and therefore, the inferior clergy will certainly build, if you reduce them to beggary'.[5]

[1] *Prose Works*, iii. 270.
[2] See *An Answer to a Letter from a Lord to a Commoner*, pp. 7, 9, 12. Cf. *Prose Works*, Davis, ix. 58; Wake Corresp. xiv, 27 Feb. 172⅘ (a report on the state of the Church of Ireland).
[3] Edward Synge, *A Brief Account of the Laws now in force in the Kingdom of Ireland . . .*, pp. 8 ff.; *A Letter from a Lord to a Commoner*, pp. 16–17.
[4] *An Answer to a Letter from a Lord to a Commoner*, p. 4.
[5] *Prose Works*, iii. 268. For accusations against bishops of non-residence, see

The controversy elicited from Swift three poems, *On the Irish Bishops*, *Judas*, and *Advice to a Parson*, in which he flays the bishops, except three:

> So God bless the Church, and three of our Mitres;
> And God bless the *Commons* for *Biting* the *Biters*.[1]

The 'three of our Mitres' who received his accolade were the only ones of the entire episcopal bench who voted against the Bills in the House of Lords. Since these were bishops of the Irish interest and the chief promoter of the Bills was an 'English' bishop, there was some attempt to gain advantage in the controversy by an appeal to nationalistic feelings.[2] Swift himself clearly endeavoured to make the proposals carry the odium of being inspired by the bishops of English birth and education, little concerned with the welfare of Ireland. He commended ironically those 'private clergymen from England' who have 'condescended to leave their native country, and come over hither to be bishops, merely to promote Christianity among us'; and he made insinuations at several points in his tract designed to appeal to the gentry in the Commons who disliked the flow of English divines into the Church of Ireland at the expense of clergymen born and educated in Ireland.[3] He continued with this anti-English note in a pamphlet entitled *A Proposal for an Act of Parliament to pay off the Debt of the Nation without Taxing the Subject* (1732).[4] Here he assumes the guise of an Englishman holding a profitable employment in Ireland, grateful to his adopted country and seeking its welfare. The proposal, set forth gravely with mathematical computations such as those used effectively in *Gulliver's Travels* and *A Modest Proposal*, is that the bishops should sell their lands and apply the funds received, except

---

James Read, *An Essay on Simony of the Bishops of Ireland* (London, 1737), pp. 82 ff. [written in 1731]; *An Answer to a Letter from a Lord to a Commoner*, p. 5; *The Reconciler*, p. 22.

[1] *Poems*, iii. 805. The three bishops were Theophilus Bolton, Archbishop of Cashel, Charles Carr, Bishop of Killaloe, and Robert Howard, Bishop of Elphin.

[2] See *The Reconciler*, pp. 29–30.   [3] *Prose Works*, iii. 251, 266.

[4] This tract was assigned to Matthew Pilkington and is listed by him in Aug. 1732 (see *Corresp.* iv. 484). It was reprinted in 1734 by A. Moore.

for a modest recompense, to the debts of Ireland. This is a suggestion, of course, for a monstrous alienation of Church lands, an inconceivable invasion of property rights. Swift intended it as an ironical counterpart of the procedure by which the bishops endeavoured to invade the property rights of the inferior clergy. The bishops found it easy, since they were not affected, to make a generous and disinterested disposition of the lives and property of the lower clergy. Here then is an equally generous and disinterested proposal, by one not affected, that the bishops should give up their wealth and luxury in a gesture of self-sacrifice and patriotism, a bland disposing of the lives and property of the higher clergy. The ironic jest lies in what Swift assumed would be obvious to all, the ingenuous assumption that a bishop sent from England was capable of transcending self-interest or serving the welfare of Ireland. The germ of this pamphlet had in fact been planted in his second pamphlet, where he had suggested that the bishops undergo a sacrifice such as they were imposing upon the lower clergy. If the parish clergy were to have their parishes—and hence their incomes—split, the bishops should likewise, in the interest of the Church, split their bishoprics—a proposal, he wrote, which would 'meet with such furious objections, that I shall not insist upon it'.[1]

III. THE SACRED TENTH

In his poem *On the Irish Bishops*, composed soon after the nefarious Church Bills of 1732 had been rejected, Swift had gratefully called for God's blessings on the Irish House of Commons. He and the body of the inferior clergy generally were pleased again when that same House in its next session 'defeated the arts and endeavours of schismatics to repeal the Sacramental Test'. It is not likely that he saw in this action an unusual affection for the Church since he expressly remarks that in both instances the proposed legislation was as detrimental to the interests of Anglican laymen as to the clergy.[2]

---

[1] *Prose Works*, iii. 268.   [2] Ibid. iii. 277.

He could not therefore have been surprised to discover that the Commons late in its session of 1733 had under consideration, with some prospect of its passing, a Bill undoubtedly detrimental to clergymen.[1] The pending Bill was designed to aid the linen industry by encouraging the cultivation of hemp and flax, and for this purpose it proposed that tithes on these two products be drastically reduced to a figure one-third of the legal prevailing rate. To the Irish clergy the proposal constituted not merely a threat to their incomes; it involved also a precedent and a principle that endangered Church property as a whole. This it was vital to combat. Faulkner reports that 'many eminent Clergymen, who opposed that Scheme, applied themselves to Dr. Swift to write against it, which he readily consented to, upon their giving him some Hints . . .'.[2] Swift's tract, entitled *Some Reasons against the Bill for settling the Tyth of Hemp, Flax, &c. by a Modus*, appeared on 8 January 173¾, as the Bill was being debated, and is presumed to have had some influence.[3] It is another of his occasional works designed to meet a particular situation in Ireland, which at the same time expresses his views on enduring problems vital to the Establishment in its temporal aspects.

The situation under discussion had a grim familiarity. Nevertheless one must have some reservations in accepting the impression Swift conveys, that the clergy had been singled out for the dubious honour of strengthening the linen industry. There appears to have been no malicious or deliberate intention to weaken the Church: the legislation was in fact part of repeated efforts to develop and maintain a flourishing linen industry in Ireland.[4] From the time that Strafford

---

[1] *Journal of the House of Commons of Ireland*, iv. 99. Leave was granted, 12 Dec. 1733, to introduce Heads of a Bill for the Further Regulation and Improvement of the Flaxen and Hempen Manufacture.

[2] *Works*, 1752, viii. 128.

[3] Advertised as 'Just published' in Faulkner's *Dublin Journal*, 8–12 Jan. 173¾.

[4] See John Hely-Hutchinson, *The Commercial Restraints of Ireland considered* (Dublin, 1789), pp. 129–51; Alice Effie Murray, *A History of the Commercial Relations between England and Ireland from the Period of the Restoration* (London, 1903),

saw the possibilities of such an industry in the third decade
of the seventeenth century to Swift's day, there had been
many executive and legislative acts concerning duties, pre-
miums, importations of machinery and labour, any one of
which inevitably affected adversely, at least for a brief time,
some segment of the population. After the Restoration, despite vigorous support from the Duke of Ormond, Sir William
Temple, and the Irish Parliament, the industry still failed
to develop satisfactorily. The appointment of the Huguenot, Louis Crommelin, to be Overseer of the Royal Linen
Manufactory in 1697 provided a great impetus, as did to a
certain extent the policy of the English government at the
end of the century to aid Irish linen as compensation for the
injury done to Irish wool. Yet too little was achieved, and it
remained for the successive Irish Parliaments in the eighteenth
century to pass a dozen or more Acts. In 1711 Swift himself
had helped by lobbying against a Bill in the English Parliament to impose a duty on Irish yarn.[1] The point relevant for
our purpose is that the pending legislation of 1733 was not
conceived as a penalty inflicted on the clergy. It was merely
part of a persistent movement to aid the Irish economy.
Inevitably the clergy as landlords and as receivers of tithes
would be vitally affected; but it was argued, a fact which
Swift recognized, that since the income of the churchmen
would increase as the industry progressed, the individual
clergyman should bear a portion of the burden needed for
its development.[2] Still, the clergy felt that they were all too
vulnerable; and in fact they had fought earlier against similar
legislation. In 1705 the Irish House of Commons considered
a Bill which limited and reduced the tithe on land sown in
flax and hemp—a forerunner of the Bill of 1733. On this
occasion the Lower House of Convocation had protested that

---

pp. 111–34; George O'Brien, *The Economic History of Ireland in the Seventeenth
Century* (Dublin and London, 1919), pp. 75–80; George O'Brien, *The Economic
History of Ireland in the Eighteenth Century* (Dublin, 1918), pp. 189–207; Conrad
Gill, *The Rise of the Irish Linen Industry* (Oxford, 1925), 61 ff.

[1] *Journal to Stella*, i. 235–7.
[2] *Prose Works*, iii. 284.

the Bill was 'very prejudiciall to the Civil Rights and propertys of the Clergy'—an invasion of freehold.[1] When a similar Bill reached the Lords, four of the spiritual peers argued that 'the Tyth or Tenth Part [is] due to the Clergy by Divine Right, which no human Law can set aside, lessen or take away'.[2]

In 1723, while defending episcopal leases, Swift took cognizance of the attempts to nibble down the tithe on hemp and flax. In that year Viscount Molesworth, the powerful Irish statesman to whom the Fifth Drapier's Letter was later addressed, directed to the House of Commons what Swift termed 'an excellent discourse for the "Encouragement of Agriculture"; full of most useful hints'.[3] Molesworth's view of the Church, however, left something to be desired, particularly his suggestion to the Commons that the cultivation of hemp and flax be encouraged by a reduction of tithes. Busily defending bishops' lands, Swift could only glance hastily at this additional attack on temporalities; but he took a moment to register disapproval of the discrimination against the clergy: 'If hops, hemp, flax, and twenty things more are to be planted, the clergy, *alone*, must reward the industrious farmer, by abatement of the tithe.'[4] He was in agreement with a 'layman' who answered Molesworth more fully, in the principle that 'a select Part of [the nation] is not to be . . . tyrannically used, deprived of their common Rights, and the Benefits of the Laws of the Land'.[5] It is this important principle, that tithes are a property right, that Swift was to argue so strenuously ten years later.

Brief as it is, *Some Reasons against the Bill for settling the*

[1] B.M., Lansdowne MS. 446, fols. 129–30 (J. Strype, Miscellaneous Collection); P.R.O., S.P. 63 (Ireland), 365. These contain a number of protests against the Bill, a memorial of the Lower Clergy, the English Privy Council's report on the clause touching tithes, and Queen Anne's promise that she would find a way to recompense the Irish clergy.

[2] *Journal of the House of Lords of Ireland*, ii. 148–9.

[3] *Prose Works*, iii. 236. Molesworth's tract was entitled *Some Considerations for the Promoting of Agriculture, and Employing the Poor*, Dublin, 1723.

[4] *Prose Works*, iii. 237.

[5] *Considerations upon Considerations for the Promoting of Agriculture and Providing for the Poor* (Dublin, [1723 ?]), p. 46.

Tyth of Hemp, Flax, &c. (to which should be added the companion piece, *Some Further Reasons*) constitutes Swift's most formidable statement on the all-important subject of tithes.[1] The tract is perhaps most interesting for its revelation of his attitude toward the exact status of tithes. Are they by divine right or legal right? This vexed question had been debated with special vehemence in the seventeenth century as a result of the Puritan attacks on tithes. The central figure in the controversy was Sir Henry Spelman, whose learned works on the subject were widely read and quoted in the eighteenth century.[2] His defence of tithes won him the affection of many Anglican clergymen, but his learned disquisitions were also a rich source tapped by Quakers, Anabaptists, and lay writers against tithes for their own purposes. Particularly he had brought discomfort to defenders of the theory that tithes are due by divine right. He was accused of being 'if not the Parent, yet the Nurse of this common and mischievous Error' that tithes are due only '*by Humane right*'.[3] At the close of the seventeenth century the supporters of divine right were rapidly becoming less numerous despite cogent arguments for their position by Thomas Comber, later Dean of Durham, in two well-known books, *The Right of Tithes Asserted and Proved* (1677) and *An Historical Vindication of the Divine Right of Tithes* (1682). Another defence, though with less authority, came from the non-Juror Charles Leslie, in his *Essay concerning the Divine Right of Tithes* (1700).

The opposed position was well stated at the same time by John Sharp, later Archbishop of York, who agreed with

[1] I would surmise that *Some Further Reasons against the Bill for settling the Tithe of Hemp and Flax, &c.* was the list compiled by the person or persons briefing counsel for the petitioners against the Bill. Swift approved and, in a sense, adopted the list as his own. He may well have had a hand in drawing it up.

[2] Spelman's *De non temerandis ecclesiis* (1613) and *Larger Treatise on Tithes* (a collection of his writings on the subject, 1647) were widely known. In 1698 Edmund Gibson, later Bishop of London, printed *Reliquiae Spelmannianae* with a eulogistic biographical preface.

[3] See the 'Epistle Dedicatory' in Thomas Comber's *An Historical Vindication of the Divine Right of Tithes*, London, 1682.

Comber that tithes are validly due to the clergy, but denied them to be so 'by the express law of God'. 'I can by no means be persuaded', Sharp wrote to Comber, 'that Christians at this day are obliged by any law of God to pay a tenth, or ninth, or eleventh, or any precise proportion of their income to the maintenance of the clergy.'[1] This position was elaborately and persuasively presented by Humphrey Prideaux, Dean of Norwich, in *The Original and Right of Tithes, for the Maintenance of the Ministry in a Christian Church, truly stated* (1710). Prideaux denied that tithes are due 'as to the *quota pars*, by a Divine Law obligatory upon all Mankind'. He urged those who contended for such a viewpoint to consider its dangerous implications. If the tenth part of every man's annual increase is due to the clergy by divine right, then all compositions for tithes, all impropriations, all settlements of any kind affecting tithes are breaches of Divine Law, and the government which arranged and permitted these practices, as well as the people concerned, has been continuously engaged in impiety and sacrilege.[2] The absurdity of this position he believed to be apparent. His own view was far more moderate. He maintained that the clergy are entitled to a 'sufficient maintenance'; that this principle is derived from scripture and ancient practice, and enforced by law. Thus tithes 'stand upon as good a bottom as if they were so due [i.e. by divine right], and it is altogether as much sin against God, as well as his Ministers, to detain them'.[3]

This attitude was the more prevalent among the early eighteenth-century clergy. Bishop Gilbert Burnet expressed the legalistic principle succinctly: 'Certainly it is a much wiser Way to assert our Right on the Bottom of Law, which here cannot be disputed, than to run into a remoter and more doubtful Argument of the *Divine Right of Tythes*: In this we are sure we have both Law and Justice on our Side.'[4] Among

---

[1] Thomas Sharp, *The Life of John Sharp*, D.D., ed. by Thomas Newcome (London, 1825), ii. 12 ff.

[2] 'To the Reader', Sig. A 3–4.   [3] p. 309.

[4] *A Sermon Preach'd, and a Charge given at the Triennial Visitation of the Diocese of Salisbury* (London, 1714), pp. 67–68.

jurists and laymen generally such a view took hold easily. W. Bohun of the Middle Temple, whose *The Law of Tithes* (1730) received respectful attention in Swift's day, asserted that tithes are '*now generally confessed to be mere* Lay Chattles, and consequently *determinable according to the Rules prescribed by our* Common *and* Statute Law'.[1] Swift's friend, Lord Carteret, remarked that it is 'a jest to affirm Bishops to be *jure divino*, or tithes to be so'. The Irish peer to whom the remark was made, Viscount Perceval, agreed, adding that many of the great divines deny the precise tenth to be *jure divino*, though they hold that the clergy have a divine right to maintenance.[2] A final statement will suffice, from one of the more learned among the Irish bishops, William Nicolson of Derry, who declared to a correspondent:

... I shall never quarrel with you about the strength or infirmities of those arguments which have been produced in maintenance of the *Jus Divinum* of Tithes; since I am abundantly convinced that the most unanswerable proof we have against the modern disputants among the Quakers and Anabaptists is, that our claim of right is founded upon the Laws of the Land. Here is the true basis of all our temporal enjoyments and possessions; and for my own part, when I am once satisfied that my rights have such a legal establishment as this, I shall never desire to fetch my title any higher.[3]

The temper of the times was more favourable to the legalistic view, but the theory of divine right had its appeal and some of the clergy clung to it, or gave it up grudgingly. Swift was among those who yielded with reluctance. In 1723, when Molesworth in his tract on agriculture objected to the view of tithes as *jure divino*, Swift refused to concede the point.[4] He admitted, however, that it is to the advantage of

---

[1] See the Preface to Bohun's *A Tithing Table*, London, 1732.

[2] *Hist. MSS. Comm. 16th R.* 1920-3: *Diary of the First Earl of Egmont*, i. 106–7. For a good statement of the view that the clergy have a divine right to maintenance, see William Webster, *The Clergy's Right of Maintenance, vindicated from Scripture and Reason* (London, 1726), pp. 20–21, 23, 28, 51.

[3] *Letters on Various Subjects* ..., i. 321, to William Forbes, author of *A Treatise on Church Lands and Tithes*, 1705.

[4] *Some Considerations* ..., pp. 42–43.

the clergy to avoid a claim for the *jus divinum* of tithes and to
maintain that they are a legal right, since 'a maxim in law hath
more weight in the world than an article of faith'.[1] In 1733
this more realistic view prevailed with him and his clerical
colleagues who fought the reduction of tithe on hemp and
flax. It is clear from the opening statement of *Some Further
Reasons* that though he was ready to avoid the plea of divine
right, he wished nevertheless to keep the idea alive for whatever value it might have: '. . . tithes are the patrimony of the
Church: And if not of Divine original, yet at least of great
antiquity'.[2] The hesitancy in giving up the concept of divine
right and yet the willingness to accept the more expedient
legalistic view did not escape notice. Such critics of the clergy
as Lord Hervey seized the point: '. . . nor will I deny the
Reverend Order this Justice, that, tenacious as they are of
the *Divine Right of Tythes*, they have never scrupled to prefer
a *Parliamentary Right to a Pound Rate*, when it promised them
a better Revenue'.[3] If this witty comment describes Swift's
dilemma, it does something less than justice to his sincerity
and his convictions. He found a certain persuasiveness in a
frequent argument offered in defence of tithes, one which had
cogency for the eighteenth-century mind, the argument from
antiquity; and he made use of that for his purposes. In *Some
Reasons* he declared that the clergy may not be deprived of
'their ancient legal dues'.[4] But the crux of his argument, the
one on which he desired to rest his case, was the concept of
tithes as property. 'The Tenth of all yearly Increase is made
the Clergyman's Estate by the same laws . . . that make the
Land the Landlord's Estate; by the same Laws the Liberty
and Property of the *one* as well as of the *other* is secured to
them.'[5] This was the principle laid down in 1723 by the
'layman' who answered Molesworth. It is the principle which
Swift recognized as having a more universal appeal. The

---

[1] *Prose Works*, iii. 237.   [2] Ibid. iii. 286.
[3] *An Answer to the Country Parson's Plea against the Quakers Tythe Bill* (Dublin,
1736), p. 63.
[4] *Prose Works*, 282, 283.
[5] *Considerations upon Considerations* . . ., pp. 46–47.

proposed legislation he termed an invasion of the property
rights of the clergy. Will it be alleged that a clergyman's
property 'is not upon an equal foot with the properties of
other men?' The clergy, he wrote, 'acquire their own small
pittance, by at least as honest means, as their neighbours,
the landlords, possess their estates; and have been always
supposed, except in rebellious or fanatical times, to have as
good a title: For, no families now in being can shew a more
ancient'.[1] Parliament, therefore, ought to guard the rights
and properties of the clergy instead of invading them. Swift
adopted a current argument to support the view that a
clergyman had a recognized property in tithes. All leases or
purchase of titheable lands have for centuries been cheaper
by virtue of their being titheable, it being understood that
the transaction is for only nine-tenths, with the remaining
one-tenth belonging to the Church. Otherwise in justice a
lessee or purchaser should have paid more. This position was
well stated in 1722 by William Taswell, who was defending
the secular foundation of tithes:

> For whether you bought your estate; or whether it came to you by
> Descent, or by Gift; the first Purchaser bought but nine Parts. For had
> the Estate been Tithe-free, it would have cost at least two Years pur-
> chase more. The tenth Part thereof you have no right to; 'tis, as a
> reserved Rent, to be paid as the Law directs; and consequently you
> ought to give it to those for whom it was reserved; otherwise you are
> unjust. . . . And the Case is the same, whether you be Landlord, or
> Tenant. For no Landlord can let to his Tenant any more than he has
> himself a Right to.[2]

Accepting this view, Swift held that if tithes are abated or
lands exempted from tithes by an Act of Parliament, 'so much
value is taken from the proprietor of the tithes, and vested
in the proprietor of the lands, or his head tenants'.[3]

It was in the light of such a conception of tithes that Swift

[1] *Prose Works*, iii. 278-9.
[2] *The Popish Priest Unmasked, or the Quaker's Plea for non-Payment of Tithes
Answer'd* (London, 1722), p. 42.
[3] *Prose Works*, iii. 286.

attacked the pending Bill as a 'violation of common justice', and this from a legislative branch which has always 'had so tender a regard to property'.[1] The situation, he believed, presented potentially a sinister precedent. If Parliament assumed the right to reduce things titheable below the tenth justly due, 'which is and ever will be the Clergy's equitable right', it could also assume the right to reduce tithes 'to a sixtieth or eightieth, and from thence to nothing'.[2] Swift recognized uneasily the weakened position of the clergy consequent on losing the sanction of divine right. If the right to tithe is grounded in common law and statute, if tithes are 'mere lay Chattles', then the civil authority is more difficult to resist. Thus we find him lamenting that the clergy had lost in recent times the right to be taxed only with its own consent.[3] Despite his insistence on the rights of the clergy, he is clearly aware of the weakness of a State Church in conflict with a civil power ready to work its will on ecclesiastical property. In fact, this tract of 1733 is not so much a proud and spirited defence as a plea that an impoverished priesthood be not further impoverished by invidious treatment. The clergy, he maintained, are already encouraging the linen industry; it is unreasonable to single them out for 'a heavy burden, which neither the nobility, nor gentry, nor trades-men, nor farmers' are expected to bear.[4]

One aspect of the legislation of 1733 Swift considered particularly dangerous—a 'terrible circumstance in this Bill . . . of turning the tithe of flax and hemp into what the lawyers call a *Modus*'.[5] Far-sighted churchmen feared the modus, or money composition, an arrangement whereby a clergyman compounded for an annual fixed sum over a long term (or forever) in lieu of a tenth part of the actual tithe-able product. In practice this expedient arrangement often

---

[1] *Prose Works*, iii. 288.   [2] Ibid. iii. 279.

[3] Ibid. iii. 287. The clergy recognized the importance of maintaining that they had 'the sole right of taxing themselves' (see *Journal of the House of Lords of Ireland*, 1779, i. 750; White Kennet, *The Case of Impropriations*, p. 120; [John Johnson], *The Clergyman's Vade Mecum*, p. 132).

[4] *Prose Works*, iii. 280, 281–2.   [5] Ibid. iii. 281.

prevailed. Its great merit, according to its supporters, was that the clergyman would avoid a constant wrangle with his parishioners. Instead of facing annually a disputatious gathering of tithes set forth in kind, selling them to the unpopular tithe-farmers, or canting them at auction, the churchman who accepted a modus found his tithing transaction simple and dignified, and he lived in amity with his parishioners. Writers on Church leases and tithes, however, pointed to a glaring weakness in the money composition: it failed to take into account the tendency of money to sink in value. Reference has already been made to Swift's use of Fleetwood's *Chronicon Preciosum* (1707), which presented the disastrous effects of inflationary tendencies on church temporalities. This work contained a strong warning to clergymen against the modus:

... if ever you design to take Orders and Obtain any *Rectory*, *Vicarage*, or higher *Dignity* in the Church, you be, above all Things, careful how you make any Composition or Agreement, for any long Space of Years, to receive a certain Price of Money, for the Corn that is due to you, altho' for the present it may seem a tempting Bargain, and a profitable Exchange, and rid you of some Trouble. You know not what Time may bring forth, nor what great Alterations may happen, nor what great Mischiefs you, unwittingly, may do your Successors.[1]

Swift had learned this lesson well. As we have seen, he had pointed out in 1723 the inflationary peril in long-term episcopal leases; and now in 1733 he utilized the same arguments against the modus. The rise in value of commodities and the corresponding fall in money was an inescapable historical fact. Though it was later amended to twenty-one years, the pending legislation at first proposed to fix the modus on flax forever.[2] Money, Swift declared, is not 'of any certain perpetual intrinsic value'. It has sunk at least nine-tenths in the last four centuries and by a third 'within our own memories,

---

[1] p. 174. For similar warnings see Thomas Comber, *An Historical Vindication of the Divine Right of Tithes* (London, 1682), p. 242, White Kennet, *Parochial Antiquities . . .*, pp. 604–5; Boulter, *Letters*, i. 234.
[2] *Journal of the House of Commons of Ireland*, iv. 113, 29 Dec. 1733.

in purchasing almost everything required for the necessities or conveniencies of life'. This gradual decline he thought would continue, and therefore a modus agreed to at the moment will year by year sink in purchasing power. Thus he enunciated as a principle that 'no corporation . . . should by any means grant away their properties in perpetuity upon any consideration whatsoever'—a principle he had enforced in 1723 with the remark already quoted, that 'a barrel of corn is of a real intrinsic value, which gold and silver are not'.[1]

As the Bill was pending, Swift and several of his clerical friends petitioned the House of Commons 'in behalf of themselves and the Rest of the Clergy of the Church of *Ireland* . . . setting forth that they will be greatly affected in their Properties by a Clause' in the Bill. On 29 December 1733, counsel for the petitioners was heard, and on that day the Commons accepted certain changes favourable to the clergy, but the proposed modus still remained.[2] On 8 January 173¾, Faulkner published Swift's *Some Reasons*. When he reprinted it later, he included an Advertisement which stated that Swift's 'Reasons were presented to several Members of Parliament, and had so good an Effect, that the Bill was dropped'.[3]

The Bill was not dropped, though the offending clause imposing a modus was expunged in the House of Lords— and on the very day that the petition of Swift and his friends was presented to that House.[4] Still Faulkner may attribute too much to Swift's efforts. He had not persuaded the Commons to eliminate the mod**us**, and it is not at all certain that the Lords needed persuasion. Before Swift took a hand in the proceedings there was strong opposition among that body. The temper of the Lords was reported to England by

---

[1] *Prose Works*, iii. 281, 229.

[2] See above, p. 133, n 2. It is possible that the petition effected the change in the duration of the modus from 'forever' to twenty-one years.

[3] *Works*, 1752, viii. 128.

[4] *Journal of the House of Lords of Ireland*, iii. 267. The Commons accepted the amendment by the Lords, 11 Jan. 173¾ (see *Journal of the House of Commons of Ireland*, iv. 120).

Marmaduke Coghill, Judge of the Prerogative Court, who wrote that the Bill could not pass since 'the whole body of the Bishops, & several of the temporall Lords' opposed it. The principal reason for the strenuous opposition of the clergy, he said, was the unreasonableness 'that the Clergy should only give that encouragement [to the sowing of flax and hemp] by abating of more than twice the value of their tythes, & the Laiety give nothing att all . . .'.[1] But whatever Swift's influence, the clergy in this instance, whose attitude he represented, prevailed.

IV. THE LEGION CLUB

In 1736 Swift reached the apogee of his pessimism concerning the Church. The temporalities were once again under attack, and he reflected sadly on the 'universal hatred which prevails against the clergy'. The history of Christianity revealed, as he glanced back to observe it, a singular persistence of 'the same principle of robbing the Church'.[2] In Ireland at the moment that principle was manifesting itself in the agistment controversy.

'Our Town is crowded with Lawyers and Country Gentlemen: agistment is the word which divides their Hopes and Fears.'[3] These words, written to Lord Orrery from a correspondent in Dublin, in April 1736, hint at the agitation which sharply divided the gentry and the clergy of Ireland and which inspired one of Swift's most famous poems, *A Character, Panegyric, and Description of the Legion Club*. Tithe agistment, the subject of this bitter controversy, was the tithe on pasturage, especially pasturage grazed by dry and barren cattle. There had been resistance to the payment of this tithe

---

[1] B.M. Add. MS. 21123.   [2] *Prose Works*, iii. 304.

[3] *The Orrery Papers*, ed. the Countess of Cork and Orrery (London, 1903), i. 155. For brief general discussions of the agistment controversy see Richard Mant, *History of the Church of Ireland*, ii. 554–8; T. Dunbar Ingram, *A Critical Examination of Irish History* (London, 1904), i. 269 ff. Boulter's *Letters*, ii. 150–1, 170, 181–5, presents it through the eyes of a churchman. See also the report on the agistment Bill, B.M. Add. MS. 21132, fols. 54, 65, 66.

as early as 1707, but the antagonism to it was more violent
and better organized in the 1720's. The rights of the clergy
were legally established in 1722 by a suit brought into the
Court of Exchequer in Ireland at the instance of Archdeacon
Neale of Leighlin, whose claim was upheld on appeal in
England. This victory was hailed by Irish churchmen as 'a
most signal Service to the Church'. Archbishop King wrote
to Neale that 'You deserve the thanks and acknowledge-
ment of every Churchman, & I doubt not but it will preserve
you a greatfull remembrance as long as Tithes are paid in
Ireland.'[1] Nevertheless lay resistance continued, and came for-
midably to a head in 1735. In December a petition was introduced into the Commons by several 'Gentlemen, in Behalf of
themselves and the Rest of the Farmers, Grasiers of Ireland',
praying for relief against suits demanding tithe agistment
'notwithstanding that according to the best Information . . .
no such Tythes have ever been paid, or even demanded in
this Kingdom until a few Years since'.[2] Three months later,
in March 173$\frac{5}{6}$, a second petition to the same purpose, by
another group of 'Gentlemen and Freeholders', was introduced.[3] The favourable reaction to this second petition
brought Swift into the situation with his poem, in which he
applied to the House of Commons the name of the biblical
unclean spirit. In his private correspondence he had earlier
referred to the Irish Parliament either as The Club or the
Legion Club,[4] but now he applied the latter title publicly for
the first time in a bitter denunciation of its members who were
active against the clergy. Sir Thomas Prendergast, the noisy
Tom of another poem by Swift, received this accolade:

> Let Sir T—, that rampant Ass,
> Stuff his Guts with Flax and Grass;

---

[1] King Corresp. 12 July 1726. See also William Nicolson, *Letters on Various Subjects . . .*, ii. 578; Edward Synge, *Two Affidavits in relation to the Demands of Tythe-Agistment in the Diocese of Leighlin* (Dublin, 1736), pp. 25 f. Archdeacon Neale won his suit in a spiritual Court in 1707; in King's Bench in 1722.

[2] *Journal of the House of Commons of Ireland*, iv. 184. See also iv. 199.

[3] Ibid. iv. 213, 214, 217, 219.

[4] *Corresp.* v. 260, 287, 295, 305.

But before the Priest he fleeces
Tear the Bible all to Pieces.

. . . .

Worthy Offspring of a Shoeboy,
Footman, Traytor, vile Seducer,
Perjur'd Rebel, brib'd Accuser;
Lay thy paltry Priviledge aside,
Sprung from Papists and a Regicide;
Fall a Working like a Mole,
Raise the Dirt about your Hole.[1]

Anthony Morgan, friendly with Swift until he acted as chairman of the committee to consider the petition, received relatively restrained treatment:

Bless us, *Morgan*! Art thou there Man?
Bless mine Eyes! Art thou the Chairman?

. . . .

Hast thou been so long at School,
Now to turn a factious Tool!
Alma Mater was thy Mother,
Every young Divine thy Brother.
Thou a disobedient Varlet,
Treat thy Mother like a Harlot!

. . . .

Send the Clergy all to graze;
And to make your Project pass,
Leave them not a Blade of Grass.

Some of the most violent language is applied to the House of Commons as a whole, which is pictured as Bedlam:

Let them, when they once get in
Sell the Nation for a Pin;
While they sit a picking Straws
Let them rave of making Laws;
While they never hold their Tongue,
Let them dabble in their Dung;
Let them form a grand Committee,
How to plague and starve the City;

[1] *Poems*, iii. 829 ff.

> Let them stare and storm and frown,
> When they see a Clergy-Gown.
> Let them, 'ere they crack a Louse,
> Call for th'Orders of the House;
> Let them with their gosling Quills,
> Scribble senseless Heads of Bills;
> We may, while they strain their Throats,
> Wipe our A——s with their V——.

This bitter invective is Swift's response to the sympathetic report in the Commons on the petition of March $173\frac{5}{6}$ and to the resolutions which followed. The resolutions maintained that the clergy is amply provided for by its glebes, undisputed tithes, and other emoluments; that its demand for tithe agistment is 'new, grievous, and burthensome to the Land-lords and Tenants' of the nation; that this new demand has impaired the Protestant interest by causing emigration; that it has occasioned Popery and infidelity by creating dissension among laity and clergy; and that the tithe should be re-sisted by all legal means pending further legislative action.[1] Encouraged by these resolutions, Gentlemen-Freeholders formed a number of associations pledged not to pay the tithe, to provide funds and legal talent to any who would resist, and to show favour to any clergyman who did not demand his due. The clergy generally watched these proceedings with great concern, and Swift expressed the prevalent attitude in his reference to the 'public associations' set up to ruin the Church.[2]

In the midst of this violent dispute his poem on the Legion Club was circulating in manuscript—'a cursed long libel', he wrote to Sheridan on 15 May 1736, is 'running about in manuscript . . . the foolish town imputes it to me'. 'I have some Club enemies', he continued, 'that would be glad to shoot me, and I do not love to be shot; it is a death I have a particular

---

[1] *Journal of the House of Commons of Ireland*, iv. pt. 2, appendix lxv; iv. 219. The report of the committee was also printed separately by order.

[2] *The Gentleman's Magazine*, vi (1736), 215–16; Boulter, *Letters*, ii. 120, 150, 182; *Corresp.* v. 402, 440.

aversion to'. He expressed his pleasure that the parliamentary session had ended and that it would be a year and a half before the Club met again, 'to be revenged farther on the clergy'.[1] His mind running on despoliations of the Church, he began at this time a tract entitled *Concerning that Universal Hatred which prevails against the Clergy*, dated 24 May 1736. In it he apparently intended to present some of the major historical despoliations, leading up to the present one by which the Irish clergy were being deprived of their rightful tithe. He turned at the beginning to 'that monster and tyrant, Henry VIII, who took away from [the clergy], against law, reason, and justice, at least two-thirds of their legal possessions . . .'.[2] It was logical that he should pay his respects to the greatest despoiler in Anglican history, as Henry was conceived to be, at a moment when the Irish Commons was imitating that 'detestable tyrant'. Unfortunately after a few pages he broke off and left incomplete what might have been an interesting attempt to show how the 'hatred of the clergy' had been fostered by those who had designs on Church possessions. As it is, we have no reasoned statement in which he discusses the issues raised by the controversy over agistment. The casual comments in his letters and *The Legion Club* are merely emotional outbursts. It may be said, however, that the basic issues were not new and that his earlier discussions of such matters as Church lands, tithes, relations of laity and clergy, apply similarly to this controversy.

In this phase of the agistment dispute, which lasted for at least four years, Swift once again found common ground with the bishops. Edward Synge, formerly a troublesome canon of St. Patrick's but now Bishop of Ferns, was staunchly defending the Church in print and refuting the arguments and resolutions which emanated from gentry in the Commons.[3]

[1] Ibid. v. 331 ff.

[2] *Prose Works*, iii. 301. See below, pp. 161 ff.

[3] See his *Two Affidavits in relation to the Demands of Tythe-Agistment in the Diocese of Leighlin* (Dublin, 1736). Eight suits for recovery of tithe-agistment filed by Synge were largely instrumental in bringing the controversy to a head (see the Report of the Committee cited above, p. 138, n. 1).

Archbishop Boulter, who rarely saw eye to eye with the Dean of St. Patrick's, wrote at length to English prelates and statesmen of the plight of the Irish Church and clergy under this new attack. Like Swift, these men were deeply disturbed by the animosity displayed toward the clergy. Boulter confirmed the prevalent fear, which Swift had remarked on earlier, that the attack on tithes would spread. To the Earl of Anglesey he wrote:

What has been already done, is but the beginning of what is intended, for several of them speak out, that the present claims of the clergy, even those about the legality of which there is no dispute, are matter of frequent controversy, and breed quarrels between the clergy and laity, and which ought to be taken away, and they mention in particular small dues, tythe of flax, and potatoes. . . .[1]

The anonymous author of a pamphlet defending the clergy declared that 'Restraint in one sort of Tithes may possibly bring in the like as to others, a Reduction of Tithes, a Division of Glebes, and that may stretch to Church Lands of every Denomination.'[2]

It was, in fact, soon recognized that the controversy over agistment transcended the validity of the one tithe under dispute, that the chief issue was the clergy's right to tithes as property, precisely the issue Swift had faced in 1733, when he defended tithes as property on the same footing as other kinds of property and therefore not subject to legislative whim. Of the several pamphlets published during the controversy Swift refers to one specifically, 'an excellent discourse in defence of the clergy, which I have read with much pleasure'.[3] This was Alexander Macaulay's *Property Inviolable* (1736), written in answer to an anonymous pamphlet entitled *Prescription Sacred: or Reasons for Opposing the New Demand of Herbage in Ireland* (1736). The latter pamphlet, though ostensibly concerned with tithe agistment, was an omnium

---

[1] *Letters*, ii. 152 and *passim*.
[2] *Reasons for the Present Clamours against the Clergy of Ireland* (Dublin, 1736), p. 23.
[3] *Corresp.* v. 335.

gatherum of charges against the clergy, among others their litigiousness, their weakening of the Protestant interest, their excessive wealth and design to increase it even farther. Its most challenging aspect was the denial that tithes are property validly grounded in either ceremonial or common law and its argument that if tithe-agistment prevailed 'a general confusion will follow from this revolution in property'. Courts of equity and Acts of Parliament, the author insisted, are the constitutional means by which tithes are determined.[1] Macaulay's answer, as its title indicates, places the emphasis where Swift and other contemporary clergymen wished it to be, on the inviolability of property whether lay or ecclesiastical. We have seen that Swift was ready to forgo, although reluctantly, any defence of tithes by the principles of divine right and immemorial custom. Macaulay announced at the outset that he proposed to consider the clergy in its temporal, not in its spiritual capacity, not as clergymen but as subjects, and in so doing to oppose the author of *Prescription Sacred*, whose views have 'a Tendency to weaken Property in general'.[2] *Property Inviolable* brought comfort to the churchmen; and from Swift it elicited praise of the author's 'truly honourable zeal in defence of the legal rights of the clergy'.[3] Macaulay's defence rested on his insistence that every beneficed clergyman in Ireland has a freehold in his benefice. Property, he wrote, is 'a Tender Thing', and the property of all the freeholders is equally secure and inviolable. If legislation can take away the right of one, it may do the same with all. Tithe agistment is due by prescription, by common law, and by statute, and as property so based the legislature is bound to protect it. This, he maintained, is the very essence of liberty; otherwise the legislature could pre-empt the right to abolish all tithes or glebes, or turn the clergy out of their houses— and could give similar treatment to every man whether lay or

[1] pp. 12 and *passim*.
[2] *Property Inviolable: or, Some Remarks upon a Pamphlet entituled, Prescription Sacred* (Dublin, 1736), p. 3.
[3] *Prose Works*, xi. 414.

clerical. He used a point of special cogency to bring home to laymen the perils involved in tampering with property rights. If the revenues of the clergy may be thus arbitrarily reduced, the same action could logically extend to impropriators and lay patrons who have estates or inheritances in tithes and advowsons held in fee simple to themselves and their heirs forever.[1] Macaulay, who was a barrister, made good use of statutes, precedents, and legal authorities, buttressing his arguments with details, to achieve a reasoned statement of a position that Swift presents only in its lineaments.

One fundamental aspect of the agistment controversy ran counter to Swift's deep conviction that the ultimate source of national welfare inhered in the land. The resistance to tithe agistment was to him more than an assault on ecclesiastical property rights; it was a further debilitation of an already enfeebled agricultural economy whose failure to flourish had so vitally affected both Church and State. In his various Irish tracts there is a constant insistence that the economic plight of Ireland can be relieved, or at least prevented from becoming more disastrous, if tillage is increased and the trend toward turning arable lands into pasturage arrested. 'Agriculture,' he wrote in 1720, 'which hath been the principal care of all wise nations . . . we countenance so well, that the landlords are everywhere by penal clauses absolutely prohibiting their tenants from ploughing . . . .'[2] In the Seventh Drapier's Letter he listed as one of 'the *Wishes* of the Nation' that 'due Encouragement should be given to *Agriculture*; and a Stop put to that pernicious Practice of Graziers, engrossing vast Quantities of Land . . . whereby the Country is extremely depopulated'.[3] These are typical of his plaints for nearly two decades as he observed a country which could ill afford to

---

[1] *Property Inviolable*, pp. 15, 30, 42 and *passim*. The importance attached to the argument concerning property is further indicated in two pamphlets, one attacking Macaulay, the other supporting him: *Property Vindicated* (1739), *Property Reasserted* (1740).

[2] *Prose Works*, vii. 17.

[3] *The Drapier's Letters to the People of Ireland*, ed. Herbert Davis (Oxford, 1935), p. 169.

import food-stuffs gradually reduce its tillage to a point
where any crop failure, however mild, was likely to bring
undernourishment or starvation. It was, of course, the crop
failures of 1727 and the following years which inspired
A Modest Proposal. Swift was only one of many who called
for relief. In 1728 Archbishop Boulter sought aid from the
English Privy Council. In pleading for favourable action on
a Bill to encourage tillage he described the situation in
Ireland as follows:

. . . many persons have hired large tracts of land, on to 3 or 4000 acres,
and have stocked them with cattle, and have no other inhabitants on
their land than so many cottiers as are necessary to look after their
sheep and black cattle; so that in some of the finest counties, in many
places there is neither house nor corn field to be seen in 10 or 15 miles
travelling; and daily in some counties, many gentlemen (as their leases
fall into their hands) tye up their tenants from tillage. . . .[1]

The Bill which Boulter commended became a law in 1728
(1 Geo. II, c. 10). It required tillage of at least five in every
one hundred acres regardless of any agreement to the contrary between landlord and tenant; but the provision proved
too mild and the penalty too weak to solve the problem. In
the decade of 1730 to 1740, with tillage steadily declining,
the urgency of the situation was widely recognized by both
laymen and churchmen.[2]

There is no reason to suspect that Swift's pleas for increased
tillage derived from anything more than a sincere desire for
the welfare of Ireland, yet he—as well as churchmen generally
—fully realized that clergy and Church were far better served
by land in tillage than in pasturage. The tithes on products of
the soil, though often difficult to collect, were usually considered valid, whereas tithes on pasturage were both less

---

[1] *Letters*, i. 178–9. See George O'Brien, *Economic History of Ireland in the
Eighteenth Century*, p. 111.
[2] See, for example, *The Present State of Tillage in Ireland Considered*, 1725;
Considerations on Agriculture, 1730; *Reflections upon the Present Unhappy Circumstances
of Ireland*, 1731; Samuel Pierson, *Farther Considerations for the Improvement of
Tillage in Ireland*, 1738; *Some Thoughts on the Tillage of Ireland*, 1738; *The Dublin
Society's Weekly Observations*, 1739.

valuable and in dispute or litigation. Swift was quite early
aware of the impoverishment of some parishes where arable
land was turned into grazing. In 1710 he remarked on certain
parishes 'sunk so low by the Increase of Graziers' that the
incumbents are unable to pay a small Crown rent.[1] A decade
later Archbishop King wrote to Wake at Canterbury in the
same vein:

... now that the plow is laid aside ... grain is dearer in Dublin than
in London. ... Land formerly plowed is now turned into grazing for
bullocks and dry cattle that yield nothing to the clergy; and benefices
that formerly were worth hundreds to incumbents hardly yield crown
rent to the king. I have seven parishes in this diocese in this circumstance, and no clergyman will accept of them; and the same is the case
in many others in the kingdom, which are either seized into the king's
hands for nonpayments or want incumbents.[2]

Such complaints multiplied. A report to England in 1727
stated that 'at present the Countrey People in Ireland do not
apply themselves so much as formerly to Tillage, from whence
the Tyths were very considerable to the Curate, but for the
Most Part they do now turn their Farms into Pastureage the
Tyths whereof are not regulated, and but little worth ...'.[3]
At the height of the controversy over tithe agistment an
'Apologist' for the clergy pointed out that if land is in corn
the parson receives his yearly tithe; if it is devoted to dry and
barren cattle, the landowner or grazier knows he may stave
off the tithes or perhaps be free of them entirely.[4] The churchmen who so strenuously opposed the legislation removing
tithe on pasturage were not concerned merely with the loss
of present tithes; they realized that any concession to pastur-

---

[1] *Journal to Stella*, ii. 680.

[2] Gilbert Collection, MS. 28, 15 Nov. 1720. In 1723 the Irish churchmen
promoted a Bill to encourage tillage (*Journal of the House of Commons of Ireland*,
iii. 356). Josiah Hort wrote to Wake that it would benefit many small benefices by
increasing tithes (Wake Corresp. xiv, 29 Nov. 1723). The complaints of the Irish
clergy against the conversion of land from tillage to pasturage were at least a
century old (see Royal Irish Academy MS. 23. F. 1, fol. 302, from 1615).

[3] P.R.O., S.P. 63 (Ireland), 388.

[4] *An Apology for the Clergy of Ireland, in respect of their Civil Rights* (Dublin,
1738), p. 8.

age, to make it more profitable, would accentuate the tendency to turn arable lands into grazing, to the detriment of those who depended on tithes. 'I have in vain represented to several of [the laity]', Boulter wrote to Sir Robert Walpole in 1737, 'that in the south and west of *Ireland* by destroying the tithe of agistment, they naturally discourage tillage . . .'.[1] In the following year Swift urged Faulkner to print Alexander Macaulay's *Some Thoughts on the Tillage of Ireland* (1738), the same Macaulay whose tract in 1736 Swift had praised so warmly. In this new tract he brought more comfort to the clergy. 'He has learnedly shown,' Swift told Faulkner, 'from the practice of all wise nations in past and later ages, that tillage was the great principle and foundation of their wealth, and recommends the practice of it to this kingdom with the most weighty reasons.' This would seem to be, Swift added wryly, the sentiment of the House of Commons, 'although the increase of tillage may be of advantage to the clergy'.[2] He could speak of this matter from his own experience. In 1730 his cathedral chapter granted him from the economy fund a sum of £20 annually to repair the deanery 'in Consideration of the great decrease in the Dean's rents by turning tillage ground into pasture in the parishes belonging to the Dean'.[3] His constant complaints from 1730 of the decrease in his tithes are certainly in part a result of the trend away from tillage. Other members of his chapter suffered individually,[4] and doubtless the cathedral economy suffered proportionately. It was this phase of the agistment controversy which prompted his words: 'by the great providence of God, it is so ordered, that if the clergy be fairly dealt with, whatever increases their maintenance will more largely increase the estates of the landed men, and the profits of their farmers'.[5]

This controversial context out of which *The Legion Club* emerged helps to explain what Sir Walter Scott called its 'extreme virulence of invective'.[6] Swift's mood of bitterness

---

[1] *Letters*, ii. 183. [2] *Corresp.* vi. 56.
[3] Chap. Min. 1720–63, 17 Apr. 1730. [4] Ibid. 17 Mar. 1740.
[5] *Corresp.* vi. 56. [6] Swift, *Works*, ed. Sir Walter Scott (1814), i. 427.

and pessimism was deepened by similar occurrences in
England tending in his opinion to undermine Church and
churchmen. Among some there was a conviction that the
attack on tithes in Ireland had been instigated in England,
and that it was part of a larger sinister design.[1] Swift himself
does not go so far, but he does remark several times on the
simultaneous attacks in the two countries. 'The people of
England', he wrote to Sheridan in May 1736, 'are copying
from us to plague the clergy, but they intend far to outdo
the original'.[2] In the following month he wrote to Charles
Ford, 'As to the Church, it is equally the aversion of both
kingdoms: you for the Quakers' tithes, and we for grass, or
agistment. . . .'[3] The allusion to the Quakers concerned a Bill
then being hotly debated in the English Parliament calling
for relief to that sect in payment of tithes. The basic issue
involved was the same as that in the agistment controversy:
the legality of tithes and their status as property. Irish
churchmen watched the English dispute with great interest,
fearing that legislation favourable to the Quakers in England
would spread to Ireland. As Archbishop Boulter wrote to
Canterbury, '. . . the Church of *England* and *Ireland* are so
interwoven in point of interest, that one cannot suffer, but
the other will soon fall into the same distress'.[4] The Quakers
were frequently in the van of any attack on tithes, and the
Irish clergy knew them as formidable opponents who had
managed to get special legislative concessions from the time
of William III and earlier.[5] They were well organized for
both religious and commercial purposes, as the Irish Convocation reported in 1711, noting that the Quakers needed 'the
watchful Eye of the Government' even more than other
sectaries because as a group they used 'a specious Pretence
of Religion [for] the Pursuit of Gain'. They 'take upon them

---

[1] Boulter, *Letters*, ii. 151, 185, 191.
[2] *Corresp.* v. 336; see also v. 331.
[3] Ibid. v. 351.
[4] *Letters*, ii. 186.
[5] See J. C. Beckett, *Protestant Dissent in Ireland, 1687–1780*, pp. 131–5.

to give a publick Opposition to the passing of any Bills, which may be to the Prejudice of their Sect'.[1]

To the Irish churchmen the increasing economic power of a group which symbolized resistance to tithes was a matter of alarm. When the Quaker relief Bill was before the English Parliament, the interest in Ireland was such that the pamphlets pro and con were reprinted in Dublin.[2] They took on added significance in the light of what was then occurring in Ireland and lent colour to the view that the simultaneous attacks on the legal rights of the clergy of the two countries were related. Swift was kept informed of the situation in England, and he doubtless saw some of the reprinted pamphlets. One of these deserves brief attention for the reinforcement it gave to the gentry who were fighting tithe agistment and as well for its unqualified assertion of a view that Swift had vigorously opposed in 1733. Erastian though he was in principle, Swift had denied that the clergy are in effect in civil employment and that a reduction of tithes was therefore nothing more than a tax on employments.[3] This seemed to him a pernicious doctrine in its insistence that tithes are salary rather than property. The pamphlet in question, published anonymously but now known to be by Lord Hervey, was entitled *An Answer to the Country Parson's Plea against the Quakers Tythe Bill*. It defended the view that 'The Tythes of the Clergy, are the Wages, which, as Servants of the Publick, they receive from the Bounty of the Laws. . .'. The right of tithes, as it depends upon the grace of the legislative power, is therefore subject to the will of that power. A legislature may with validity convert them into lay fees if it so desires. Lord Hervey distinguished between a layman's freehold inherited from his father and a clergyman's freehold which 'accrues to him by Gift of the Publick, on such Conditions as are or shall be declared to qualify the Tenure

[1] *The Present State of Religion in Ireland* (London, [1712]), pp. 8–9. See also B.M. Add. MS. 28948, fols. 128–9; *Corresp.* i. 283.
[2] *Papers relating to the Quakers Tythe Bill*, Dublin, 1736. This consists of six pamphlets.
[3] *Prose Works*, iii. 282.

of the Possession, or the Recovery of any Rights incident to it'. Ecclesiastical property, he argued, is therefore a trust subject to regulation and is not inviolable property.[1] As for tithes, they are a 'prodigious Usurpation upon the Property of Mankind'; they are, he continued eloquently,

> ... the East-Wind that withers the Fruit, the Caterpillar that destroys the Harvest in the Ear, the Locust that preys upon the Property of the Rich, and eats up the Bread of the Poor, an Harpy that carries Law-Suits in one Claw, and Famine in Another, that devours, what the Publick Taxes spare, and is more inexorable than an Excise.[2]

The pamphlet is further remarkable for its clear intimation that the conflict was not between Quakers and clergy but between the landed gentry and the clergy, and for its generally violent and abusive tone.[3] References to the insolence of the clergy, to their 'litigious insatiably covetous Temper', to the priests who neither plough nor sow yet claim oppressive sums from those who do—these and other such statements help to define the atmosphere which brought from Swift his reflections on the prevalent hatred of the clergy and the aversion to the Church.

Even more was happening in England. Swift wrote to Sheridan that 'their Parliament are following our steps, only with two or three steps for our one'.[4] The allusion is to another assault on ecclesiastical property in the form of a mortmain Bill. Introduced into the English House of Commons in March 1736, it proposed that subjects should be restrained in the future from granting land or money by will to religious uses. Its supporters argued that men should give, if they wished, during their lives, so as to avoid prejudic-

---

[1] p. 34. Lord Hervey's pamphlet was an answer to Dr. Sherlock's *The Country Parson's Plea*, also published anonymously. For the conflict in England over the Quaker tithe Bill, see Norman Sykes, *Edmund Gibson: Bishop of London, 1669–1748* (Oxford, 1926), 163 ff.; *Hist. MSS. Comm. 16th R. 1920–3: Diary of the First Earl of Egmont*, ii. 254, 266: Queen Caroline at first thought the bill reasonable but came to the conclusion that 'it touched upon the clergy's property'.

[2] *An Answer to the Country Parson's Plea against the Quakers Tythe Bill*, p. 64.

[3] Ibid. pp. 63 ff.

[4] *Corresp.* v. 331.

ing their heirs.[1] Like most churchmen of his day, Swift felt
that statutes of mortmain penalized the Church undeservedly.
In 1708 he annotated with an angry comment Matthew
Tindal's *The Rights of the Christian Church* at the point
where Tindal defended statutes of mortmain.[2] In 1713 and
1723 he commented further on the unfairness of such
statutes. They seemed to him to bear hard on the Church,
which was vulnerable to despoliations but 'barred by a *dead
hand*' from augmenting its possessions.[3] The Quaker tithe
Bill and the mortmain Bill were obviously related pieces of
legislation designed against the clergy; in fact, the two Bills
were linked in the pamphlets reprinted in Dublin. Exclaim-
ing against the power and wealth of the Church, Lord Hervey
warned that this power was 'daily increasing from the
Capacities of that Corporation . . . to purchase all the Lands
of *England* in *Mortmain*'.[4] He pleaded that it be checked;
otherwise it would in the course of time 'extend its Sway
over all the Property of the Kingdom . . . tending to the
Destruction of this free Government'.

From England Swift received word sadly of the rancour
against the Church shown by his old friends Bathurst and
Carteret; and soon the impact of English affairs was forcibly
brought home when the Irish House of Commons, following
in the steps of the English House, introduced a mortmain
Bill, in November 1737. To one of the Commoners he sent a
complaint: 'I hear your House is forming a Bill against all
legacies to the church, or any public charity, which puts me
under a great difficulty; because, by my will, I have be-
queathed my whole fortune to build and endow an hospital
for lunatics and idiots'.[5] A few days later he petitioned that
his bequest be excepted from the provisions of the Bill.[6]

Thus the temper and tendencies of the times in both
England and Ireland accentuated his belief that the history

[1] See *Hist. MSS. Comm. 16th R. 1920–3: Diary of the First Earl of Egmont*, ii.
242.
[2] *Prose Works*, iii. 105.   [3] Ibid. iii. 143, 230.
[4] *An Answer to the Country Parson's Plea* . . . p. 52.
[5] *Corresp.* vi. 48.   [6] Ibid. vi. 49.

of Christianity revealed a pattern of plundering. It was in June 1736, as he took stock of the situation in both countries —'of the worst times and peoples, and oppressions that history can show in either kingdom'—that he declared gloomily: 'I have long given up all hopes of Church or Christianity.'[1]

[1] Ibid. v. 350 f.

I. THE LAITY

SWIFT was never able to resign himself to the inevitable conflict between churchmen and laity. From his violent language one might assume that the Anglican gentry of Ireland—the landowners and squires—were unrelenting enemies to the Establishment no less than the Nonconformists. He did not forget, it is true, their importance to the Church in its struggle with dissent and Catholicism. Similarly, as we have seen, he knew that they could be depended upon at times in the Commons to support the inferior clergy against the bishops, whose strength was in the House of Lords. Nevertheless he was aware of too many instances when the gentry sought its own interest; and after 1720 he described them increasingly in caustic language. His tracts and letters are filled with references to the 'insolent ignorant oppressive squire', the 'screwing landlords of this impoverished kingdom', the 'base corrupt spirits of too many of the chief gentry'.[1] One of his chief grievances against these landed men, who were so vital to the welfare of the clergy, was their stubborn resistance to payment of tithes. Their recalcitrance revealed itself not merely on special occasions, as in the agistment controversy; more harmful in the long range was their responsibility for economic attrition, their steady nibbling away at the incomes of the clergy and their complacent acceptance of clerical poverty. In 1734, in one of his wrathful attacks on the landlords, Swift wrote that 'the payment of

[1] See *Corresp.* iii. 245, 310; iv. 118–19, 312, 328; v. 160, 387, 430; *Prose Works*, vii. 25, 110, 122; xi. 193.

tithes in this kingdom, is subject to so many frauds, brangles, and other difficulties, not only from Papists and Dissenters, but even from those who profess themselves Protestants; that by the expense, the trouble, and vexation of collecting, or bargaining for them, they are, of all other rents, the most precarious, uncertain, and ill paid'.[1]

If the subject of tithes looms disproportionately large in Swift's eyes, we must remember its vast importance to the eighteenth-century clergyman. Nothing reveals his attitude quite so clearly as the good counsel he gave to Thomas Sheridan who, at Swift's recommendation to Lord Carteret, was given a living in 1725:

I often advised you to get some knowledge of tithes and Church livings. You must learn the extent of your parish, the general quantity of arable land and pasture in your parish, the common rate of tithes for an acre of the several sorts of corn, and of fleeces and lambs, and to see whether you have any glebe . . . being so far off, you must not let your living as I do, to the several farmers, but to one man; but by all means do not let it for more than one year, till you are surely apprised of the real worth, and even then never let it for above three. . . . You may learn all on the spot, and your neighbouring parsons may be very useful, if they please, but do not let them be your tenants. . . . Take care of the principal squire or squires; they will all tell you the worst of your living; so will the proctors and tithe-jobbers; but you will pick out truth from among them.[2]

He spoke out of the depths of his own experience, well illustrated in his reply to Robert Percival, who was showing the usual resistance of his class to tithes. Swift accused Percival of exercising 'the terror of squireship' on the tithe collector, frightening him into taking half the tithes due:

This odd way of dealing among you folks of great estate in Land and money, although I have been used to, I cannot well reconcile my Self with, especially when you never give me above a quarter value for your tythes—on which account alone you should not brangle with me. It is strange that Clergymen have more trouble with one or two Squires, and meet with more injustice from them than with fifty farmers. If

---

[1] *Prose Works*, iii. 278.   [2] *Corresp*. iii. 244–5.

your Tenants payd your Rents as you pay your Tythe, you would have cause to complain terribly.[1]

It was in this mood that Swift wrote wittily though feelingly to Pope that 'although tithes be of divine institution, they are of diabolical execution'.[2] The gentry were not alone culpable. The poorest cottier and the most substantial farmer alike, he complained, regularly take advantage of the clergyman, who is fortunate if he receives half of his legal tithes.[3] Nevertheless he places the onus on the gentry, the large landowners and the squires who, more powerful than lesser cultivators of the soil, resisted more successfully and set a bad example. It was evident to the discerning that laity and clergy were in a ceaseless struggle over the proportion of income from land to accrue to each. Landowners in granting leases often felt that rents could be higher if tithes were lower; and they not infrequently caused discontent among their tenants by inveighing against 'the sacred tenth'. Archbishop Boulter complained to the government that the gentry put 'it into the heads of their tenants, that it was not their rents, but the paying of the tythes that made them find it hard to live on their farms'. 'The controversy here', he wrote to Walpole, is 'whether the parson shall have his due, or the landlord a greater rent.'[4] Swift saw in these tactics a selfish desire by the landlords to grasp more than their share. He argued that even if tithes were removed or lowered, the tenant or industrious farmer would not profit since the landlord would raise the rent in an equal proportion. The tenant would therefore not 'sit easier in his rent'; the landlord would merely achieve his intention, to become 'lord of the soil and of the tithe together'.[5]

---

[1] B.M. Add. MS. 38671, 11 Dec. 1729 (printed in A. Martin Freeman, *Vanessa and Her Correspondence with Jonathan Swift*, London, 1921, p. 200). See also *Corresp.* iv. 118–20.

[2] Ibid. iv. 127.   [3] *Prose Works*, iii. 262, 280; vii. 122.

[4] *Letters*, i. 229, 234–5; ii. 184, See also *Considerations upon Considerations for the Promoting of Agriculture . . .*, p. 52.

[5] *Prose Works*, vii. 123; iii. 283. That the landlords would use the removal of tithes as a pretext for raising rents—this was an argument of long standing among

The resistance to tithes took many forms and brought forth many bitter charges. One of the most damaging, greatly perturbing to the clergy, was that tithes were responsible for the mounting emigration. Since emigration weakened the Protestant interest and removed cultivators of the soil, from whence the Church chiefly drew its wealth, many churchmen attempted to refute this serious accusation. The steady increase of emigrants in the first decades of the century caused concern in all quarters, lay and clerical. In times of bad crops, as the numbers leaving Ireland multiplied, the problem became more acute. Thus it was in the years 1726 to 1729—those lean and famine years which inspired *A Modest Proposal*—that an unusually large increase in emigration occurred. Boulter reported this melancholy situation to the English government:

... above 4200 men, women, and children have been shipped off ... within three years, and of these above 3100 this last summer. ... The whole north is in a ferment at present, and people every day engaging one another to go next year to the *West Indies*. The humour has spread like a contagious distemper. ... [1]

There were two disturbing aspects to the problem, economic and religious, though in some respects these were inseparable. In eighteenth-century mercantilist theory it was agreed 'that the natural Strength of a Nation consists in the Number' and increase of its inhabitants. [2] This succinct statement of an economic natural law (so it was considered) suggests the seriousness with which contemporaries viewed any loss in population. People were thought to be, as one writer stated, 'the chiefest, most fundamental, and precious commodity'. [3] The political arithmeticians maintained that each person

---

the Irish clergy: see, e.g. *Some Observations . . . upon the Paper . . . intituled, A State of the Case of the Inhabitants of . . . Ulster, in relation to . . . small Tythes*, 1695, p. 22.

[1] *Letters*, i. 210; see also i. 230–1.

[2] *The Tribune* (Dublin), no. 17, 1729. For other statements of this 'natural' law and Swift's use of it, see Louis A. Landa, '*A Modest Proposal* and Populousness', *Modern Philology*, xl (1942), 161–70.

[3] William Petyt (?) *Britania Langeuns*, in *A Select Collection of Early English Tracts on Commerce*, ed. J. R. McCullough (London, 1856), p. 458.

constituted an economic unit whose annual value to the nation could be exactly computed—'thirty pounds a head, valuing them as little better than slaves or negroes', according to Swift's contemporary Samuel Madden, who addressed himself urgently to the Irish public on the disturbing subject of emigration.[1] Thus the departure of any considerable number of people was thought to be a real economic loss to the country. The clergy felt perhaps more keenly another kind of loss—to Protestantism. As an Anglican layman concerned for the welfare of the Church, Madden also called attention to this danger: 'it has weakened', he wrote, 'and is weakening the Protestant interest . . . remedies should be thought of as soon as possible'.[2] The attitude of the clergy was expressed by Archbishop Boulter, who reported to England that the worst aspect of the emigration 'is that it affects only protestants, and reigns chiefly in the north, which is the seat of our linen manufacture'.[3]

Laity and clergy could agree that emigration was an evil, but they violently disagreed as to causes. The dissenters, eager to discountenance a system that forced them to support a despised religious establishment, proclaimed tithes as one of the chief causes. They also attacked the machinery for the collection and enforced payment of tithes—the tithe farmers and the bishops' courts. This encouraged the ship agents, who recruited emigrants at markets and fairs, to use freedom from tithes as a magnet to prospective emigrees.[4] In 1729 the dissenting ministers issued a memorial blaming tithes and ecclesiastical courts as a cause 'of a great desertion in the north', and the Irish gentlemen in London took advantage of the situation to spread the same views.[5] Later in the agistment controversy emigration became an issue. The 'Gentlemen and Landholders' who petitioned for relief from tithe of

---

[1] *Reflections and Resolutions proper for the Gentlemen of Ireland* (Dublin, 1738), pp. 27 ff.   [2] Ibid.   [3] *Letters*, i. 210.

[4] P.R.O. Northern Ireland: *The Report of the Deputy Keeper of the Records for the Year 1933* (Belfast, 1934), p. 22 (for the original manuscript here summarized, see P.R.O., S.P. 63 [Ireland], 391).

[5] Boulter, *Letters*, i. 231 f.

pasturage brought persons to testify in the Commons that the tithe had determined them and others to emigrate. The committee's report embodied a statement that the new and burdensome tithe aggravated the tendency among Protestants to go to America, which 'must inevitably prejudice and endanger the Protestant Religion, Interest, and Strength of this Kingdom'; and this view was reflected in the resolutions adopted by the full House.[1] It is of special note that the committee named Co. Meath in particular as one from which many Protestants had emigrated, thus bringing the matter home to Swift, whose parishes in Meath could originally boast only few Protestant families. In the succeeding pamphlet warfare over tithe agistment the spokesmen for the landowners continued to accuse the clergy of responsibility for driving Protestants abroad, to the detriment of the Protestant interest.[2]

The churchmen denied this—and blamed the landowning class and its short-sighted, oppressive policies. As early as 1718 Bishop Evans wrote to Archbishop Wake: 'I hear 1000 of Protestants go to America, because their Landlords every where bear hard upon them & Papists succeed them in the Farms in severall parts of the Kingdom.'[3] In the following year Archbishop King wrote to Wake in a similar vein; and in 1729 Lord Carteret submitted to the English Privy Council a report on the causes of Irish emigration as formulated by the justices of the north-western and north-eastern circuits.[4] Although the justices made some criticisms of the clergy, they supported the contention of the churchmen that the landlords were guilty of certain policies clearly detrimental to the Protestant interest. Bishop Synge of Ferns

[1] *Journal of the House of Commons of Ireland,* iv. pt. ii, appendix lxv.
[2] *Prescription Sacred: or, Reasons for opposing the new Demand of Herbage in Ireland* ([Dublin], 1736), p. 14; [Samuel Blacker?], *Property Vindicated: or, Some Remarks upon a Late Pamphlet, intitled, Property Inviolable* (Dublin, 1739), pp. 30–31.
[3] Wake Corresp. xii, 20 May 1718.
[4] Gilbert Collection, MS. 28, King to Wake, 2 June 1719; P.R.O. Northern Ireland: *The Report of the Deputy Keeper . . . 1934,* p. 23.

and Leighlin, who answered the landowners in detail, categorically denied that tithe agistment or tithes in general could validly be held responsible for emigration. He blamed instead 'the Exactions of Landlords', as well as the current practice among the gentry who 'chuse to stock their Lands with *Beasts* rather than *Men*'.[1] Other controversialists who defended the clergy took the same view. The 'Apologist' for the clergy of Ireland maintained that the landlords who turned arable lands into pasturage were driving the labouring man to America; and Alexander Macaulay added his voice, insisting that there is a direct relationship between tillage and emigration: encouragement of the one discourages the other.[2]

Thus the issue of emigration, with its implications concerning the relative strength of the Protestant and Catholic populations, was part and parcel of a larger problem affecting Ireland's economy—the state of tillage. No clergyman could be indifferent to the produce of the soil; his individual welfare and that of the Church depended to a large extent on a flourishing agricultural condition. It is in this larger context that Swift views the subject of emigration, with tithes, tillage, and departing Protestants as interdependent elements. One of his persistent themes in the Irish tracts is the depopulation of the countryside and the forced emigration of farmers and cottagers. He unhesitatingly blamed the squires and the landlords—'. . . to them is owing the depopulating of the country'.[3] In a number of his comments on emigration there is an ironic pretence that it is a solution for Ireland's ills. He had often wished, he wrote in 1724, 'for some years past, that instead of discouraging our people from seeking foreign soil, the public would rather pay for transporting all our unnecessary mortals, whether Papists or Protestants, to America'.[4] And again in 1728: '. . . it is a comfortable circumstance' that some thousand families were departing for America.[5] But in their proper setting these and similar state-

---

[1] *Two Affidavits in relation to the Demands of Tythe-Agistment. . . .*, pp. 21 ff.
[2] *An Apology for the Clergy of Ireland*, p. 7; see also *Property Inviolable*, pp. 34–35.
[3] *Prose Works*, vii. 110.   [4] Ibid. vii. 70.   [5] Ibid. ix. 328.

ments are seen to be bitter ironic reflections on the misery of a land whose people must emigrate. His real attitude is revealed in one of the true causes that any country flourishes and grows rich, which he listed in 1727: '... by improvement of land, encouragement of agriculture, and thereby increasing the number of their people, without which any country, however blessed by Nature, must continue poor'.[1] He seems not to have doubted the mercantilist maxim that people are wealth; he merely argued that this universal economic law is vitiated in Ireland by the landowning class through its fatal policy of increasing pasturage at the expense of tillage:

... the unhappy practice of stocking such vast quantities of land with sheep and other cattle, which reduceth twenty families to one: these events ... have exceedingly depopulated this kingdom. ... There is not an older or more uncontroverted maxim in the politics of all wise nations, than that of encouraging agriculture. ... If labour and people make the true riches of a nation, what must be the issue where one part of the people are forced away, and the other part have nothing to do?[2]

Why all this concern for the poor? he asked. Let them 'seek their bread abroad'. 'Where the plough has no work, one family can do the business of fifty, and you may send away the other forty-nine.' This, he added, is an 'admirable piece of husbandry, never known or practised by the wisest nations, who erroneously thought people to be the riches of a country!'[3] It is in the *Answer to the Craftsman* (1730) that he most effectively and characteristically reveals the link between tithes, tillage, and emigration. With fine irony in the manner of *A Modest Proposal* (itself an ironic discussion of the theme that people constitute wealth) he proposes among the solutions to Ireland's ills that an annual quota of natives be transported to America and that all profitable lands be turned into pasturage. For the second of these proposals he has a special commendation:

... the article of paying tithe for supporting speculative opinions in religion ... will be very much lessened by this expedient; because dry

[1] *Prose Works*, vii. 84.   [2] Ibid. vii. 133–4; see also iii. 225.
[3] Ibid. vii. 114.

cattle pay nothing to the spiritual hireling . . . so that the industrious shepherd and cowherd may sit every man under his own blackberry bush, and on his own potato-bed, whereby this happy island will become a new Arcadia.[1]

Nor did Swift spare the landlords on that other offence—their responsibility for emigration because they exacted excessive rents and thus created a dispossessed class who sought a new life in America. Even in a sermon he inveighed against 'that *Aegyptian* Bondage of cruel, oppressing, covetous Landlords' who are 'every Day unpeopling their Kingdom'.[2] In his various tracts, economic and religious, there are many similar references. One of his most vigorous protests on the subject was directed to his friend John Barber, then an Alderman of London, to whom Swift pointed out that the Irish Society's policy of raising rents exorbitantly—'beyond all I have ever heard even among the most screwing landlords of this impoverished kingdom'—has caused its tenants to consider 'removal to the Plantations in America'.[3]

Thus Swift added his voice in refutation of those who complained that tithes were responsible for emigration and sought to place the blame. This was, as he recognized, only one issue in the conflict of interests between laity and churchmen—an issue which he conceived to involve peril to the nation as a whole, not merely to the Church. Nevertheless it was symptomatic of the general resistance to tithes, and as such it deepened his sense of the insecurity of the Establishment.

II. IMPROPRIATIONS

Swift's jealous, possessive attitude toward tithes and Church lands had historical roots. His bristling reaction to any threat, fancied or real, to the temporalities is understandable in one who looked into the past and saw the

---

[1] Ibid. vii. 222–3.   [2] *Prose Works*, Davis, ix. 201.
[3] *Corresp.* v. 430. For the Irish Society see *A Concise View of the Origin, Constitution, and Proceedings of the Honourable Society of the Governor and Assistants of London of the New Plantation in Ulster . . . commonly called The Irish Society*, 1832.

persistent alienations of Church property from the time of Henry VIII to his own day. The Irish Establishment appeared in his eyes to have been specially vulnerable throughout most of its long history, chiefly as a result of the troubled and unsettled state of the country. His awareness of the past being strong, he tended to see the contemporary attacks in terms of similar attacks in earlier periods. There was a long line from past to present, all part of a process of attrition sapping the Church of its vitality and power to endure. We must remember that he was historically close to some of the great despoliations he felt so keenly, that he grew to manhood in the seventeenth century—a period of turbulence for the Irish Church and of major alienations of its possessions, whose effects he witnessed. The ill consequences carried over into the eighteenth century and had an immediacy which no contemporary clergyman could escape. These facts make more understandable Swift's kindly feelings for certain seventeenth-century personages who behaved well toward the Irish Establishment, as James I, who granted lands to the clergy, and the Earl of Strafford, who showed a determination to stop the evil traffic in ecclesiastical properties and to restore the patrimony of the Church.[1]

'The depredations of 1641 and 1688'—these Swift particularly mentions as causing confusion in tithes and glebes.[2] In the Rebellion of 1641 the Catholics quickly seized the possessions of the Church of Ireland, adding more and more as their victories grew.[3] These seizures were given official sanction in 1642 by two separate assemblies of Catholic churchmen and laymen meeting at Kells and at Kilkenny, who authorized the Roman Catholic secular clergy to retain and enjoy the 'profits, emoluments, and rights of the churches and Church livings in as large and ample

---

[1] *Prose Works*, iii. 253, 292; v. 434; x. 295; xi. 174; *Prose Works*, Davis, ix. 46.
[2] Ibid. iii. 253.
[3] See W. A. Phillips, *History of the Church of Ireland*, iii. 95 ff., 107 ff., 129, 149 ff.; *Books of Survey and Distribution* (Irish Manuscripts Commission), vol. i: *County of Roscommon*, ed. Robert C. Simington (Dublin, Stationery Office, 1949), Introduction, ix ff.

manner as the late Protestant clergy did . . .'. When the Articles of Peace were signed in 1649 between the Catholic Federation and the Duke of Ormond there was an intention to rectify the seizures, but actually certain concessions made to the Catholics left some Church lands, leases, livings, and tithes in dispute and confusion. Commonwealth policies and the Cromwellian Settlement compounded the confusion; and the Act of Settlement in 1662, which purported to restore Church properties to the original status of 1641, failed of its intention, largely because of the claims of the Soldiers and Adventurers. Even this partial restoration of the Church patrimony was upset at the time of the Revolution: when James II gained a measure of control in Ireland, the Act of Settlement was nullified, once again to the confusion of the temporalities. There was a final attempt under William and Mary, by another Act of Settlement and Explanation, to deal with the forfeited estates and to rectify as far as possible the confusion in Church possessions. Thus it is that Swift writes: 'The greatest part of the Clergy throughout this kingdom, have been stripped of their glebes by the confusion of times, by violence, fraud, oppression, and other unlawful means'.[1] To him 'the depredations of 1641 and 1688' were not isolated events so much as a continuation of the enfeebling historical forces to which the Irish Church was doomed; and as he examined the alienations of his own time, he saw the relevance of past events.

Swift's attitude toward Henry VIII is revealing. He traces to that monarch the ultimate source of the weakness and poverty of the Church. Henry was the original despoiler, a 'sacrilegious tyrant', who is never mentioned without excoriation—'an infernal beast', 'a monster', 'a wicked prince', 'a detestable tyrant'.[2] This view prevailed widely among contemporary Anglican clergymen, who held that Henry had culpably committed extended sacrilege in disposing as he did of the seized monastic possessions. At the

---

[1] *Prose Works*, iii. 279; cf. iii. 140 ff.
[2] Ibid. iii. 252, 301 ff.; iv. 191.

suppression of the religious houses in Ireland the tithes and other temporalities were vested in the Crown by certain Acts (28 Hen. VIII, c. 16; 33 Hen. VIII, c. 5) which also provided that these temporalities could be disposed of by Letters Patent.[1] Under this legislation the king, although he retained much for himself, made extensive grants to his favourites. Thus laymen entered into what was formerly Church property. Men without the capacity for performing ecclesiastical duties came to possess ecclesiastical estates and were invested with titles to tithes. This misappropriation, Anglican historians frequently pointed out, had a shameful precedent: the Church of Rome had transferred lands and tithes originally intended for the parochial clergy to the monasteries. Eighteenth-century clergymen professed themselves shocked at this occurrence. Swift referred to it as 'a scandalous usurpation even in popish times'; and he and others concerned with Church history maintained that Henry's behaviour to the English parochial clergy was no less brazen and sacrilegious.[2] They never ceased to resent his niggardly provision for the Establishment or his failure to restore to the parishes the lands and tithes which under Catholicism had been alienated to the monasteries. This sacrilege coloured their view of the Reformation. White Kennet, whose study of impropriations was the most exhaustive in Swift's day, represents the consensus of Anglican churchmen. Discussing the passing of Church possessions into lay hands—'this great change in the Propriety of Tythes'—he said of the Reformation:

The King and a great Majority of the Two Houses were still zealous for the Doctrines of Popery, and establish'd the most absurd Articles of it. They did indeed in some Sense reform the Discipline and

---

[1] See W. A. Phillips, *History of the Church of Ireland*, ii. 231 ff.; the Appendix to the Report of Her Majesty's Commissioners of the Revenue and Condition of the Established Church (Ireland), Dublin, 1868, Appendix No. 20 and *passim*; see also Henry Holloway, *The Reformation in Ireland: a Study of Ecclesiastical Legislation* (London, 1919), pp. 112 ff.

[2] *Prose Works*, iii. 141. White Kennet and James Read, quoted immediately below, are typical.

the Revenues of the Church; but this too, not altogether to suppress the Usurpations of the Pope and the Monks, but rather chiefly to encrease their own Secular Authority and Interest.[1]

James Read, a contemporary Irish cleric writing on the same subject and drawing support from Sir Henry Spelman, Whitgift, and Dr. Robert South, wrote:

I must own I should have thought the Reformation . . . so much the more graceful, lovely and unexceptionable, if the Appropriations, that were then resumed [i.e. the tithes misappropriated to the monasteries], had been restored to their respective Churches, from which they had been Sacrilegiously alienated, by the Pope and Regular Clergy.[2]

There were others even less willing to give Henry credit, harking back to Thomas Ryves, who had declared bluntly that 'he reformed not religion'.[3]

Swift reflects these attitudes in unrestrained language. He maintained that Henry VIII had robbed the Anglican Establishment in England and Ireland of at least two-thirds of its legal possessions. He granted that the seizure of the extensive abbey lands under parliamentary authority had been justified; but since these lands had been given to the abbeys by pious men, princes, and laymen for sacred uses, their retention for profane use was 'absolute sacrilege, in the strongest sense of the word'. He was ready to admit, though grudgingly, that Henry had abolished the power of the Pope as a universal bishop, yet this was not done for love of a true religion. The king's motives were vicious—to gratify an irregular appetite and give himself liberty to commit sacrilege. Henry's peculiar talents were cruelty, lust, rapine, and atheism. These are sentiments Swift set down in 1736.[4] Nevertheless they were not views formulated under the stress of recent events. During his residence with Sir William

[1] White Kennet, *The Case of Impropriations and of the Augmentation of Vicarages* (London, 1704), p. 128; see also pp. 120 ff. and *passim*.

[2] *An Essay on Simony of the Bishops of Ireland* (London, 1737), p. 79; see also pp. 153 ff.

[3] *The Poor Vicar's Plea for Tythes* (London, 1704), p. 98; 1st ed. 1620.

[4] *Prose Works*, iii. 301 ff.

Temple he had read Lord Herbert's *Life and Raigne of Henry VIII* (1649) and had registered in its margins his opinions of 'the profligate Dog of a King'. 'Nero was Emperour of Rome and was a Saint in comparison of this dying dog Henry.' Henry 'robbed the Church and then defended himself with the Spoyls'; and when Lord Herbert ends the history, leaving the king in his grave, Swift writes:

And I wish he had been Flead, his skin stuffed and hangd on a Gibbet, His bulky guts and Flesh left to be devoured by Birds and Beasts, for a warning to his Successors for ever. Amen.[1]

Again in 1713 he had discussed Henry and the Reformation in the same vein.[2] The Reformation, he maintained, owed nothing to Henry's good intentions. The king was merely the accidental instrument by which it was effected in England; his purpose was to gratify 'his insatiable love of power, cruelty, oppression, and other appetites'. 'Neither hath any thing disgusted me more in reading the histories of those times, than to see one of the worst princes of any age or country, celebrated as an instrument in that glorious work of the Reformation.' Similarly Swift took the prevalent view that the king had not effected a reformation in religion; he had continued to defend all the Popish doctrines and to persecute those who professed Protestantism.[3]

Henry's retention of abbey lands, of cathedral properties, and of the estates of bishops was not his worst offence.[4] The greater crime, with more dire effects in subsequent generations, was the misappropriation of tithes to secular persons— 'a most flagrant act of injustice and oppression', Swift terms

---

[1] Lyon, Hawkesworth: among the preliminary material is a list of Swift's reading for one year, from 7 Jan. 169⅔. See Lord Rothschild, *Some Unpublished Marginalia of Jonathan Swift* (Cambridge, 1945), pp. 7–8, for these comments on Henry VIII.
[2] *Prose Works*, iii. 150.   [3] Ibid. iii. 149 f., 303.
[4] After some resistance to seizure, St. Patrick's fell into the hands of the king in 1547. The chapter assented under force. Dean Edward Bassenet is blamed for surrendering (see Lawlor, *Fasti*, p. 12). Swift's only known reference to the event was a comment written on a lease of deanery property which had come down in Bassenet's family. Swift wrote: 'This Bassenett was related to the Scoundrel of the same name, who surrendered the Deanry to that beast, H.8.' (Monck Mason, p. 26, note d).

it.[1] He believed that the poverty of the Irish Church could be traced in large measure to the extensive lay possession of tithes. It was the inferior clergy who had suffered most. The granting away of tithes meant that 'the parishes were left destituted or very meanly provided of any maintenance for a pastor'. In many parishes, Swift points out, not only the tithes but 'the whole ecclesiastical dues, even to mortuaries, Easter-offerings, and the like, are in lay hands, and the incumbent lies wholly at the mercy of his patron for his daily bread'.[2] The problem of impropriations occasioned perhaps more discussion among Swift's contemporaries than any other problem touching temporalities. This particular diversion of its patrimony seemed to many the worst evil the Church had inherited from the past. Both the higher and the inferior clergy constantly ascribed the present shortcomings of the Establishment to the widespread existence of impropriate parishes. A typical complaint came in 1711 from both Houses of Convocation, who explained that the persistence of Popery in Ireland resulted from an insufficiency of Protestant clergymen to supply the parishes and combat Romish doctrines: there is not adequate support, the report said, for the parochial clergy, 'the Reason of which is, that, upon the *Dissolution of Abbies and Monasteries*, the Tythes then appropriated for their Support, were granted to *Laymen*. . . . These *Impropriations* being a considerable Part of the *Tythe* of the whole Kingdom. . . .'[3] In the same year Archbishop King described the grim state of the diocese of Ferns, where 71 of 131 parishes were impropriate;[4] and, to give one more instance, in 1736 Bishop Synge blamed

---

[1] *Prose Works*, iii. 141.

[2] Ibid. At the Dissolution of the monasteries, Acts of the Irish Parliament (28 Henry VIII, c. 16 and 33 Henry VIII, c. 5) provided that laymen who were granted Church lands and tithes were obliged to support the parish clergy. It was the constant complaint of the churchmen that this obligation was ignored (see King Corresp., King to Thomas Wentworth, 7 July 1722; W. A. Phillips, *History of the Church of Ireland*, ii. 232–3).

[3] *The Present State of Religion in Ireland* [1712], p. 17.

[4] See C. S. King, *A Great Archbishop of Dublin, William King, 1650–1729* (London, 1906), pp. 148–9.

impropriations for the dire conditions in the diocese of Leighlin, tithes in 24 of 82 parishes being in the hands of laymen.
With no tithes to provide incumbents, he observed, 'the
Number of Clergy are not proportion'd to the Exigencies of
the People. *The People are destroy'd for lack of knowledge.*'[1]
These complaints in fact were echoes of numberless such
complaints from Irish clergymen in the seventeenth century,
when a commission investigating 'the decay and ruinous
state of the parish churches' blamed 'the multitude of impropriations'.[2] It was a rare churchman who was not in
some respects affected by this inherited evil. Swift himself,
as we have already seen, possessed only a portion of the tithes
of his parishes, the remainder being in lay possession; and it
will also be recalled that he purchased the impropriate tithes
of Effernock to improve the income of the vicars of Laracor.[3]
There was no question in his mind of forcing the return of
impropriations to the Church. The rights of the churchmen
had been lost in the series of settlements, and he knew the
difficulties and dangers of disturbing property rights. The
method he approved was by purchase, as he did with Effernock, and by pious donations.[4] There was another school of
thought on the subject, represented by Archbishop King,
which held that lay possession of tithes was not necessarily
harmful. In fact it might be highly beneficial, since impropriators would resist any attacks on that part of clerical income
and would refuse support to dangerous legislation. Thus
impropriations, in this view, cemented the alliance between
laity and clergy. In 1711, soon after Swift had successfully
negotiated the return of the First Fruits for the purchase of
glebeland and impropriate tithes, King wrote to him that the
money would be better spent for glebeland alone: 'I look
upon it as a security to tithes, that the laity have a share in
them; and therefore I am not for purchasing them, but where

---

[1] *Two Affidavits in relation to the Demand of Tithe-Agistment . . .*, p. 18.
[2] W. A. Phillips, *History of the Church of Ireland*, ii. 542.
[3] See above, p. 41.
[4] *Prose Works*, iii. 141.

they are absolutely necessary.'[1] Swift seems not to have shared this view, at least not wholly.

When he prepared the First Fruits Memorial for Harley in 1710, Swift included at the very beginning, thus indicating its importance in his eyes, a statement concerning impropriations and their evil consequences: 'There are in Proportion more Impropriations in Ireland than England, which added to the Poverty of the Country, makes the Livings of very small and uncertain Value, so that five or six united do often hardly amount to 50 ll *p* ann. . . .'[2] His allusion is to the many pluralities, the simultaneous tenure by a single clergyman of more than one cure of souls, made necessary by impropriations. If tithes from a particular parish were diverted to a layman, leaving an insufficiency to support an incumbent, then there was little to be done except to unite several parishes in order to provide a competency. Once again Swift was concerned with an inherited evil, one of the most persistent and vexing problems facing the Church, in this instance predating the Reformation. The medieval Church had often legislated against pluralities. Popes and Councils had attacked pluralists; canons and decretals were issued to cope with the problem, and skilled canonists had given it their attention.[3] Yet the abuse continued into the Reformation and to Swift's time, a matter of constant concern and ineffectual regulation. It was perhaps most difficult to deal with in those dioceses having a high proportion of impropriations, such as Swift's own diocese of Meath. Bishop Evans reported to Archbishop Wake in 1717 that 'the Multitude of Impropriations in Meath gives me great disturbance, many churches (even where there are Protestants) being unserv'd for want of a Competent maintenance . . .'. Dispensations, he added, had been granted to clergymen to hold benefices widely separated—'even to a 100 miles distance'.[4] The result, as

---

[1] *Corresp.* i. 273.   [2] *Journal to Stella*, ii. 679.

[3] See F. W. Maitland, *Roman Canon Law in the Church of England* (London, 1898), pp. 20 ff., 148–9; A. Hamilton Thompson, *The English Clergy and their Organization in the Later Middle Ages*, pp. 12 f., 104–5, 246–7.

[4] Wake Corresp. xii, Evans to Wake, 10 July 1717; see also Nicolson to Wake,

might be expected, was non-residence. Attacks on pluralities came unceasingly from every direction; but there were
strenuous defenders as well, among them Swift—himself a
pluralist—who felt that impropriations and economic conditions in Ireland made them necessary. There might be a
long-range plan, he thought, to eliminate them, but an impoverished Church in an impoverished country must at least
permit pluralism as an expedient. He showed some sensitive-
ness to those who criticized the clergy for the practice. In
1723, when the author of *The History of the Popish Clergy*
demanded that 'there be no Pleuralities', Swift replied that
'pluralities ... is a word of ill fame, but not well understood';

> The clergy having been stripped of the greatest part of their revenues,
> the glebes being generally lost, the tithes in the hands of laymen, the
> churches demolished, and the country depopulated; in order to preserve
> a face of Christianity, it was necessary to unite small vicarages, suffi-
> cient to make a tolerable maintenance for a minister.[1]

He was fully aware that there were abuses among the
clergy of the 'privilege' of pluralities and that some of the
more valuable ought to be broken up to provide for several
incumbents; but he thought it graceless of laymen, whose
possession of Church patrimony was ultimately responsible,
to blame the clergy. If impropriate tithes could be regained,
the problem might be solved, or at least eased. He had therefore recommended in the Memorial of 1710 that the rents on
parishes impropriate to the Crown be returned to the clergy
for the purchase, among other things, of impropriate tithes.[2]
For Swift, pluralism was implicit in the history of a Church
which had fought without success to retain its worldly goods
from a greedy laity. When Bishop Burnet wrote that sacrilege

---

17 June 1718. The number of impropriate parishes in Ireland in the period has been
variously estimated (see W. A. Phillips, *History of the Church of Ireland*, iii. 278–9:
of 2,436 parishes 562 were in lay hands; in 118 the whole of the tithes were impropriate). See also J. C. Beckett, 'The Government and the Church of Ireland under
William III and Anne', *Irish Historical Studies*, ii. (1941), 284.

[1] *Prose Works*, iii. 235–6; cf. iii. 270.
[2] *Journal to Stella*, ii. 680.

in the Church of Rome is a mortal sin, Swift wished to know whether it was 'only so in the church of Rome'. Is it, he asked, 'but a venial sin in the Church of England.'[1]

III. THE IRISH INTEREST

However much he despaired of 'the base corrupt spirits' of the gentry, Swift did not lose sight of their importance to the Church of Ireland. The welfare of the Establishment could be achieved, if at all, only with the co-operation and good-will of this powerful group, and he was ready to support any honourable measures which might effect a stronger alliance between gentry and churchmen. Thus it became one of his persistent endeavours to build up a Church interest among the gentry of Ireland. In practice this meant that he espoused the Irish (i.e. Anglo-Irish) interest in the Church as opposed to the English interest—that is, he wished preferment to be given more liberally to sons and relatives of the Anglo-Irish gentry and less so to Englishmen. The matter transcended merely clerical appointments. There was mounting dissatisfaction among the gentry over the disproportionate patronage given to the English in civil and military as well as in ecclesiastical offices. Swift wrote to a friend in 1725 that 'the people of Ireland have just found out that their fathers, sons, and brothers, are not made bishops, judges, or officers . . . and begin to think it should be otherwise'.[2] The gentry, he believed, had a legitimate grievance, and increasingly from 1720 he dwelt on the importance of making Irish appointments in all fields, though his special efforts were concerned with the Church. It was a policy he thought necessary to bring the gentry and the churchmen into common cause such as would result in stronger lay support for the Establishment.

[1] *Prose Works*, iii. 142.

[2] *Corresp.* iii. 289. See King's letter to Edward Southwell, 29 Dec. 1725 (King Corresp.), in which he complains of the disproportionate preferment bestowed on the clergy sent in from England, and then concludes: 'The Case is in effect the same as to the Army, Revenue and Civil employments, the disposal of these affect the Lawiors and Gentlemen, and tho' the resentment of the Clergy may not be valued, yet it seems not politic to provoke those that make up the House of Commons.'

The urgent need for such an alliance was advocated, particularly in critical moments, by moderate men who sought to ease the tension between laity and clergy. In 1732, when the two unfavourable Church bills were pending, one of the most telling arguments advanced against their passage was that they 'would hinder sons of the nobility and gentry from being bred up to the church and entering holy orders'.[1] Similarly at the time of the agistment controversy in 1736, when feeling against the clergy was running high, a spokesman for the gentry accused the churchmen of remissness in encouraging 'Gentlemen of Birth and Honourable Parentage to enter into Holy Orders'.[2] These had been discouraged by the practice of preferring 'Strangers to Dignities Ecclesiastical above Natives', to the point that the gentry must send their sons into trade.[3] It is therefore not surprising, he remarked, that an anti-Church faction exists which resents the power of the Church and resists the payment of tithes. He pleaded for an alliance between the gentry and the clergy based upon self-interest. If the gentry were permitted to profit from leases on Church lands and their sons were given good clerical livings, then the gentry could be depended upon to befriend the clergy and the Church:

If our Gentry were to partake according to their Proportion of the Profits of the Church . . . either in Leases from the Bishops as formerly, whereby many good Families were maintained in Gentility and Hospitality under their Wings, and consequently were always their Humbler Servants in Causes, wherein the Church was any way interested, both in Country and Parliament, and also in a proper and fair Distribution of Promotions and Dignities Ecclesiastical amongst their Sons, answerable to the Number of Graduates of Birth and Distinction bred in our own University, then they wou'd see their Interest in supporting the Church and Clergy. . . .[4]

This frank appeal, stressing mutual economic advantage, was

---

[1] *An Answer to a Letter from a Lord to a Commoner*, p. 33. Cf. *Prose Works*, iii. 266.

[2] *Reasons for the Present Clamours against the Clergy of Ireland* (Dublin, 1736), p. 6.

[3] Ibid. pp. 8, 16, and *passim*.   [4] Ibid. pp. 25 f.

precisely the position of clerics such as Swift, who recognized the value of a Church interest among the Irish gentry.

The attempt to develop an Irish interest ran counter to the policy of the English government, whose intention from the accession of George I was to build up in the Irish Establishment a dependable Whiggish episcopal bench. It was felt that such a policy was needed to offset Tory and High-Church sentiments among the gentry and the inferior clergy of Ireland and such Tory appointments—the Primate Lindsay, for instance—as carried over from the reign of Anne. In practice this meant the appointment from England of trusted Low Churchmen—among them, Evans of Meath, Goodwin of Kilmore, Nicolson of Derry, and above all, Archbishop Boulter, along with Evans the most intransigent in demanding that only those in the English interest be given preferment or appointments. The government's policy appears to have moderated somewhat in 1724. Grafton wrote to Townshend that 'the King thinks it entirely right that Englishmen should be preferred to the Bishopricks in Ireland. Yet his Majesty takes it to be as wrong that the Deaneries and other inferior preferments there, should not be given to the Irish clergy'.[1] But this more balanced policy was not apparent to the Irish clergy and gentry; and in fact it seems not to have been effectual since the Whig bishops, who controlled much of the patronage, were not sympathetic. The Irish clergy were not wholly ignored, yet they were at a great disadvantage. They complained frequently that the Lord Lieutenants, the English Lord Justices, and the English bishops regularly preferred their imported chaplains to the better livings, leaving only the lesser places to the Irish clergy. As Swift said, 'nothing left for the younger sons of Irishmen but vicarages'.[2]

The cleavage between English and Irish interest was unusually bitter at the episcopal level, with Archbishop King the most powerful figure among the latter. In this respect

---

[1] P.R.O., S.P. 63 (Ireland), 383, 4 Mar. 172¾.
[2] *Prose Works*, iii. 287.

Swift and King saw eye to eye. Swift's remark about the 'many worthless bishops [from England], all bedangled with their pert illiterate relations and flatterers', finds its parallel in King's reference to the clerics sent from England as being not 'the brightest generally speaking [though] they seem notably dexterous and industrious to make money for wives and children'.[1] In 1717 the archbishop had written acidly to Canterbury: 'The Lord Lieutenant has 3 chaplains from England which I doubt will be as many as he can provide with preferments according to their expectations for ordinary benefits will not satisfy the merits of any that comes from your side of the water.'[2] Swift's alignment with King was remarked on in a letter of Bishop Goodwin to Wake in 1720: 'The A[rch] B[ishop] & the Dean are now join'd in great amity. But how they will do to stop this inundation of English Bishops I know not.'[3] By this time the division was already deep and bitter. Bishop Evans constituted himself a watchdog over the Irish bishops, whose leanings toward appointments of their own kindred and countrymen he reported regularly to Canterbury in the years 1716 to 1718. He referred to them as 'these (nationally) mad People'; and he broke openly with King in 1718 over the appointment of an Englishman to the see of Derry, left vacant by the death of Swift's friend and former tutor, Bishop Ashe.[4] Both King and Edward Synge, Archbishop of Tuam, had strongly urged for the vacant see a person born or educated in Ireland. Although Synge was less violent in his espousal of the Irish interest than King, Bishop Goodwin could report to Canterbury on this occasion that 'even my good Lord of Tuam thinks there are enough of us already & suspects that we lay schemes for bringing over more . . . [he] seems to think it hard that English Bishops should take the best Bishopricks

[1] *Corresp.* iv. 349; King to Charlett, 17 June 1721, quoted in C. S. King, *A Great Archbishop. . . ,* p. 228 (cf. pp. 202, 252–3).

[2] Wake Corresp. xii, 20 Aug. 1717.

[3] Ibid. xiii, 28 Dec. 1720.

[4] Ibid. xii, Evans to Wake, 30 Oct. 1716; 1, 6 Feb., 8 Mar. 171$\frac{6}{7}$; 31 Mar., 30 Apr. 1717; 28 Mar., 24 July 1718; 28 Mar. 1720.

here'.[1] When Bishop William Nicolson of Carlisle was given Derry and the right (so it was thought) to retain Carlisle as well, the rupture between the two factions was complete, and resentment in Ireland spread beyond the episcopal bench to the laity. 'The Coffee-Houses & Town ring with it & they say the Cath[edral] ought to be pull'd down &c since all the best Preferments are confer'd on Englishmen'—so Evans reported to Wake. He added that 'Dublyn ... is Horn-mad ... & said many Spightful things....'[2] It is hardly surprising that Nicolson under the circumstances found his reception in Ireland 'as an English Foreigner' somewhat discouraging.[3] Nor is it surprising that shortly afterward King was omitted from the list of Lord Justices, or that the bishops of the English interest opposed him for the Primacy in 1723 when the Tory Lindsay was dying, although in point of experience, distinction, and loyalty to the Whig cause, he was the logical successor. On this important occasion Evans wrote to Canterbury that King must not be made Primate because 'he loves neither our Name, or Nation'; and the Duke of Grafton, echoing the English bishops in Ireland, complained to Walpole: 'He is ... to a ridiculous extent, national.'[4]

The opposition was successful. Armagh was conferred on Hugh Boulter, whose announced policy was 'to break the present *Dublin* faction on the bench'.[5] We are not concerned here with the details of Boulter's campaign to strengthen the English interest at the expense of 'the Archbishop of *Dublin*'s party'; the account already given indicates the nature of the conflict and identifies the parties involved. It also serves as a

[1] Ibid. xiii, 13 Feb. 171⁷⁄₈. See also Goodwin to an unnamed English official, 19 Oct. 1717 (P.R.O., S.P. 63 [Ireland], 375).

[2] Wake Corresp. xii, 25 Mar. 1718. See also the bitter, ironic letters of King to Wake, Gilbert Collection, MS. 28, 25 Mar., 12 Apr., 10 May 1718, and Synge's restrained protest, Wake Corresp. xii, 29 Apr. 1718.

[3] Wake Corresp. xiii, Nicolson to Wake, 3 Apr. 1720; Gilbert Collection, MS. 27, Nicolson to Wake, 19 Mar. 172⁰⁄₁.

[4] See *Letters ... to and from William Nicolson,* ii. 497; Wake Corresp. xiv, Evans to Wake, 22 Aug. 1723; Goodwin to Wake, 13 July 1723; C. S. King, *A Great Archbishop ...,* p. 275 (quotes Grafton).

[5] *Letters,* i. 12; see also i. 13, 17, 26, 115–16, and *passim.*

background for Swift's own efforts in the Irish interest. It is clear enough that his endeavours were part of a factional, internal struggle for power and position within the Church, but it is equally clear that Swift saw the matter more magnanimously as a means of improving the welfare of the Irish Establishment. In the years following 1720 Swift's 'nationalism' and his resentment of the discrimination against the Anglo-Irish clergy are often revealed in his tracts and his correspondence. When Carteret was Lord Lieutenant, relying on friendship and that nobleman's good sense, Swift appealed for an end to the evil policy. He stressed the benefits of an alliance between clergy and gentry cemented by the presence of younger sons in Orders, who he hoped would hereafter share more liberally in Church patronage. He wrote to Carteret that the bestowal of the best ecclesiastical preferment on strangers had created discontent and discouraged learning and the study of divinity in Ireland. '. . . the young men sent into the Church from the University here, have no better prospect than to be curates, or small country vicars, for life. It will become so excellent a governor as you, a little to moderate this great partiality, wherein . . . you will . . . take away one great cause of universal discontent.'[1] Swift's efforts in this instance had a small measure of success but not so great as implied in Carteret's light remark of later years: 'When people ask me, how I governed Ireland, I say that I pleased Dr. Swift.'[2] Friendship between the Dean of St. Patrick's and a Lord Lieutenant subject to Walpole may have done Carteret little good. It is of interest that the government, wary of Carteret for several reasons, limited his Church patronage at his second appointment as viceroy in 1727.[3] As a matter of course the bishops of the English interest were not satisfied with some of his appointments. Bishop Goodwin observed to Canterbury that the men Carteret chose for

---

[1] *Corresp*. iii. 248.

[2] Ibid. v. 429.

[3] P.R.O., S.P. 63 (Ireland) 288; Boulter, *Letters*, i. 280; Basil Williams, *Carteret and Newcastle: a Contrast in Contemporaries* (Cambridge, 1943), pp. 70–80.

preferment never 'went under the denomination of Whiggs'.[1]
Reports circulated that he favoured the Tories. To answer
this 'calumny' Swift issued a mock defence: *A Vindication of
his Excellency The Lord C——t, from the Charge of favouring none but Tories, High-Churchmen and Jacobites* (1730).
The pamphlet contains a Tory Account and a Whig Account,
with the ledger showing a heavy favourable balance on the
Whig side. Thus Swift can conclude:

. . . so, I do not find how his Excellency can be justly censured for
favouring none but High-Church, high-fliers, termagants, Laudists,
Sacheverellians, tip-top-gallant-men, Jacobites, tantivies, anti-Hano-
verians, friends to Popery and the Pretender, and to arbitrary power,
disobligers of England, breakers of Dependency, inflamers of quarrels
between the two nations, public incendiaries, enemies to the King and
Kingdoms, haters of True Protestants, laurelmen, Annists, com-
plainers of the Nation's poverty, Ormondians, iconoclasts, anti-
Glorious-memorists, white-rosalists, tenth-a-Junians, and the like:
when by a fair state of the account, the balance, I conceive, plainly lies
on the other side.[2]

This pamphlet, which has characteristic ironic touches, is
one of Swift's more effective contributions to the support of
the Irish interest.

The 'English foreigners' kept Swift under close observation. When his plan to go to England in 1726 was known, no
less a personage than Archbishop Boulter sent a warning to
the Duke of Newcastle, then Secretary of State: '. . . we do
not question his endeavours to misrepresent his Majesty's
friends here, wherever he finds an opportunity'.[3] The Primate
requested that the dean be watched closely. This wariness
had a certain justification in view of Swift's intention to set
before the government the injury being done to Ireland by
the support given to the English interest. It was for this
purpose that the Earl of Peterborough arranged the famous

[1] Wake Corresp. xiv, Goodwin to Wake, 14 July 1725. Cf. Baron Pocklington to
Wake, expressing surprise that Sheridan, 'second to Swift in the Battle about the
halfpence', had been given a living by Carteret (1 July 1725).
[2] *Prose Works*, vii. 249.
[3] *Letters*, i. 51.

meeting with Walpole at Swift's request, in which he set forth to an impervious listener some of the grievances of Ireland. Foremost among these was the disproportionate patronage given to those born and educated in England, to the great discouragement of the native born and to such an extent, Swift declared, that 'the whole body of the gentry feel the effects in a very sensible part, being utterly destitute of all means to make provision for their younger sons, either in the Church, the law, the revenue, or, of late, in the army . . .'.[1] Undaunted by the futile meeting with Walpole Swift tried again—with the Duke of Dorset, who became Lord Lieutenant of Ireland in 1730. He believed that his long friendship with Dorset would prove valuable, but his expectations were not fulfilled. Dorset was not so helpful as Carteret. By 1735, despite their pleasant personal relations, Swift could complain of Dorset's remissness, his failure to 'consider that people here might have some small share in employments civil and ecclesiastic, wherein my Lord Carteret acted a more popular part'.[2] A year later, despairing of achieving his purposes, he dismissed Lady Betty Germain, who had been acting as his intercessor with the Lord Lieutenant: 'Henceforth', he wrote, 'I shall only grieve in silence, when I hear of employments disposed to the discontent of his Grace's best friends in this kingdom. . . .'[3]

Swift was eager to be thought, in his own phrase, a 'judicial recommender' of worthy clergymen, particularly since his Tory sympathies made anyone he suggested suspect. He insisted to Carteret, Dorset, and others that he recommended 'without regard to party'; and even his strong desire to advance the Irish interest did not influence him, so far as can be judged, to name unworthy men or ask excessive favours.[4] Certainly he would have preferred to preserve the Tory complexion of the inferior clergy as an offset to the preponderantly Whig episcopal bench, yet this appears to have

[1] *Corresp*. iii. 309–10.   [2] Ibid. v. 178.
[3] Ibid. 413–14; see also v. 295, 325, and *passim*.
[4] *Corresp*. iv. 144; v. 187, 324, 407–8, 413.

been a lesser consideration than a sincere desire that competent young men among the gentry be brought into the Establishment. This policy could be expected in time to moderate 'the contempt of the clergy', satisfy the gentry in one of its legitimate grievances, and establish a more useful relationship between laity and clergy, to the advantage of the Church. If Swift was frequently at odds with the gentry, here at least his views harmonized with theirs. It should be emphasized that he did not view this matter narrowly; more was involved than merely the welfare of the Establishment. The larger issue was to wrest from the English government a measure of justice for Ireland and to secure relief from certain oppressive practices which kept the country from flourishing. In his tracts Swift linked support of the Irish interest in the Church with the broader plea that 'the British native' be given 'a share of preferments in all kinds'—civil, military, and ecclesiastical. This in a sense is the burden of his remarkable letter to Peterborough in 1726, following the futile interview, which he hoped would be passed on to Walpole. Apart from the outrage on justice and merit, he believed that the policy of the English government was unwise since one of 'the true causes of any country's flourishing and growing rich' is 'by disposing all offices of honour, profit or trust, only to the natives, or at least with very few exceptions'.[1] Here too Swift's efforts were largely nullified and his hopes for the Irish Church defeated.

IV. THE BISHOPS

Swift's relations with the bishops contributed to his unhappiness over the state of the Irish Church. In the First Fruits affair he had reacted with bitterness to their lack of tact and their ingratitude, and his experiences with them as the years passed did little to soften his opinion. In the last three decades of his life he enjoyed expressing his contempt

---

[1] *Prose Works*, vii. 84. See also vii. 21, 22, 87–88, 99, 121, 222, 248; *Drapier's Letters*, ed. Davis, 156, 162.

N

for the entire episcopal bench and boasting that he neither knew nor had 'commerce with persons of such prodigious grandeur'. 'I do not stoop so low as to be visited by Irish Lords or Bishops.'[1] These sentiments, though they reflect his general disillusionment, were not uttered with complete seriousness. He was never charitable, it is true, in his attitude toward the 'worthless bishops' sent over from England; but his relations with those of the Irish interest, King, Stearne, Bolton, and others, though by no means free from irritations, improved in the later years. If no real intimacy existed between these men and Swift, there was at least something more than a mere *modus vivendi*. They recognized and appreciated his merits, and valued his support in the conflict with the English appointments.

The relationship between Swift and Archbishop King over the extensive period of their parallel clerical careers is a long chapter in itself, only a small part of which has emerged here. In certain of his dealings with Swift the great archbishop revealed some of the less commendable aspects of his character, for example in 1715, when he connived at the seizure of Swift's correspondence and displayed a readiness to believe him guilty of Jacobitism.[2] At rare moments, however, their intercourse and collaboration achieved a cordiality and understanding that verged on friendship, yet it never quite came to that. Between these two proud men there was always a barrier which prevented these better occasions, as in 1721 and 1724, from developing into intimacy. After 1724, when Swift became the Hibernian Patriot, there is (except occasionally) a warmer note in their relations, best illustrated by King's appreciative comment to a friend in England at the time of Swift's visit in 1726. This was the occasion of Boulter's letter asking that Swift be kept under surveillance.[3] King wrote in a different vein:

As to our Irish Copper Farthen Dean, he has behaved him Self very well in his Station, very agreeable to me, and been useful to the Publick

---

[1] *Corresp.* v. 18, 223.   [2] Ibid. ii. 421 ff.
[3] See above, p. 175.

both by his Charity and his Labours, all that I wish in his behalf is that you wou'd not spoile him in London.[1]

The long friendship between Swift and John Stearne, dating from the time they had occupied the adjacent cures of Laracor and Trim, had its fluctuations. It was first severely tried in 1713. Stearne had earlier, in 1708, failed to keep his promise to bestow on Swift the cure of St. Nicholas Without, in the gift of the dean and chapter of St. Patrick's.[2] In 1713, when Swift prepared to succeed Stearne as dean of St. Patrick's, he urged that the cure be left to his disposal; but once again his wish was slighted.[3] Before departing for his bishopric Stearne acted hastily to nominate Theophilus Bolton. The slight to Swift was not intentional, and the action was in a good cause—to prevent the Crown from seizing the right of nomination, then in dispute.[4] Nevertheless Swift, who desired the benefice for the poet Parnell, was angry and resentful. He felt that he deserved more consideration from one who had risen to dean and bishop by his instrumentality. Although he did not permit this incident to destroy the friendship, he was not able wholly to forget it. Twenty years later, in 1733, he recalled it to Stearne in a letter recounting the decline of their relationship.[5] On this later occasion it was Stearne's support of the Bills of Residence and Division—'those two abominable Bills, for enslaving and beggaring the clergy'—that strained the friendship. But to Swift's angry letter and bitter accusations Stearne, who had no wish to quarrel, replied in a tone of moderation, concluding with an invitation to Swift to visit him.[6]

The willingness of the Irish bishops to propitiate Swift is also observable in Theophilus Bolton, who had risen by 1730 from a disputatious prebendary at St. Patrick's to the archbishopric of Cashel. Though he was one of the Irish 'nationals'

[1] King Corresp., King to Frances Annesley, 30 May 1726 (quoted in *Corresp.* iii. 391 n).

[2] *Corresp.* i. 72, 73, 79, 117; *Journal to Stella*, i. 70–71.

[3] *Corresp.* ii. 51 n., 257 n.; *Journal to Stella*, ii. 668.

[4] Chap. Min. 1690–1719, fols. 228, 231, 2 May 1713; see also fol. 236.

[5] *Corresp.* v. 16–17.   [6] Ibid. 72–73.

—'as dangerous an *Irishman* as any on the bench', Boulter reported to the Archbishop of Canterbury—he had the rare gift of maintaining friendly relations with both parties to the conflict.[1] In the same year, 1723, that he received as his guest in Clonfert the controversial Dean of St. Patrick's, he won the English government's recommendation, transmitted by Grafton to Carteret, for the vacant see of Elphin: '. . . tho' he be a native [he] may be very safely and usefully intrusted with power'.[2] In the following year he showed his independence and his Irish sympathies by opposing in the Privy Council the proclamation against the Drapier, a gesture that would not be lost on Swift.[3] As Chancellor of St. Patrick's he had not pleased Swift, but he redeemed himself in 1732. Unlike Stearne, he opposed the two abominable Bills'. In 1735 he wrote to Swift in a manner further calculated to win approval, announcing that he proposed to be 'a true Irish bishop'.[4] Swift's last letter to him, in that year, reveals a genial relationship. The same desire to live in amity is seen in Edward Synge, at one stage an active opponent at St. Patrick's and later by virtue of his Whig connexions the Bishop of Ferns and Leighlin. He too made overtures to Swift, to whom he wrote in 1738: '. . . when I grew a great man, and by the by you helped to make me so, you turned me off. If you are pleased again to employ me, I shall be as faithful and observant as ever'.[5] There is no reason to believe that Swift felt any personal friendliness for Synge, yet in 1724 or 1725 he had recommended him to Lord Carteret as one of several Dublin clergymen 'who are generally understood by their brethren to be the most distinguished for their learning and piety'. These men, he added, were named 'without any regard to friendship' and only for 'the universal character they bear'.[6]

Swift's relations with the bishops of the English interest

---

[1] *Letters*, i. 134; cf. Wake Corresp. xiv, Goodwin to Wake, 30 July 1722, King to Wake, July 1722.

[2] P.R.O., S.P. 63 (Ireland), 383, Mar., 172$\frac{2}{3}$.

[3] *Corresp.* iii. 235 n.   [4] Ibid. v. 172–3; see also v. 157.

[5] Ibid. vi. 99.   [6] Ibid. iii. 248.

were of another complexion. They knew what to expect from one who had been so closely related to Queen Anne's last ministry and a personal friend of Harley, Bolingbroke, Atterbury, and the Duke of Ormond. The Jacobite intrigue of the last three of these did not make Swift's lot any easier; and the English bishops of the Church of Ireland, at least the more violent ones, never ceased to think of him as a disaffected person, to be constantly watched. In 1718 Bishop Evans began a zealous campaign to impress Wake with Swift's unreliability and disaffection, verging, as he conceived it, towards open treason;[1] and naturally he did not miss the opportunity in 1723, when Atterbury was attainted for treason, to announce (possibly for Swift's special benefit) that 'The Bishop of Rochester was always a silly fellow.'[2] Swift himself felt that the very fact of his friendship had been a hindrance to the promotion of certain people; indeed others held to the same view. It is conceivable that Berkeley suffered in this respect. When Queen Caroline inquired of Lord Wilmington in 1732 the reason that Berkeley was 'disagreeable' to the kingdom of Ireland, Wilmington replied that 'he could not tell, unless that he was very great with Dean Swift'.[3] It was Evans, appointed to the see of Meath in 1716, who was the most uncompromising of the English appointments and the least willing to live on amicable terms. From the beginning he was more than ready to quarrel, as he had already quarrelled when Bishop of Bangor with members of the High Church party. On the bishop's arrival in the diocese Swift had been attentive and friendly—to use his own phrase, 'more than ordinary officious in my respects'.[4] This brief, placid relationship was soon broken when Evans refused to license a curate Swift proposed for one of his livings in Meath. The excuse he gave is not known, but the political motive is revealed in a letter to Wake, where he declared that he did

---

[1] Wake Corresp. xii, 28 Feb. 171⅞ and *passim*.
[2] *Corresp*. iii. 166.
[3] *Hist. MSS. Comm. 16th R.* 1920–3: *Diary of the First Earl of Egmont*, i. 238, 15 Mar. 173½.
[4] *Corresp*. iii. 37.

not propose to license a man who would assist 'the Dean in keeping up the spirit of Faction among the neighbouring clergy'.[1] The friction between the two was not eased by the violent eruption of party spirit consequent on Bishop Hoadly's famous Erastian sermon in 1717. The Whig bishops in Ireland watched with great concern the resurgence of Tory sentiment; and they feared that the meeting of Convocation, proposed in connexion with the parliamentary session of 1717, would bring trouble from the Tory clergy in the Lower House. Evans requested Wake to use his influence against a Convocation at this juncture, particularly calling attention to the rumour that Swift might be prolocutor if a session were held.[2] This was in July. Two months later he reported to Canterbury that 'Dr. Swift with other Dignitaries &c in Severall Parts of this Kingdom endeavour to keep up the Spirits of their Party by assuring them that the Whigs will soon be down & that their Friends will sway &c.'[3] In the following years he continued to keep Swift under surveillance and to make regular reports to Wake. The dean preached 'a Strange Sermon' before the State in February 1718: 'It was somewhat like one of Montaign's Essays, making very free with all orders and degrees of men amongst us. Lords, Bishops, &c. men in Power, the pretended Subjects were Pride, and humiliation'.[4] When rumour indicated that Stearne was to be translated to the important see of Derry, Evans, shocked at the prospect, wrote urgently to Wake a discreditable fact—'Jonathan Swift, and that Tribe are his particular Friends and Correspondents . . . in short, he is thought to be Tory . . . all over, which (here) is reckon'd by every honest man Jacobite'.[5] At the same time

---

[1] Wake Corresp. xii, 24 June 1717.
[2] Ibid. Evans to Wake, 13, 16, 19 July 1717.   [3] Ibid. 23 Sept. [1717].
[4] Ibid. 28 Feb. 171⅞. The sermon is not extant.
[5] Ibid. 22 Apr. [1718]: Evans does not mention Stearne by name here, but it is clear from the facts stated that Stearne is the person referred to. See also 18 Jan. 171⅞, 21 Jan. 171⅞, when Evans reports: 'I am told Swift made him Bishop to come into the Deanery & is very great with him. . . . The most knowing and honest among our Friends assure me that his Bias is toward the disaffected.'

he discovered to his sorrow that the Chancellor of his diocese 'is entirely govern'd by Swift'.[1]

These matters set the tone for the more striking public quarrel between the bishop and the dean which occurred at Evans's visitation in June 1718. On this occasion Swift rose to the defence of three clergymen whom Evans censured. 'I could entertain your Grace', the latter wrote to Wake, 'with the insolent rudeness of Dr. Swift att my Visitation last week where he had never appear'd before, he endeavour'd to arraign me before my Clergy for my unkind carriage towards 3 of them, who were all of them very criminall as plainly appear'd when I stated the Severall cases.'[2] From this time bishop and dean were openly at odds. They quarrelled again in 1719 when Evans refused to accept a proxy for Swift's appearance at the diocesan visitation.[3] In 1720, on the publication of the *Proposal for the Universal Use of Irish Manufacture*, Evans reported this to Wake as a 'Vile Pamphlet' said to be by Swift, openly preaching treason.[4] In the following year he blamed Swift for a 'very scandalous, silly Letter' which appeared in the *St. James's Post* of 6–8 September, attacking his character and political principles;[5] and soon after Swift accused Evans of making 'personal reflections' upon him at a visitation and again refusing to accept a valid proxy.[6] In 1723 Evans informed Wake that Swift had ridiculed 'terribly' some forms of prayer presented at a public meeting of the bishops.[7] Thus the enmity persisted until the death of Evans in 1724. The details of the quarrels depict the atmosphere surrounding Swift as a churchman and make more intelligible his behaviour and his pessimism concerning the Church of Ireland. They afford us as well a glimpse of him as he appeared from the vantage point of his

---

[1] Ibid. xiii, 5 Feb. 171⅞.

[2] Ibid. xii, 20 June [1718]. See also Nicolson to Wake, 8 July 1718; Delany, *Observations*, 216–17; *MLN*, lxviii (1953), 223–6.

[3] *Corresp.* iii. 36–37.

[4] Wake Corresp. xiii, 19 June 1720; cf. 7 May 1720.

[5] Ibid. 19 Sept. 1721; *Corresp.* iii. 87 n.

[6] *Corresp.* iii. 86–87.   [7] Wake Corresp. xiv, 30 Mar. 1723.

enemies. In Swift's defence it may be said that Evans appears to have been the most disliked and, as already remarked, the most irreconcilable of the English appointments.

As was not unexpected, the recommendations of the English interest prevailed in the appointment of Evans's successor, Henry Downes.[1] Swift, possibly hoping for good relations with his new diocesan, showed himself attentive and gracious, as he had when Evans came into Meath. The new bishop was struck by the 'unexpected goodness' and 'uncommon civilities' of the Dean of St. Patrick's, 'as if he had a mind to atone ... for the uncommon trouble he had given to my predecessor'.[2] Swift's relations with Downes and with the succeeding bishops of Meath—details are scanty—do not change the general impression. Partisan differences kept them separated, and indeed with Ralph Lambert (succeeded in 1727) and Welbore Ellis (succeeded in 1732) there were conflicts and dislikes of long standing. In 1708 Swift had himself expected to be made chaplain to the Earl of Wharton, newly appointed Lord Lieutenant of Ireland, yet he had accepted with good grace the choice of Lambert. But he would not be likely to forget Lambert's opposition to the inferior clergy in the bitter convocation disputes of 1709. 'Pox on your convocations, and your Lamberts; they write with a vengeance'—he had remarked to Stella at the time.[3] His attitude towards Ellis was doubtless coloured by the events of 1710 when, as emissary of the Irish bishops to negotiate for the First Fruits, he had been treated with discourtesy by Ellis, then Bishop of Kildare.[4] So far as is known, there was no open quarrelling with either Lambert or Ellis, nor the element of personal rancour which characterized the relations with Evans. All of the Whig bishops watched Swift closely and duly reported his activities to one another or to Canterbury. William Nicolson, Bishop of Derry, is characteristic. In

[1] Wake Corresp. xiv, Nicolson to Wake, 3 Mar. 172¾; Goodwin to Wake, 4 Mar. 172¾.

[2] Letters ... to and from William Nicolson, ii. 574.

[3] Journal to Stella, i. 127. See also Corresp. i. 124 n.

[4] Corresp. i. 219.

1719, when Archbishop King and Swift came to Ireland's defence against attack from England, Nicolson named them to Wake as members of 'Our new Sect of State-Independents', describing King as an 'Ecclesiastical Grandee' and Swift as the 'Angel of St. Patricks . . . now the Guardian of the Kingdom'. Soon afterwards he carefully culled for Wake's benefit the 'choicest Beauty-Spots' from Swift's 'seditious libel'—*A Proposal for the Universal Use of Irish Manufacture*; and four years later he observed with irritation the dean's part in the controversy over Wood's copper coinage—'our Spiritual Draper', he sarcastically called Swift.[1] There were also eruptions of a different kind, such as the dispute which occurred in 1729 at the enthronement of John Hoadly, the newly appointed Archbishop of Dublin. Tempers flared and sharp words were spoken when the archbishop and his vicar-general denied Swift's right to administer the oaths. This denial of the dean's jurisdiction resulted in nothing more than Swift's refusal for the moment to dine with Hoadly.[2] In 1730, when Gay invited Swift to visit him near Salisbury, he offered as inducement the proximity of its bishop—that is, Benjamin Hoadly, the famous brother of the new Archbishop of Dublin.[3] In reply Swift thanked Gay for offering him the 'neighbourhood of another Hoadly'. 'I have enough of one', he wrote. 'Our gardens join, but I never see him except on business.'[4] Yet Swift and Hoadly appear to have managed their common affairs in the spirit of reasonableness, perhaps even in amity, induced to a certain extent by Swift's affection for Hoadly's

[1] Gilbert Collection, MS. 27, 31 Oct. 1719; 9 June 1720; 27 Aug., 12 Oct. 1724; Wake Corresp. xiv, 21 Aug., 30 Oct., 4 Nov. 1724. Despite his bitter attacks, Nicolson presented Swift with a copy of *The Irish Historical Library* (1724). Swift was critical of it (see *Corresp*. iii. 428).

[2] B.M. Add. MS. 21122; *Corresp*. v. 71–72 n. This was a jurisdictional dispute begun, it appears, by William King, who insisted that he be enthroned in both Christ Church and St. Patrick's, whereas by custom earlier archbishops of Dublin were enthroned only in St. Patrick's. The deans of the two cathedrals resisted the innovation (see *A Short State of the Case of the Dean and Chapter of Christ Church, Dublin* [Dublin, 1704]; Bodleian, Ballard MS. 8, fols. 128–9).

[3] *Corresp*. iv. 158.

[4] Ibid. 174–5; see also v. 70.

daughter. There were, however, occasional eruptions of political differences, as in 1737, when Hoadly attacked Swift for opposing (once again) the importation of halfpence from England. 'My neighbour Prelate,' Swift wrote to the Earl of Orrery, 'who politicly makes his court to Sir Robert Walpole by imitating that great Minister in every minute pulling up his breeches ... harangued my neighbours against me under the name of some wicked man about the new halfpence, but received no other answers than "God bless the [Drapier]".'[1]

With one Whig prelate sent from England Swift had amiable relations from the beginning: Thomas Rundle, translated to the rich see of Derry in 1735. Rundle's nomination to a bishopric in England, where his Arian opinions made him suspect, was successfully opposed. As a solace he was appointed to Derry, whereupon William Pulteney wrote to Swift: 'What do you say to the bustle made here to prevent the man from being an English bishop, and afterward allowing him to be good Christian enough for an Irish one?'[2] Rundle's friendship with Alexander Pope would have won him Swift's indulgence, but in his own right Rundle immediately won sympathy from the Irish interest by bringing with him as chaplain an Irish clergyman—'a very wise and popular action', Swift wrote approvingly to Pope.[3] In view of the circumstances in England, there was naturally some dissatisfaction over the appointment among the bishops in Ireland. To Swift this holier-than-thou attitude was an appropriate subject for a satiric poem, in which he pays his respects to the English bishops who have come to Ireland 'to plunder and enslave'; and he finds that Rundle is more Christian than his detractors who never

> own'd a pow'r Divine,
> But *Mammon*, and the G[er]m[a]n Line.[4]

[1] *Corresp.* v. 433.

[2] Ibid. v. 147; *Hist. MSS. Comm. 16th R. 1920–3: Diary of the First Earl of Egmont*, ii. 23, 151, and *passim*; Mant, *Hist. of the Church of Ireland*, ii. 540–1; Phillips, *Hist. of the Church of Ireland*, iii. 215–17; Norman Sykes, *Edmund Gibson: Bishop of London, 1669–1748*, pp. 156 ff.

[3] *Corresp.* v. 227.   [4] *Poems*, iii. 820.

As he came to know Rundle better, he approved him more. Rundle, he wrote to Pope,

is esteemed here as a person of learning, and conversation, and humanity; but he is beloved by all people. He is a most excessive Whig, but without any appearing rancour, and his idol is King William; besides three thousand a year is an invincible sweetener.[1]

It must be admitted, as at least a possibility, that some of his denigration of bishops derived from personal bitterness and disappointments; nevertheless Swift was sincerely disturbed over the low level of episcopal appointments. There is another factor, difficult to assess but playing a part—the traditional distrust among the inferior clergy of the powerful bishops, rooted in the many conflicts over jurisdiction. Swift, as we have already seen, was particularly sensitive to any attempt by the bishops to enlarge their power at the expense of the lower clergy. But the Whig complexion of the episcopal bench in Ireland was perhaps the chief factor in his differences with them. Their abuse of ecclesiastical patronage for personal and party interest, without respect to merit or the welfare of the Church—this seemed to him the worst of their offences. There were of course a number of issues which influenced his feelings about particular bishops, as for example Lambert's subscription to the Bank in 1721, which Swift strongly opposed, or Boulter's part in the attempted removal of the Test Act in 1732 and in the regulation of the coin in 1736–7. It was on this latter occasion that Boulter reported several times to the English government 'the opposition and clamour of Dean *Swift*, the papists, and other discontented or whimsical persons'.[2] Thus, in addition to their policy of anglicizing the Irish Establishment, the English Whig prelates supported other measures which Swift thought injurious to the clergy, the Church, and the country. The complexity and variety of his differences with the bishops should be recognized, growing as they did out of causes that

---

[1] *Corresp.* v. 303.

[2] See *Prose Works*, Davis, ix. 313; Boulter, *Letters*, ii. 162, 172, 192; *Corresp.* vi. 47–48; B.M. Add. MS. 32690 (Newcastle Papers), fol. 356.

at times cannot easily be disentangled—personal, political, ecclesiastical, patriotic. The general effect, however, is clear enough—to intensify his pessimistic view of the Church of Ireland, which could never prosper either temporally or spiritually under the guidance of prelates so 'puft up with Wealth and with Pride'.[1]

[1] *Poems*, iii. 804.

Conclusion

OTHER observers of more sanguine disposition than Swift were no less unhappy at the low state of the Irish Establishment. Writing to William soon after the Battle of the Boyne, Queen Mary urged him to give the Church of Ireland the benefit of his special care. 'Every body agrees', she said, 'that it is the worst in Christendom.'[1] In this sentiment she was merely echoing what others had reported earlier—the Earl of Clarendon, for example, Lord Lieutenant in 1686, who sent word to Canterbury that 'the state of the Church is very miserable'.[2] These typical observations are of the second half of the seventeenth century when Swift's attitudes were being formed; and there is little to indicate that conditions improved sufficiently in the early eighteenth century (if indeed they were not aggravated) to bring about any change in the chorus of despair. Every Irish bishop of the day wrote eloquently of the sorry conditions in his diocese. The doleful facts, set down conscientiously year after year, need not be given in detail. The story was always the same: too many Papists and too few Protestants; a scarcity of endowed vicarages; a great lack of churches, and of those in use many 'far inferior to the Stables and Barns of our Gentry';[3] glebes and parsonages seldom to be found; non-residence, the rule rather than the exception, encouraged by the landed gentry because these 'selfish men hardly sincerely desire [resident clergy], well

[1] Sir John Dalrymple, *Memoirs of Great Britain and Ireland* (London, 1773), ii, appendix ii. 132, 17 July 1690.

[2] Quoted by W. D. Killen, *Ecclesiastical History of Ireland* (London, 1875), ii. 160.

[3] Wake Corresp. xiv, a report to Wake on the state of the Church of Ireland, 27 Feb. 172$\frac{4}{5}$.

knowing the clergy wou'd draw their Tithes & wou'd not perhaps so easily compound for them as they are now forced to do living at a distance'.[1]

In one opinion the Irish clergy, so often divided, found common agreement, that the Church of Ireland was moribund. It was a view that many of the laity shared. 'The Present E[stablishmen]t seems to me in a tottering Way, and things ripening gradually to its Dissolution.' Thus in 1737 wrote the anonymous author of a tract with a revealing title, *A Letter from a Gentleman in the Country to His Son at the University, dissuading Him from going into Holy Orders*.[2] The clergy in Ireland, this writer declared, are doomed, its members already mere drudges 'in Penury and Contempt' and constantly diminishing in temporal and spiritual power. The landlords, he added, are 'daily clipping and circumcising the Church's Property':

. . . it is not altogether improbable, but that in the Course of a few Years, they may reduce it to nothing, or to what the Clergy will think to the full as bad, a fixed *Stipend*: For then they will be mere Creatures of the State, without Votes or Privileges. . . .[3]

With views such as these issuing from both clergy and laity, Swift's own sentiments are revealed as typical rather than unusual, although he felt more strongly perhaps than most contemporary clergymen that the Establishment was 'tottering' and 'ripening gradually to its Dissolution'.

He believed that 'clipping and circumcising the Church's Property' had been going forward inexorably throughout the centuries, initiated by Henry VIII. In one of his many references to that 'Profligate Dog of a King' who had robbed the Church of its possessions Swift remarked that 'power . . . always follows property' (i.e. land).[4] This commonplace of the age had for him the force of a social law. Commenting at several points in his tracts on constitutional changes in

---

[1] Wake Corresp. xiv, a report to Wake on the state of the Church of Ireland, 27 Feb. 172⅘.   [2] p. 13.   [3] Ibid.

[4] *Prose Works*, Davis, ix. 220; but see *The Examiner*, no. 13, where Swift writes: '*Power*, which, according to the old Maxim, was used to follow *Land*, is now gone over to *Money*. . . .'

English history and great shifts in political and social power, he tended to view these movements as a result of the transference of property from one group to another.[1] This process he conceived to be still running its violent and prolonged course in the Irish Establishment; to a large extent it explained, he thought, the decline of the Church, its lost vigour, and the waning power of the clergy.

Swift's personal situation intensified his pessimism. His ill health, his inability to collect his due in tithes, his bitter impotence as he failed time and again to secure preferment for deserving clergymen—these certainly played a part. But there were also other matters, less personal though affecting him as a churchman, such as the prevalent 'contempt of the clergy', the increasing support of dissent manifested in attempts to repeal the Test Act, the attack on ecclesiastical courts, and in England various unfavourable tithe bills, accompanied by cries that the State was in danger from excessive Church power. From 1730 Swift's tone grew sharper, his hopelessness more apparent. In the midst of the recurrent assaults on clergy and Church he expressed to Sheridan the wish that he could be born in the next century, 'when we shall be utterly rid of parsons'.[2] This and similar sentiments belong to 1736, the year of *The Legion Club*—an occasional poem, it is true, but in implication far more than occasional. It is less a sudden eruption over a particular event than the expression of long-accumulated bitterness and despair. Even when allowance is made for Swift's tendency to overstatement, there is clearly apparent in this decade his strong sense that the Irish Church would continue to sink in power and prestige.

It is hardly necessary to mention again that his concern was less with spiritual or doctrinal affairs than with temporal. The state of the Church, its weaknesses, its inherited and contemporary difficulties—these are the matters that principally

[1] The significance of this view in Swift was pointed out to me by Mr. Myrddin Jones of Oxford, whose study is as yet unpublished.

[2] *Corresp.* v. 336.

preoccupied him, and to an extent not generally recognized. Swift accepted the Erastian principle, yet he did not like the consequences. He believed in a Church strong through its alliance with the State and powerful in its exclusive position. He could not, however, view with equanimity the lessons which history taught of the English and Irish Establishments, that the clergy of an Erastian church paid for its privileged status by vulnerability to political authority and by some loss of independence. The strains to which the Church of Ireland was subjected from both internal and external sources, the buffetings it received, are set forth in Swift's various Church tracts, which collectively are a long lament for its weakness.

Tension and struggle were by no means the whole story of Swift's clerical career. In a sense he himself gives a misleading impression since he wrote most often, and most indignantly, about his striking experiences as a churchman and had relatively less to say of the routine aspects of clerical life. Yet these quieter moments predominated and played their part. They reveal what tends to be ignored, the extent to which as dean he devoted himself year in and year out to humdrum matters —humdrum, that is, in contrast to the dramatic controversies but still necessary for the proper functioning of the Church. Week after week he presided over chapter meetings in which the detailed business of the cathedral received attention—the approval of a lease, a decision to repair the fabric, the purchase of new prayer books, the replacement of a verger. Not even Swift's enemies accused him of neglecting his stewardship of St. Patrick's; and all of the early biographers testify to his scrupulous and pious management. In the midst of adverse comment Orrery inserts a line of praise: 'he performed the duties of the church with great punctuality, and a decent degree of devotion'.[1] 'His cathedral of St. Patrick's', wrote Delany, 'is the only church [in Dublin], wherein the primitive practice of receiving the Sacrament every Lord's Day, was renewed. . . . And it is most certain, that he constantly

----

[1] *Remarks*, p. 5.

attended that Holy Office: consecrated and administered the Sacrament, in person.'[1] This level of his achievement as a dean is well known—the conscientious supervision of the preaching, of the decorum and usage of the cathedral, and of the choir. Swift listening critically to a clergyman in the pulpit and being ready with his criticism as soon as the preacher came into the chapter house;[2] Swift following the anthems with music book before him (though unable to read the notes) to make certain that the choir omitted none of the words[3]—these and similar vignettes handed down by observers exhibit him vividly and characteristically performing his duties as ordinary of a great cathedral.

Swift had his personal shortcomings—and they have been subjected to elaborate scrutiny throughout the decades. He did not wholly escape, particularly in his early career, that curious complacency of the age with respect to place-seeking. During the eighteenth century clerical preferment was a thing of the market-place. In 1715, when the rising John Evans, then Bishop of Bangor, was rumoured to have his choice of either of two vacant bishoprics, one valued at £1,100, the other at £3,000, his good friend Edmund Gibson observed: 'I am apt to think he understands Arithmetic better than not to know the great difference between £1100 and £3000.'[4] Now Swift, it must be granted, was in most respects a worldly man. Although the imputations of avarice levelled against him need not be taken seriously, he had, unquestionably, a respectful attitude toward worldly goods. In those early years when he was eager to settle himself, when he was most ambitiously striving to find a place in the Church, he accepted without demur the political traffic in clerical offices; yet he was not himself willing to compromise with his convictions and his principles. Deeply disillusioned, he was nevertheless not so cynical as his age. He had, in fact,

---

[1] *Observations*, pp. 46–47; cf. Lyon, Hawkesworth, p. 75.
[2] *Observations*, p. 206; Lyon, Hawkesworth, p. 155.
[3] Lyon, Hawkesworth, pp. 76, 155.
[4] Bodleian, MS. Add. A 269, Gibson to Nicolson, 15 Dec. 1715.

an ingrained respect for the clerical function. He had indeed
a great contempt for many individual clergymen, but not for
the order. No one was more bitter, shocked, and indignant
that so few who wore the cloth wore it becomingly. And there
was increasingly apparent in him as the years passed a sense
of the dignity of the priesthood and a zealous commitment to
work for its improvement. It is quite true that he never lost
his taste for politics. Some have professed to see in his
character contradictory elements—the divine at odds with the
politician. 'No Cloyster', he wrote to Charles Ford in 1719,
'is retired enough to keep Politicks out, and I will own they
raise my Passions whenever they come in my way. . . .'[1] But
who can ascertain that thin line which divided Church
and State in the period? An eighteenth-century clergyman
often needed the temperament and skill of the politician to
achieve success in Church affairs. The qualities in Swift
which he brought to political controversy did not, certainly,
make him less effective as he moved into those embattled and
litigious areas where the Establishment cried out for defence.

His effectiveness, however, derived chiefly from another
obvious fact—his serious and full acceptance of the duty
and obligation imposed on a distinguished clergyman whose
institution ramified into every aspect of the life of the nation.
Swift took for granted that a churchman of his status must
act in a larger sphere, that the dignity of a dean embodied a
certain social and cultural eminence as well as religious and
political power. This suggests a further, and final, point.
What did Swift signify for the Church of Ireland? The
answer can be given only very generally, but with a certain
assurance. Without question he gained for the Establishment respect, regard, and appreciation. The variety of his
activities has significance. The man was not disassociated
from the churchman. It was the Anglican dean, not merely
Jonathan Swift, who performed extensive charities, who
founded a small alms-house for widows, who was a governor

---

[1] *Letters of Jonathan Swift to Charles Ford*, ed. D. Nichol Smith (Oxford, 1935),
p. 82.

of charity hospitals, who devised his fortune to the afflicted. There were few public matters which did not engage his attention, local or national, whether it was the election of a Lord Mayor of Dublin or the lowering of the coin. It was the Anglican dean who was blessed as the Drapier, who became the Hibernian Patriot, who received a silver box and the freedom of the City of Cork. It was the Dean of St. Patrick's who was gazed on affectionately as he walked through the alleys and streets of his Liberty, and who found thirty of its gentlemen and principal residents ready to defend him against the threats of 'that Booby Bettesworth'.[1] The man was not distinguished from his clerical status as he sent forth tract after tract in an effort to mitigate the ills of the country and to encourage it against oppression and misrule from England. And to mention one more of many possible instances, it was the Anglican churchman who lived in easy intercourse with the great, the Lord Lieutenants and other statesmen, and whose literary genius was the admiration of friend and enemy alike.

Swift's influence in these various capacities cannot of course be stated in precise words. His conception of pastoral care, as Herbert Davis has remarked, widened out to embrace the nation. If Ireland irritated and displeased him in many respects, it also received gratefully his warm commiseration, as of a pastor to his flock. And unquestionably as a living symbol of the Anglican Establishment in Ireland, he gave it moment and distinction.

[1] *Prose Works,* iv. 261 ff.; *Corresp.* v. 53 ff.

Index

Abercorn, James Hamilton, 6th Earl of, 75.

absences, 46, 47.

Achonry, Archdeacon of, *see* Walls, Thomas.

Act of Settlement, 40, 161; of Uniformity, 8.

Addison, Joseph, 79.

Advice to a Parson, poem, 122.

advowsons, 10.

Agher or Agherpallis, parish, 27, 34, 36; account of, 42.

agistment controversy, 135–50, 155.

agriculture, Swift on, 142–3, 142 ff.

Aiton, Andrew, 15 n. 2.

alienation of Church lands, 100–1, 107, 122–3.

Anabaptists, 127, 129.

Anglesey, Arthur Annesley, 5th Earl of, 140.

Anglo-Irish, 169–77.

Anne, Queen, xv, 40, 52–54, 62–66, 171, 181.

Answer to the Craftsman, 158–9.

'Antibill, The', 108–9.

Antrim, county, 10–11, 16, 20–21.

Armagh, diocese of, 39.

— Archbishops of, *see* Boulter, Hugh; Hoadly, John; Lindsay, Thomas; Marsh, Narcissus; Usher, James.

— Dean of, *see* Reeves, William.

Ashe, St. George, Swift's tutor and friend, Bishop of Clogher, 9, 10, 35, 172.

Atterbury, Francis, Bishop of Rochester, 84–87, 181.

Ball, F. Elrington, 28–29.

Ballycarry, village or small town, 23.

Ballynure, parish, 15 n. 2, 16 and nn. 2, 3; Swift rector in, 17; area of, 17; dissenters in, 18–21; church at, 22–23.

Ballyprior, parish, 16 n. 2.

Bangor, Bishop of, *see* Evans, John.

Barber, John, London printer and alderman, friend of Swift, 159.

Bassenet, Edward, Dean of St. Patrick's, 164 n. 4.

Bath, Sir William Pulteney, Earl of, 186.

Bathurst, Allen, 1st Earl, 149.

Berkeley, Charles, 2nd Earl of, Lord Justice of Ireland, 26, 38, 45, 47, 58, 195; and the deanery of Derry, 27–34.

Berkeley, Dr. George, Bishop of Cloyne, 181.

Bettesworth, Richard, 195.

Bindon, Francis, painter of Swift's portrait, 95.

bishops: and landowners, 99–111; and clergy, 111–23; Swift's relations with, 177–88; *On the Irish Bishops* (1732), 111.

Blackburne, Lancelot, Bishop of Exeter, 110.

Bohun, W., of the Middle Temple, writer on tithes, 129.

Bolingbroke, Henry St. John, 1st Viscount, 88, 181.

Bolton, John, vicar of Ratoath and prebendary of Dunlavin, later Dean of Derry, 29–34, 37, 45.

Bolton, Theophilus, prebendary of Stagonil, Chancellor of St. Patrick's, Bishop of Clonfert, Archbishop of Cashel, 78–80, 83–84, 92–93, 122; relations with Swift, 178–80.

Boulter, Hugh, Archbishop of Armagh, 119, 140, 143, 145–6, 153–5, 171, 173, 175, 180; relations with Swift, 140, 175, 178, 187.

Brett, Jasper, 14 n. 1.

Brice, Edward, first Presbyterian minister at Templecorran, later prebendary of Kilroot, 19.

Brodrick, Alan, Speaker of the Irish House of Commons, 56.

Browne, Peter, Provost of Trinity College, Dublin, 60.

Burnet, Gilbert, Bishop of Salisbury, 25, 52, 105, 128, 168.

Bushe, Arthur, secretary to the Earl of Berkeley, 28, 29, 32, 33.

Calhoun, James, curate, 15 n. 2, 23 n. 5.

Canterbury: Swift may have expected a prebend in, 5, 7.

— Archbishop of, see Wake, William.

Capel, Sir Henry, Baron Capel, Lord Deputy of Ireland, 8, 15.

Carlisle, Bishop of, see Nicolson, William.

Carnmoney, rector of, see Winder, John.

Caroline, Queen, 181.

Carr, Charles, Bishop of Killaloe, 122.

Carteret, John, 2nd Baron Carteret, afterwards Earl Granville, 129, 149, 152, 156, 174, 175, 180; *Vindication of Lord C[artere]t*, 175.

Case of the Laity, with some Queries (1723), 107.

Cashel, Archbishop of, see Bolton, Theophilus.

Cathedral of the Holy Saviour, 8, 10; Chancellor of (Enoch Reader), 49–50.

Catholics, 35, 151, 156, 160, 189.

Chamberlain, Philip, Canon of St. Patrick's, prebendary of St. Audoen, 79–82.

Character of an Irish Squire, 104.

Character of P[rimate] M[arsh], 45.

Charles I, King, 76, 100, 101, 105.

Charles II, King, 106.

Charlett, Arthur, Master of University College, Oxford (The Gazeteer or the Oxford Intelligencer), 73.

Chetwode, Knightley, 76.

Chichester family, 17.

Christ Church Cathedral, see Dublin.

Chronicon Preciosum (Fleetwood), 105–6, 133.

churches, lack of, 189.

Clarendon, Henry Hyde, 2nd Earl of, 189.

Clements, Henry, 15 n. 2.

clergy: and landlords, 97–111, 148; and bishops, 111–23; and laity, 151–9; and gentry, 169–77.

Clogher, Archdeacon of (Thomas Parnell), 179.

— Bishop of, see Ashe, St. George.

Clonfert, Archbishop of, see Bolton, Theophilus.

Cloyne, Bishop of, see Crow, Charles; George Berkeley.

Coghill, Marmaduke, Judge of the Prerogative Court, 135.

Colpe, Monastery of, 43.

Comber, Thomas, Dean of Durham, 127–8.

congregations, size of, 21.

Connor, 49; parish church, 15 n. 2.

Cope, Robert, friend of Swift, 78–79.

Cowper, William, 1st Earl, 61.

Craik, Henry, and the deanery of Derry, 28.

Crommelin, Louis, Huguenot Overseer of the Royal Linen Manufactory, 125.

Crow, Charles, Bishop of Cloyne, 52, 53.

Crown rents, 36, 53–54, 62, 66.

Cunningham, William, 15 n. 2.

curates, 15 n. 2, 23 and n. 5, 36, 38–39, 44; see also Swift, J.

Darensis Episcopus, 7 n. 2.

Davis, Herbert, 195.

'Dearly beloved Roger', 21 n. 2, 38.

Deece, Barony of, 42.

Degge, Sir Simon, 118.

Delany, Patrick, Chancellor of St. Patrick's, Dublin, biographer of Swift, 74, 93, 192.

depreciation of value, 105–6, 133–4.

deprivation, power of, 71.

Derensis Episcopus, 7 n. 2.

Derry: Bishops of, see King, William; Nicolson, William; Rundle, Thomas.

— deanery of, 27–34, 45.

Derry: Deans of, Bolton, John; Ormsby, Coote.

Discovery, The, poem, 34.

dissenters, 18–21, 28, 56, 58, 99, 151, 155, 191.

Division, Bill of, 116–17, 179, 180.

Dobbs, Richard, of Antrim, 15 n. 2, 19, 22; Mrs. Dobbs, 19.

Donegal, Arthur Chichester, 3rd Earl of, 16.

Dopping, Anthony, Bishop of Meath, 12, 13, 14 n. 2, 35, 40, 88; his brother Samuel, 88.

Dorset, Lionel Cranfield Sackville, 1st Duke of, 176.

Dougatt, Robert, prebendary of Swords, Archdeacon of Dublin, Precentor of St. Patrick's, Dublin, 74, 83–84, 89, 92.

Down, county, state of the Church in, 11; Archdeacon of, *see* Mathews, Lemuel; Cathedral, 10.

Down and Connor, diocese of, 10, 13–15, 34; Bishops of, *see* Hackett, Thomas, and Taylor, Jeremy.

Downes, Henry, Bishop of Elphin, Bishop of Meath, 98, 99, 102, 184.

Drapier, the, 180, 186, 195.

Drapier's Letters, 110, 126, 142.

Drogheda, Henry Moore, 3rd Earl of, 43, 44 n.

Dromore, 48.

Dublin: Archbishops of, *see* Hoadly, John; King, William; Marsh, Francis; Marsh, Narcissus.

— Archdeacons of, *see* Dougatt, Robert; Reader, Enoch; Whittingham, Charles.

— Castle, Swift at, 27.

— Christ Church Cathedral: Deans of, *see* Ellis, Welbore; Moreton, William.

— — independence of Christ Church and St. Patrick's, 72–73.

— St. Anne's Church, 87–90; vicar of (Robert Howard), 87–93.

— St. Bride's Church, 87–92; vicars of (Robert Grattan), 47, 91, 92, 94; (James Duncan), 87.

Dublin: St. Nicholas Without, church of, 79–80, 179; vicar of (John Grattan), 47, 94.

— St. Patrick's Cathedral: disputes between chapter and Crown, 48; independence of St. Patrick's and Christ Church, 72–73; Swift on the constitution of, 86; younger prebendaries, 94; surrender of the deanery to Henry VIII, 164 n. 4.

— — Liberty of, 68–69.

— — Prebend of Dunlavin, 27, 30, 34, 44–47; date of Swift's appointment, 44, 45.

— St. Sepulchre, palace of, 50, 68.

— St. Thomas, Monastery of, 36.

— Trinity College (College of Dublin), 3.

Dunboyne, rector of (Thomas Forbes), 88.

Duncan, James, vicar of St. Bride's, Dublin, 87.

Dunlavin, parish of, 46; *see also* Bolton, John, and Dublin (St. Patrick's Cathedral).

Durham, Dean of (Thomas Comber), 127–8.

ecclesiastical commission (William III), 26; economics, 97; landowners, 102–3.

Effernock, tithes of, 41, 166.

Elizabeth I, Queen, 72, 83.

Ellis, Henry, 15 n. 2.

Ellis, Welbore, Bishop of Kildare, Dean of Christ Church, Dublin, 65, 72, 73, 184.

Elphin, Bishops of, *see* Downes, Henry; Howard, Robert.

Ely, Bishop of, *see* Fleetwood, William.

emigration, tithes and, 154–7; tillage and, 157–9.

Emly, Dean of (Enoch Reader), 49–50.

Erastian principle, 192.

Eugenius IV, Pope, 10.

Evans, John, Bishop of Bangor, later of Meath, 35, 65, 100, 102, 108, 118–19, 156, 167, 171–3, 193; relations with Swift, 181–3.

Excellent New Song, poem, 110–11.

Exeter, Bishop of (Lancelot Blackburne), 110.

Faulkner, George, Swift's publisher, 114, 134, 145.

Ferns, Bishop of, *see* Synge, Edward; diocese of, 165.

First Fruits for the Church of Ireland: Swift and, 40, 44, 46, 50–56, 60–65, 166; Queen Anne and, 52–54, 62–66; Irish bishops and, 60–65, 73.

— Board for Funds, 40, 65.

— Memorial (1710), 40, 66, 67, 167, 168.

'First Fruits of Ingratitude', 66.

Fishamble Street, Dublin, 94.

Fitzpatrick, Simon, 15 n. 2.

flax, tithes, 124–35.

Fleetwood, William, Bishop of Ely, *Chronicon Preciosum* (1707), 105–6, 133.

Forbes, Thomas, chaplain to the Duke of Shrewsbury, rector of Dunboyne, 88.

Ford, Charles, 146, 194.

Galway, Henri de Massue de Ruvigny, 1st Earl of, and the deanery of Derry, 29, 31, 32.

Gay, John, 185.

Gazeteer, The, *see* Charlett, Arthur.

gentry and churchmen, 107, 169–77.

George, Prince Consort of Queen Anne, 57.

George I, King, 78, 171; Acts of, 120, 143.

Germain, Lady Elizabeth (Betty), 176.

Gibson, Edmund, 193.

glebes, 10, 11, 18, 21, 22, 35, 67, 112, 114, 116, 118–20, 166, 189; Laracor, 39–41, 65; Agher, 42; Rathbeggan, 43.

Godolphin, Sidney, 1st Earl of, 56, 57, 59, 61.

Goodwin, Timothy, Bishop of Kilmore, 109, 171, 172, 174.

Grafton, Charles Fitzroy, 2nd Duke of, 171, 173, 180.

Granville, Earl, *see* Carteret, John, 2nd Baron.

Grattan, John, prebendary of St. Patrick's, Dublin, vicar of St. Nicholas Without, 47, 94.

Grattan, Robert, prebendary of St. Patrick's, Dublin, vicar of St. Bride's, 47, 91, 92, 94.

'great prerogatives', 70.

Hackett, Thomas, Bishop of Down and Connor ('Bishop of Hammersmith'), 13.

Halifax, Charles Montagu, 1st Earl of, 52, 55, 61.

Hamilton, Ezekiel, 73 n. 3.

'Hammersmith, Bishop of', *see* Hackett, Thomas.

Harley Cabinet, 44, 46, 74.

Harley, Robert, 1st Earl of Oxford, 61–67, 181.

Hart Hall, Oxford, 2, 4.

Hawkesworth, John, and the deanery of Derry, 28.

hemp, tithes, 124–35.

Henry VI, King, 105, 106.

Henry VIII, King, 53, 139, 160–4, 190.

Herbert, Edward, 1st Baron Herbert of Cherbury, 164.

Hervey, John, Baron Hervey, 130, 147–9.

Hibernian Patriot, xv, 178, 195.

Hoadly, Benjamin, Bishop of Salisbury, 73, 182, 185.

Hoadly, John, Archbishop of Dublin, later of Armagh, 69, 93, 185–6; his daughter, 186.

Holt, Samuel, prebendary of Maynooth, 92.

Holy Saviour, Cathedral of, Connor diocese, 8, 10, 17.

Honest Jo, in Swift's poem, 110.

Hort, Joseph, 144 n. 2.

Howard, Robert, prebendary of Maynooth, St. Patrick's; vicar of St. Anne's, Dublin; Chancellor of St. Patrick's, Bishop of Killala, Bishop of Elphin, 87–93, 122.

impropriations, 159–69.

incomes, clerical, 109, 114.

Insula (Island Magee), parish, 12 n. 1, 16 n. 2.

Ireland, Church of, xv, 35.

Irish bishops, and First Fruits, 60–65, 73; money paid to, 66.

— Church, corrupt state of, 13; possessions, 16; poor state of, 189–91.

— The Irish Interest, 169–77.

— *Irish Manufacture*, 185.

— The Irish Society, 159.

— Parliament and the agistment controversy, 135–50.

— Presbyterians, 56.

Island Magee (Insula), parish, 12 n. 1, 16 n. 2.

Jacobitism, 182.

James I, King, 10, 160.

James II, King, 161.

Johnson, Esther (Stella), xv, 49, 61–66, 184.

Jones, John, 50 n. 1.

Jones, Myrddin, 191 n. 1.

Judas, poem, 122.

Kells, 160.

Kennet, White, 162–3.

Ketteringham, Osborne, 15 n. 2.

Kildare, Bishops of, *see* Ellis, Welbore; Moreton, William.

Kilkenny, 160.

Killala, Bishop of (Robert Howard), 87–93, 122.

Killaloe, Bishop of (1710), 60–61, 66; *see also* Carr, Charles.

Kilmore, Bishop of, *see* Goodwin, Timothy.

Kilpatrick, Simon, 15 n. 2.

Kilroot: Swift appointed prebendary of, 8; who was his sponsor? 8–10; account of Kilroot, 10–12; Swift's impressions, 11, 15; his predecessor (William Milne), 12–15; prebend a union of three parishes, 16; income, 16 and n. 3; a diocesan residence, 17; antiquarian and historic interest, 17; area of, 18; state of in the 17th century, 18; dissenters in, 18–20; size of Swift's congregations, 21; where did he reside? 21, 22; where did he preach? 21–23; no church at Kilroot, 22; Swift's resignation, 24.

King, James, prebendary of St. Patrick's, Dublin, 94.

King, William, Bishop of Derry, Archbishop of Dublin: and Swift, xiv, xv, 7 n. 2, 41, 48, 58, 65; on commission of 1693, 13; and the deanery of Derry, 28–31; and Swift at St. Patrick's, 51, 69, 74, 75, 77–84, 87–91, 178, 185; the First Fruits, 52, 53, 55, 57, 60–64, 66; reconciliation with Swift, 81–82, 92; and the prebend of Tymothan, 83, 84; his death, 93; on Irish Papists and dissenters, 107; his Antibill, 108–9; and tithe agistment, 136, 144; and emigration, 156; and impropriations, 165; and glebe-land, 166; and disproportionate English clerical preferment, 169 n. 2, 172; why opposed for Lord Justice and Primacy, 173.

laity, the, 151–9.

Lambert, Ralph, Wharton's chaplain, Bishop of Meath, 35, 60, 184, 187.

Land Acts, 98, 100, 101, 105.

landowners, bishops and, 98, 100–11.

Laracor, 21 n. 2, 27–44, 74; Swift's appointment, 27; benefice united with Agher and Rathbeggan, 27, 34, 36; expectations disappointed, 27; date of Swift's institution, 36; income from, 36; crown rent, 36; a vicarage, 36; area, 36; Swift's curates, 36, 38, 39, 44; account of the church, 37; the glebe and church building, 37, 39–41; parsonage built, 37; interest in tithes, 41, 166; Swift's clerical life at, 38, 39, 44.

Laughnalitten, church or chapel, 16 n. 2.

leases: Swift's tract on letting of, 97, 99; Act governing, 100; length of, 100–1, 104–5, 107.

Legion Club, the (Irish Parliament), 135–50, 191.

Leigh, Thomas, Canon of St. Patrick's, Dublin, 50 n. 1.

Leighlin: Archdeacon of (Benjamin Neale), 136; Bishop of, *see* Synge, Edward; diocese of, 166.

Leslie, Charles, non-Juror, 127.

Lightburne, Stafford, Swift's curate at Laracor, 38–39.

Limitation Act, 105.

Lindsay, Thomas, Archbishop of Armagh, 171, 173.

linen industry, 124, 125.

Lisburn, parish church of, 10; Swift at, 15–16.

Lord Mayor, 68, 71, 195.

Lyon, Rev. Dr. John, antiquary, 2, 69, 74.

Macaulay, Alexander, *Property Inviolable*, 140–2, 157; *Tillage of Ireland*, 145.

Madden, Samuel, Irish divine, writer, and philanthropist, 155.

Maitland, Frederic William, on 'temporal' and 'spiritual', 96.

manse houses, 10, 18, 21, 22, 35, 41–43, 67, 112, 116, 118–21, 189.

Marsh, Francis, Archbishop of Dublin, 49.

Marsh, Jeremiah, Treasurer of St. Patrick's, Dublin, 49.

Marsh, Narcissus, Archbishop of Dublin, later Archbishop of Armagh, 6; and the deanery of Derry, 29, 30, 31, 44; and Dunlavin, 44, 45; his library, 50–51.

Mary, Queen, 189.

Mason, Monck, and the deanery of Derry, 28.

Master of the Rolls in Ireland, 1, 2.

Mathews, Lemuel, Archdeacon of Down, 15.

Maynooth, St. Patrick's, Dublin, prebend of, *see* Holt, Samuel; Howard, Robert.

Meath; Bishops of, *see* Dopping,

Meath—*cont.*
Anthony; Downes, Henry; Evans, John; Lambert, Ralph; Moreton, William; Tennison, Richard.

— county, emigration from, 156.

— diocese of, 34, 35, 167.

Milne, William, prebendary of Kilroot, Swift's predecessor, 12–15, 19.

Modest Proposal, A, 143, 154.

modus, 124, 132–4.

Molesworth, Robert, 1st Viscount, xv, 126, 129, 130.

money, value of, 105–6.

Moor Park, Sir William Temple's seat in Surrey, 55.

Moreton, William, Bishop of Kildare, Dean of Christ Church Cathedral, Dublin, Bishop of Meath, 7, 8.

Morgan, Anthony, Irish M.P., 137.

mortmain, 148–9.

Mossom, Dr. Robert, Dean of Ossory, 86–87.

Moyfenragh, Barony of, 36.

Mulhuddart, prebend of, *see* Whittingham, Charles.

Naboth's vineyard, 37.

national debt, 111, 122.

Neale, Benjamin, Archdeacon of Leighlin, 136.

Neal's Town, 40.

Newcastle, John Holles, Duke of, 61.

Newcastle, Thomas Pelham-Holles, Duke of, 175.

Nicolson, William, Bishop of Carlisle, Bishop of Derry, 99, 102, 110, 119, 129, 171, 173; relations with Swift, 184, 185.

nonconformity, 19–22, 151.

non-cures, 119.

non-residence, 22, 35, 118–21, 168, 189.

On the Irish Bishops, 111, 122, 123.

Ormond, James Butler, 1st Duke of, 125, 161.

Ormond, James Butler, 2nd Duke of, 54, 55, 63–66, 181.

Ormsby, Coote, Dean of Derry, death of, 27, 29.

Orrery, John Boyle, 5th Earl of, 5, 74, 135, 186, 192.

Ossory, Bishop of (John Hartstonge), 60–61, 66.

— Dean of (Robert Mossom), 86–87.

Oxford Intelligencer (Arthur Charlett), 73.

Oxford University: Hart Hall, 2, 4.

— University College, Master of (Arthur Charlett), 73.

Palmerston, Henry Temple, 1st Viscount, 9 n. 3.

parishes, division of, 112, 114, 116, 117, 123.

Parnell, Thomas, poet, Archdeacon of Clogher, 179.

Partiality Detected, 60.

pasturage, 135–50.

Pembroke, Thomas Herbert, 8th Earl of, 55, 56, 59.

'penitential letter' to Sir William Temple, 6, 7, 9.

Perceval, John, Viscount, afterwards 1st Earl of Egmont, 129.

Percival, John, Swift's neighbour at Laracor, 40, 41.

Percival, Robert, 152.

Perkinson, Mr., and the deanery of Derry, 30.

Peterborough, Charles Mordaunt, 3rd Earl of, 52, 175–7.

place-seeking, 193.

pluralism, 31, 35, 46, 67, 167, 168.

Pocklington, Baron, 175 n. 1.

Pope, Alexander, xiii, 68, 82, 93, 97, 109, 153, 186.

population, 154.

Portugal, 7.

preaching, 21, 46.

prebends, royal, 5, 26; equality of status, 45.

Prendergast, Sir Thomas, Irish M.P., 136–7.

Presbyterians, 19–21, 35.

Prescription Sacred, 140–2.

Prideaux, Humphrey, Dean of Norwich, 128.

Property Inviolable (Macaulay), 140–2.

Protestants, 43, 44, 155–6, 189.

Pulteney, Sir William, Earl of Bath, 186.

Quakers, 127, 129, 146–9.

Raphoe, see of, 49.

Rathbeggan, 27, 34, 36, 42–43.

Ratoath, parish, 30–2, 34, 37, 45; see also Bolton, John.

Read, James, 163.

Reader, Enoch, Dean of Emly, Archdeacon of Dublin, Chancellor of Connor, 49–50.

Reconciler, The, 116, 118.

rectorial tithes, 16, 17, 36, 43.

Reeves, William, Dean of Armagh, 7 n. 2.

Reformation, the, 160–4, 167.

rents, 101 ff.

residence, 111–23; requirements concerning, 46.

Residence, Bill of, 112, 179, 180.

Rochester, Bishop of (Francis Atterbury), 84–87, 181.

Romney, Henry Sidney, Earl of, 25–26.

Rundle, Thomas, Bishop of Derry, 186–7.

Ryves, Jerome, Dean of St. Patrick's, Dublin, 48.

Ryves, Thomas, 163.

Sacramental Test, 56–59, 123; Letter concerning, 59.

Sacred Tenth, the, 123–35.

sacrilege, 168–9.

St. Ailbe, 17.

St. Anne's Church, see Dublin.

St. Audoen, prebendary of (Philip Chamberlain), 79–82.

St. Bride's Church, see Dublin.

St. Colman, 17.

St. Nicholas Without, Church of, see Dublin.

St. Patrick's Cathedral, see Dublin.

St. Patrick's Day, cathedral feast on, 95.

St. Thomas, Dublin, Monastery of, 36.

Salisbury, Bishops of, *see* Burnet, Gilbert; Hoadly, Benjamin.
— Dean of, *see* Younger, John.
Scott, Temple, 115.
Scott, Sir Walter, 38; on *The Legion Club*, 145.
Scottish Presbyterians, 19–21.
sermons, Swift's, 21.
Sharp, John, Archbishop of York, 127–8.
Sheridan, Thomas, friend of Swift, 138, 146, 148, 152, 175 n. 1, 191.
Sheridan, Thomas, Swift's biographer, 28.
Shrewsbury, Charles Talbot, 12th Earl and Duke of, 88.
Smith, Mr., Swift's curate at Laracor, 38.
Somers, John, Lord, 52, 55–57, 59, 61.
South, Robert, 163.
Southwell, Edward, 169 n. 2.
Southwell, Sir William, Secretary of State for Ireland, 3.
Span, Mr., and the deanery of Derry, 30.
Speaker, Irish, 56–57.
Spelman, Sir Henry, historian and antiquary, 127, 163.
spiritualities, 10.
Stagonil, prebendary of, *see* Bolton, Theophilus.
Stearne, John, Chancellor and Dean of St. Patrick's, Dublin, Bishop of Clogher, 30, 48, 49, 61, 85, 112; relations with Swift, 178–9, 182.
Stella, *see* Johnson, Esther.
Stephen, Sir Leslie, and the deanery of Derry, 28.
Stewart, Alexander, 15 n. 2.
Stewart, Mrs., 19.
Strafford, Thomas Wentworth, 1st Earl of, 124, 160.
Sumerhill, chapel at, 37.
Sumervall (Sumerall?), Edward, 15 n. 2.
Sunderland, Charles Spencer, 3rd Earl of, 55, 59, 61, 78.
Sunderland, Robert Spencer, 2nd Earl of, 24.

suspension, power of, 71.
Swift, Deane, cousin of Swift, 2–3.
Swift, Hannah, wife of Stafford Lightburne, 39.
Swift, Jonathan: not 'the gravest of Divines', xiii; character as clergyman and churchman, xiii, xv; political enemies, xiv, xv; discontent, xv; Hibernian Patriot, xv, 178, 195; long ministry, xv, xvi; *Gulliver's Travels*, xvi; pessimism concerning the Irish Establishment, xvi, 58, 189–92; realistic appraisal of the Church of Ireland, xvi; ordained in 1694, xvi; M.A. 1692, 2; concern for physical possessions of the Church, 11; rector and vicar in Ballynure, 17; lifelong struggle against dissent, 19, 21; sermons, 21; opinion of the Earl of Romney, 26; and the deanery of Derry, 27–34, 45; and the Earl of Berkeley, 26–27, 36–38, 58; and the First Fruits, 40, 44, 46, 50–56, 60–67, 166; *Character of P[rimate] M[arsh]*, 45; preaching duties, 46; D.D., 47; in disputes between chapter and Crown, 48; early friends at St. Patrick's, 49; Parliamentary activities, 50; and Marsh's library, 50; proctor in the lower House of Convocation, 50; guardian of the rights of churchmen, 51; dean, 52; and Crown rents, 53–55; *Tale of a Tub*, 55; and Wharton, 59–60; in Dublin, 59–60; returns to England, 60–61; and Godolphin, 61; contempt for Irish bishops, 63; joins the Tories, 66.
— *Ordination*, 1–8: reasons for taking orders in Ireland, 1–5; other posts offered to him, 1, 2; University career, 3–4; ordination and preferment, 4–6; leaves the Temple household, 5; certificate of good behaviour insisted on, 6; leaves England for Ireland, 6; 'penitential' letter to Sir William Temple, 6, 7, 9; ordained deacon in Dublin, 7; ordained priest in Dublin, 8.

Swift, Jonathan: *Dunlavin*, 44–7: *see under* Dunlavin.
— *Kilroot*, 8–24: *see under* Kilroot.
— *Laracor*, 25–44: *see under* Laracor.
— *The Dean and his Chapter*, 68–95: his powers and rights, 68–71; incidents with Archbishop Hoadly, 69, 186; 'great prerogatives', 70; power of visitation, 70–71; and the independence of St. Patrick's and Christ Church, 72–73; King's opposition, 74; relations with his chapter, 68–73; reconciliation with King, 81–82; on the constitution of St. Patrick's, 86; and the Dean of Ossory, 86–87; proctor, 94; portrait painted by Francis Bindon, 95.
— his opponents: Edward Synge, 30, 31, 49, 76, 84–85, 88–89; John Hoadly, 69, 186; Vicars Choral of St. Patrick's, 71, 75–76, 94; Arthur Charlett, 73; Ezekiel Hamilton, 73; Robert Dougatt, 74, 83–84, 89, 92–93; William King, *see* King, William; Earl of Abercorn, 75; John Worral, 75; Theophilus Bolton, 78–80, 83–84, 92–93; Philip Chamberlain, 79–82; Charles Whittingham, 82–83, 92–93; Edward Synge (2), 93; John Wynne, 93–94.
— *Temporalities*, 96–150: his views on their importance, 96–97.
1. The Clerical Landlord, 97–111: Swift's tract on letting of leases, 97–111; on greed of country landowners, 98, 110–11; on value of money, 105–6; sympathies for Irish-born bishops, 108; *An Excellent New Song upon His Grace Our Good Lord Archbishop of Dublin*, 110–11.
2. Residence, 111–23: *On the Irish Bishops*, 111, 122–3; *On the Bill for the Clergy's residing on their livings*, 113–16; *Considerations upon Two Bills* ..., 114–16; on Non-Residence, 120–1; *Judas*, 122; *Advice to a Parson*, 122.
3. The Sacred Tenth, 123–35: *Some*

Swift, Jonathan—*cont.*
Reasons against the Bill for settling the Tyth of Hemp, Flax, &c., by a Modus, 124–7, 134; *Some Further Reasons*, 127, 130; Swift's views on tithes, 124–7, 129–34.
4. The Legion Club, 135–50: *A Character, Panegyric, and Description of the Legion Club*, 135 ff.; *Concerning that Universal Hatred which prevails against the Clergy*, 139; *A Modest Proposal*, 143; Swift on the decrease of his tithes, 145; on mortmain, 149; 'I have long given up all hopes of Church or Christianity', 150.
— *The State of the Establishment*, 151–88.
1. The Laity, 151–9: *A Modest Proposal*, 154, 158; *Answer to the Craftsman*, 158–9.
2. Impropriations, 159–69.
3. Irish Interest, gentry, and clergy, 169–77; *Vindication of Lord C[artere]t*, 175.
4. Bishops, 177–88.
— *Conclusion*, 189–95: on the decline of the Irish Church, xvi, 189–92; 'power always follows property', 190–1; Swift's pessimism, 190–1; ill-health, 191; sincerity of his clerical life, 192–3; personal shortcomings, 193; politics and religion, 194; the man and his office, 194–5.
Swift, Thomas, cousin of Swift, 1, 5.
Swift, William, uncle of Swift, 4.
Swords, prebendary of, *see* Dougatt, Robert.
Synge, Edward, Chancellor of St. Patrick's, Dublin, later Bishop of Raphoe and Archbishop of Tuam, 30, 31, 49, 76, 78 n. 1, 84–86, 88, 89, 98, 108–9, 119, 121 n. 3, 172.
Synge, Edward, son of the Archbishop of Tuam, Chancellor of St. Patrick's, Dublin, Bishop of Ferns and Leighlin, 89, 93, 139, 156–7, 165; relations with Swift, 180.
Synge, Samuel, Precentor of St. Patrick's, Dublin, 49, 50.

Tale of a Tub, 21, 55.

Taswell, William, on tithes, 131.

Taylor, Jeremy, Bishop of Down and Connor, 12 n. 1.

Temple, Sir William, statesman, 1–3, 5–9, 24, 25, 47, 125, 163–4.

Templecorran, parish, 15 n. 2, 16 and n. 2, 17, 21 n. 2, 23.

Temple Igormagan, parish, 16 n. 2.

temporalities, 10, 11, 35, 96–150.

Tennison, Richard, Bishop of Meath, 35.

Test Act, 56–60, 187, 191.

tillage, 67, 143–5; and emigration, 157–9.

Tillage of Ireland (Macaulay), 145.

Tindal, Matthew, *Rights of the Christian Church*, 149.

tithes, 10, 16–18, 35, 43, 46, 67, 114, 124–35, 151–3, 190–1; and emigration, 154–8; modus, 124, 132–4; Sir Henry Spelman and others on, 127–31; divine right, 127–30, 153; secular foundation, 131; agistment controversy, 135–50; in lay hands, 165–6; as wages, 147.

Towers, John, prebendary of St. Patrick's, Dublin, 94.

Townshend, Charles, 2nd Viscount, 171.

Trim, parish, 30, 40, 41.

Trotter, Thomas, N.P., 50.

Tuam, Archbishop of, *see* Synge, Edward.

Twentieth parts, 53–55, 62, 66; *see also* First Fruits.

Tymothan, prebend of, 83, 84.

University College, Oxford, Master of, 73.

Ussher, James, Archbishop of Armagh, 17.

vicarages, 10.

vicarial tithes, 16–18, 43.

Vicars Choral of St. Patrick's, 71, 75–76, 94.

Vienna, 58.

visitation, power of, 70–71; proxy for, 92.

Wake, William, Archbishop of Canterbury, 48, 98, 99, 119, 144, 156, 167, 172–5, 180–3, 185.

Walkington, Edward, Bishop of Down and Connor, 12–14.

Walls, Thomas, Master of St. Patrick's School and Archdeacon of Achonry, 47, 48, 79–82, 90, 91, 94.

Walpole, Sir Robert, 145, 153, 173, 174, 176–7, 186.

Warburton, Thomas, Swift's curate at Laracor, 38–39.

Ward, Thomas, Dean of Connor, 13, 19.

West Indies, 154.

Westminster, prebend in, 5, 7.

Wharton, Thomas, Earl of, 58–60, 118, 184; his chaplain, 60.

Whitgift, John, Archbishop of Canterbury, 163.

Whittingham, Charles, prebendary of Mulhuddart, Archdeacon of Dublin, 82–83, 92.

William III, King, 1, 5, 20, 25, 26, 146, 161, 189.

Wilmington, Spencer Compton, Earl of, 181.

Wilson, Francis, prebendary of St. Patrick's, Dublin, 94.

Winder, John, rector of Carnmoney, 13–14, 19; Swift's successor at Kilroot, 24.

Wood's copper coinage (Wood's Halfpence), 92, 110, 185, 186.

Worral, John, Dean's Vicar at St. Patrick's, Dublin, 47, 75.

Wynne, John, Sub-Dean of St. Patrick's, Dublin, 93, 95.

York, Archbishop of (John Sharp), 127–8.

Younger, John, Dean of Salisbury, 85.

PRINTED IN
GREAT BRITAIN
AT THE
UNIVERSITY PRESS
OXFORD
BY
CHARLES BATEY
PRINTER
TO THE
UNIVERSITY